SENTENCING REFORM

Books in this Series:

Volume 17. **Sage** Criminal Justice System Annuals

SENTENCING REFORM:
Experiments in Reducing Disparity

Martin L. Forst
Editor

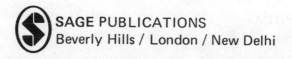

SAGE PUBLICATIONS
Beverly Hills / London / New Delhi

For information address:

SAGE Publications, Inc.
275 South Beverly Drive
Beverly Hills, California 90212

SAGE Publications India Pvt. Ltd. SAGE Publications Ltd
C-236 Defence Colony 28 Banner Street
New Delhi 110 024, India London EC1Y 8QE, England

Printed in the United States of America

Library of Congress Cataloging in Publication Data

Main entry under title:

Sentencing Reform.

(Sage criminal justice system annuals; 17)
Includes index.
1. Sentences (Criminal procedure)-- United States.
2. Sentences (Criminal procedure)--California.
I. Forst, Martin Lyle. II. Series.
KF9685.S45   1982   345.73'0772   82-10369
ISBN 0-8039-1858-5   347.305772
ISBN 0-8039-1859-3 (pbk.)

FIRST PRINTING

CONTENTS

ACKNOWLEDGMENTS

A great number of people deserve credit for their contributions to this book. I would particularly like to thank the many criminal justice practitioners who helped me understand the complexities of the sentencing process over the past several years. They gave freely of their time, though faced with more pressing duties, and they showed extraordinary patience with my research efforts. Because part of the research that led to this book was conducted under a grant from the National Institute of Justice (grant 78-NI-AX-0081/2), I would also like to express my gratitude to that agency for its generous support.

Chapter 1

SENTENCING DISPARITY:
An Overview of Research and Issues

MARTIN L. FORST

Sentencing disparity has, for most of this century, concerned diverse groups: legal scholars, criminal justice practitioners, and perhaps most importantly, the offenders themselves. On occasion, sentences handed down by judges or prison terms set by parole boards[1] appear so discrepant and inequitable as to offend fundamental notions of justice. Until recently, however, the evidence of sentencing disparity uncovered by researchers has not spurred criminal justice policymakers to take corrective action. This can be explained partially by the methodological difficulties in "proving" the existence and extent of disparity. More importantly, however, policymakers have not acted because of their adherence to an "individualized" sentencing model. Observed variations in sentences were justified by a commitment to take into account each offender's needs for rehabilitation and potential for successful adjustment in society.

To the extent that a "justice" model of sentencing has been embraced during the past decade, policymakers have shown a greater interest in eliminating inequitable sentencing. Research on sentencing disparity is increasing. Scholars, practitioners, and politicians of all persuasions are advocating measures to reduce sentencing disparity. In many jurisdictions throughout the country, efforts are being made to alter the traditional sentencing procedures.

Recent research undertaken to provide an empirical basis for changing sentencing policy has revealed weaknesses in research methodology as well as in conceptualizing and defining disparity. The chapters in this book focus on these basic issues; they address conceptual issues in developing a framework for research, methodological issues in identifying disparity, and practical problems in implementing programs. Before progress can be made in preventing or rectifying injustices in sentencing, researchers and policymakers must examine more carefully their assumptions about the nature and meaning of disparity.

A SURVEY OF RESEARCH ON SENTENCING DISPARITY

Past research into sentencing disparity has produced a body of literature richly diverse in focus as well as in methodological approach. Yet some generalizations can be made. Researchers have typically focused their attention either on the *person* imposing the sanction (judge or parole board member) or on some aspect of the *case,* frequently on extralegal factors associated with the defendant.

The earliest studies sought to show that disparities resulted from the individual characteristics of the decisionmaker. Everson's (1919) study of New York City judges, generally accepted as the first empirical study of sentencing disparity, exemplifies this orientation. Everson examined the cases of approximately 155,000 defendants whose violations of local ordinances (primarily drunkenness, vagrancy, and disorderly conduct) were disposed of in 1914 and 1916 by 42 magistrates. He discovered large variations in the ways the cases were handled and the sanctions meted out by the various judges, leading him to conclude that justice "is disconcertingly human, reflecting to an astonishing extent the personalities of the judges" (Everson, 1919: 90).

Since Everson published his pioneering work, many other researchers have focused on variations in judicial sentencing practices, and most have concluded that the individual characteristics of judges were largely responsible for the observed inequities. Sellin (1935: 217), for example, explained disparities in terms of the "human equation in judicial administration." McGuire and Holtzoff (1940a: 428) concluded that "the severity or lightness of the punishment depends in each instance very largely on the personality of the trial judge" (1940a: 428). Similarly, Gaudet (1949) argued that the disparities they uncovered resulted in part from the "capriciousness" of the trial judges.

One of the central deficiencies of these early studies lies in their lack of conceptual clarity. What was meant by the "human equation in judicial administration" and similar vague phrases? These studies did not specify what these human elements consist of or what effect they have on the sentencing decision. As Hood and Sparks (1970: 154) point out, these "explanations" are often so nebulous that they explain nothing at all.

Recently, some researchers have begun to address this deficiency. Hogarth (1971), for example, in his study of the sentencing process in Ontario, Canada, was interested in the specific individual characteristics that affect the observed sentencing patterns. He found that magistrates from working class backgrounds tended to be more punitive than those from professional backgrounds, who were more committed to the rehabilitative ideal. Moreover, the most punitive judges "were found to be young, well-educated urban magistrates. The least punitive group were young, well-educated rural magistrates" (1971: 371). Gradually, researchers following Hogarth's lead are more clearly defining what it is about judges' backgrounds—their education, social status, legal training, political affiliations—that helps determine their sentencing patterns (e.g., Nagel, 1963; Gibson, 1980).

The focus of the second line of research is not on the decisionmaker but on some aspect of the case. Commonly, this type of study shows that the sentencing decision is based at least in part on one or more "extra-legal" factors relating to the defendant, such as race, socioeconomic status, sex, or age. Numerous studies have attempted, for example, to show racial discrimination in the sentencing process. Bullock (1961: 417), in one of the most frequently cited studies, found that the race of the defendent was significantly associated with the length of sentence and concluded that those "who enforce the law conform to norms of their local society concerning racial prejudices, thus denying equality before the law" (see also Green, 1964; Washington Law Review, 1973).

A second extralegal factor frequently investigated is the geographic area in which the case was decided. A succession of studies has shown significant variations in the sentencing patterns of judges in different judicial districts within the same political jurisdiction, giving rise to the phrase "the geography of justice" (Harries and Lura, 1974; Lanpher, 1945; Seymour, 1973). Other studies have examined variations in sentences imposed in different regions in the same state, but the majority of studies have compared sentences handed down for the same offense in federal district courts in various regions of the United States. Most of these studies have reached the same conclusions: "What counts against the offender is not only *what* he does but also *where* he does it" (Journal of Criminal Law and Criminology, 1952: 362).

The relationship between the decisionmaking *process* and sentencing disparity has also been researched. Some studies have examined whether the type of counsel representing the defendant accounted for variations in sentencing (Texas Law Review, 1967); others have shown that the method of conviction is related to the nature of the sentence imposed (Tiffany et al., 1975). Hogarth (1971: 369) even found that the workload of judges was strongly related to sentencing practices. Magistrates who had heavy workloads tended to have "a rigid, expedient penal philosophy" and engaged in "punitive behavior."

Whether the studies focus on the decisionmaker or on some aspect of the case, researchers have used a variety of methodological approaches to "prove" the existence and extent of sentencing disparity. The methods have ranged from crude comparisons of a small sample of individual cases to sophisticated statistical techniques analyzing large numbers of variables. Unfortunately, most of these studies have been unconvincing, in part because of the methodological problems encountered in studying the sentencing process.

One of the crudest methodological approaches in disparity research involves comparing a small sample (as few as two) of "similar" cases. The method of analysis in this approach is extremely limited, consisting of a subjective, even anecdotal comparison of cases. McGuire and Holtzoff (1940b), for instance, briefly describe the cases of two defendants convicted of auto theft, giving capsular statements of the offense and the background of the offenders. The more culpable of the two defendants, and the one who had the more serious prior record, received a lighter sentence than the other. McGuire and Holtzoff cited these cases as evidence of sentencing disparity. But this example in particular, and this approach in general, has two significant weaknesses. First, it does not convince the critical reader that the sentences are disparate, because the researchers do not control all of the variables that may enter into the sentencing decision. Perhaps the more culpable defendant who received the lighter sentence cooperated with the district attorney and the judge took that into consideration. Perhaps the evidence against the defendant was weak, and the district attorney made a calculated decision to offer a relatively light sentence in return for a guilty plea rather than risk an acquittal at trial. A variety of rational explanations and legal justifications might be found to account for such seemingly disparate sentences. Second, even if these anecdotes convinced the reader of disparity in the sentences cited, this approach fails to provide a sense of the *extent* of the disparity—that is, what proportion of the total number of sentences in the jurisdiction are disparate.

The sample sizes of most earlier studies were fortunately much larger, although the methodology for comparing these cases was not much more sophisticated. A common approach examined the variations in sentences of judges within the same judicial district or in different judicial districts within the same jurisdiction. A study cited by Cantor (1938-39: 53), for instance, showed wide variations in the sentences imposed among several district courts in Boston in 1934: "The Boston Municipal Court fined slightly over 2 percent of the defendants convicted of drunkenness and sentenced over 48 percent to jail. The West Roxbury Court fined nearly 34 percent and the Brighton Court imposed jail sentences upon a little over 6 percent." Such evidence does not prove disparity. There are many possible explanations for the observed variations. Possibly the Boston Municipal Court sentenced more persons convicted of drunkenness to jail because the cases were more serious or the defendants appearing before the court had more serious prior records; either factor could justify harsher sentences.

For such studies to be more compelling, the researcher must not only discover variations in sentencing but must also find ways to show that the courts are sentencing roughly comparable cases. Early researchers tried to solve this methodological problem in one of two ways: by studying courts in which the cases were assigned to the sentencing judges on a "random basis" or by researching jurisdictions where the judges rotated from court to court over time (Everson, 1919; Gaudet, 1946; President's Commission, 1967). In either instance, the researcher assumed that all judges would be exposed to similar cases, equalizing the sample. Both of these approaches have been tried many times, largely with the same results—substantial variations in imposed sentences, called sentencing disparities by the researchers. These studies, however, have been criticized because the researchers only *assumed* that the sample under study was random; an independent, scientific selection of cases was not conducted. Thus researchers cannot even be sure they are controlling for "offense," to say nothing of all the other important variables in the sentencing decision. Without controlling the variables, the conclusions of the researchers are suspect. As Hogarth (1971: 7) maintains, "Without adequate statistical control over the types of cases appearing before the courts, it would be wrong to assume that there is a genuine lack of uniformity in sentencing."

One way to confront the problem of controlling variables is to simulate the sentencing process. In this approach, researchers present the same fact situation to a number of judges and ask them what sentence they would impose. Such studies have generally revealed wide variations in the types and duration of sentences imposed for identical cases (Partridge and Eldridge, 1974; Austin and Williams, 1977). But these studies are not immune from criticism. Sentencing simulation often takes place at sentencing institutes or judges' conferences; the judges must make the sentencing decisions by themselves, without the advice of other actors in the criminal justice system. In the daily administration of justice, however, sentencing does not take place in a vacuum; judges normally do not make sentencing decisions by themselves. Rather, they have probation officers to aid them and, perhaps more importantly, they have the prosecuting and defense attorneys informing the court what sentences similarly situated offenders have received in the past. The validity of simulation studies is therefore suspect because they are not realistic—they do not simulate the routine decisionmaking processes of the criminal courts.

The development of modern, quantitative statistical techniques has provided researchers with a new means to control variables. Although a variety of methods have been used, researchers commonly use some form of multivariate analysis, most frequently linear multiple regression analysis. This allows the researcher to determine the relative effects on predicted sentence severity of variations within each sentencing variable, holding other known variables constant.

Using multivariate analysis, researchers generally approach the study of disparity in one of two ways. In the first, the researcher develops a predictive model of sentencing severity, for example, seriousness of offense and the nature of the offender's prior record. Those cases not explained by the predictive model, called "residual cases," are defined as disparate on the assumption that extralegal variables accounted for the sentences imposed. In the second and more common approach, the researcher codes both legal and extralegal variables, and with multivariate analysis determines which factors predict sentence severity. If, after holding the legally relevant variables constant, the length of sentence is associated with extralegal variables, such as the race of the defendant, the researcher *infers* disparity.

A recent example of this type of research is Thornberry's (1979) study of disparities in the juvenile justice system. Employing log-linear analysis (a multivariate technique used to assess the independent effect of a number of qualitative independent variables on a qualitative dependent variable), Thornberry sought to determine the relative effects of four independent variables (two legal and two extralegal) on the length of sentence. His study revealed that blacks and members of the lower socioeconomic groups received more severe sanctions after the legally relevant variables of offense severity and prior records were held constant.

Even these sophisticated statistical techniques confront major methodological problems. One serious obstacle inherent in this approach is that of coding all of the relevant variables that the court or parole board take into consideration when imposing a sanction. Many of the variables included in the analysis are difficult to code. For example, artificial scales have been devised to code offense severity, but these scales are crude considering the broad range of fact situations that can fall within any one offense category. The variables that are *not* coded and included in the analysis present an even greater barrier to good research. Most studies, for example, do not attempt to code such factors as the vulnerability of the victim, harm done to the victim, culpability of the defendant, degree of the defendant's criminal sophistication, and many other aggravating and mitigating circumstances that judges and parole boards can legally consider in the sentencing process. Moreover, most studies do not code factors such as the strength of the prosecutor's case, the quality of the evidence, the degree of the defendant's cooperation with the authorities, and other factors that play an important role in the sentencing decision. Without including all relevant variables in the analysis, the nature and extent of sentencing disparity cannot be fully explored.

As great as these methodological deficiencies are, they do not constitute the major weakness in disparity research to date. Rather, the greatest barrier to strong and convincing research is the inability to conceptualize and define sentencing disparity clearly. The problems of conceptualization and definition will be discussed in detail later in this chapter.

DISPARITY AND INDIVIDUALIZED SENTENCING

Over sixty years of research consistently indicating disparities in sentencing has had, until recently, relatively little influence on criminal justice policymakers. Authorities have offered several explanations for the placid acceptance of seemingly wide variations in sentencing practices, but the central reason is found in the adherence to a model of "individualized" sentencing, a system of imposing sanctions that has long been part of the American system of criminal justice.

Based in part on humanitarian ideology and the tenets of positive criminology, this new approach for dealing with the lawbreaker was advocated by correctional reformers as early as 1870. Reformers wanted to abandon the nonutilitarian concept of vindictive punishment and sought instead to reform or rehabilitate the offender. According to the new rehabilitative philosophy, it was no longer sufficient to consider solely the defendant's offense. To effect an offender's rehabilitation, the person imposing the sentence must consider his or her personality, social background, motivation for crimes, and potential for reintegration into society. As Sheldon Glueck, one of the principal spokesmen for this new approach, stated in 1927:

> The legal and institutional provisions for the protection of society must be based not so much upon the gravity of the particular act for which an offender happens to be tried, as upon his personality, that is, upon his dangerousness, his personal assets, and his responsiveness to peno-correctional treatment [p. 469].

In short, the new model of justice meant a shift in emphasis from the crime to the criminal.

To the extent that correctional philosophy was changing from punishment to rehabilitation, the old methods of sentencing, reformers argued, also needed modification. Rigid sentences fixed by the courts had to be replaced with a more flexible sanctioning system, one allowing for the individual differences in offenders. Recommendations to "individualize" the sentencing process have been made for more than a century. As far back as 1870, Zebulon Brockway proposed to the National Prison Association that the authority to release offenders from prison should be vested in a "Board of Guardians" instead of the courts, and that the board should base its release decisions on the readiness of the prisoner to return to society.

> When it appears to the said Board that there is a reasonable probability that any ward possesses a sincere purpose to become a good citizen, and the requisite moral power and self-control to live at liberty without violating the law, and that such ward will become a fair member of society, then they shall issue to such ward an absolute release [Brockway, 1912: 131].

In 1927 the American Psychiatric Association (APA) formed a committee to inform the legal profession about recent developments in the field of psychiatry and to make recommendations for dealing with criminal offenders. The APA recommended "the permanent legal detention of the inadequate, incompetent, and anti-social offenders irrespective of the particular offense committed" (Menninger, 1928: 376). The 1962 draft of the Model Penal Code, written by the American Law Institute, declared that the major purpose of its sentencing and treatment provisions is rehabilitation, although other objectives are also mentioned. And as recently as 1972, the Model Sentencing Act, legislation drafted under the auspices of the National Council on Crime and Delinquency, stated that "persons convicted of crime shall be dealt with in accordance with their potential for rehabilitation, considering their individual characteristics, circumstances and needs."

The indeterminate sentence, first passed in Ohio in 1885 and later adopted in some form by all states, was developed to provide officials with the means to tailor the length of sentence to the needs of the individual. Because of its many statutory variations, the indeterminate sentence is difficult to define precisely, but it is characterized by broad legislative limits for sanctions. Judges are typically given broad discretion to choose the type of sentence and, within minimum and maximum statutory provisions, to determine the length of sentence. Reformers have argued that it is impossible for the sentencing judge to know what forms of treatment would be most effective for each defendant committed to state prison or how long the rehabilitative process might take. It would therefore be most sensible to wait until after an offender has served part of his or her sentence before selecting the exact release date. The authority to release offenders from prison is usually given to an administrative agency, a parole board. With the advice of the correctional staff, the parole board is ostensibly in the best position to determine when a prisoner is ready to return to society.

Individualized sentencing, with its rehabilitative foundation, became well accepted by the judiciary, giving legitimacy to the vast discretion accorded trial court judges and parole boards. As early as 1932, the U.S. Supreme Court sanctioned the enormous discretion needed to individualize sentences. "It is necessary to individualize each case, to give that careful, humane and comprehensive consideration to the particular situation of each offender which would be possible only in the exercise of broad discretion" (Burns v. United States, 1932). By 1949, the Supreme Court acknowledged in Williams v. New York the formal change in the philosophy of criminal sentencing. "Retribution is no longer the dominant objective of the criminal law. Reformation and rehabilitation of offenders have become the important goals of criminal jurisprudence" (p. 248). With but a few minor exceptions, the appellate courts have continued to uphold this enormous discretion.

Acceptance of the individualized sentencing model did not make judges immune to criticism for some variations in sentencing. Even the strongest supporters of individualized justice condemned sentencing inequalities that derived from bias against race, religion, social class, nationality, and similar factors not related to the aims of the rehabilitative philosophy. Supporters of individualized sentencing, however, viewed most sentencing variations as legitimate, justified by individual differences in offenders that were related to rational correctional goals. If critics pointed to sentencing "disparity," apologists would counter that the observed differences in sentences resulted from the diversified needs of individual offenders. One authority stated that "variations in sentencing are justifiable and desirable when they reflect this concept of individualized justice, of tailoring the treatment to the offender rather than to the offense" (Davis, 1956: 385). To the extent that there was a rational relationship between the individualized sentences and the espoused objective of rehabilitating the offender, enormous variations in sentences imposed on offenders convicted of the same offense were considered legally and morally justified.

DISPARITY AND JUSTICE

Over the past ten to fifteen years, an assault has been launched on the individualized sentencing model—particularly on its theoretical underpinnings. The attacks, coming from academics, the judiciary, correctional administrators, a wide spectrum of politicians, and even from prisoners, have had two main thrusts. The first prong of the attack has centered on the seeming ineffectiveness of the rehabilitative or treatment approach. Prisoners, the argument goes, are subjected to arbitrary decisionmaking, intrusive therapeutic programs, and disparate sentences—all to no functional end. That is, mounting evidence over the last decade has indicated that rehabilitative programs do not rehabilitate (Martinson, 1974). It is claimed that the recidivism rate would be the same with or without participation in rehabilitative programs. Why, critics wondered, should prisoners face these injustices if the espoused correctional aims are not being met? Other critics felt it was a waste of taxpayers' money to fund rehabilitative programs if they failed to achieve the practical result of controlling crime.

The second line of criticism has provided an even more effective attack on individualized sentencing. Critics have begun to question the justice and fairness of individualized sentencing, the broad discretion accorded criminal justice officials, and the attenuation of due process rights. They have argued that even if rehabilitative programs were effective, it would be unjust and unfair to base the sentencing decision on the successful completion of those programs.

Pinpointing the origins of these attacks is difficult, but credit is generally given to the publication of *Struggle for Justice,* a report written by a working party of the American Friends Service Committee in 1970. The report decries the discretion given to judges to consider a variety of extralegal factors when imposing sentence. The authors "suggest that the law should deal only with a narrow aspect of the individual, that is, his criminal act or acts." Presaging a return to a classical model of criminal justice, the authors advocate abandoning the rehabilitative approach and substituting the principle of "desert," urging that "the law be applied uniformly to all offenders" (p. 145).

Following the publication of *Struggle for Justice*, several works on the philosophy of punishment have appeared, and they have generally concluded that the principle of "just desert" should form the basis of the criminal sanction, thus advocating a return to the classical approach to wrongdoing—deserved punishment. Andrew von Hirsch (1976), in *Doing Justice*, emphasizes the importance of desert in the criminal law:

> Someone who infringes the rights of others . . . does wrong and deserves blame for his conduct. It is because he deserves blame that the sanction authority is entitled to choose a response that expresses moral disapproval: namely, punishment [pp. 48-49].

According to this new approach to sentencing, commonly called the "justice" model, the punishments inflicted on convicted offenders must be proportionate to the seriousness of the offense, or as von Hirsch says, "commensurate with the seriousness of the wrong" (p. 66). The authors of *Fair and Certain Punishment*, the report of the Twentieth Century Fund, make a similar recommendation, calling for a system in which the penalties should correspond to "the relative degrees of culpability and the risk of harm represented by each offense" (Dershowitz, 1976: 24). Presumably, if all defendants received sanctions proportionate to the seriousness of their offenses, sentencing disparity would decrease because similarly situated offenders would receive the same punishments.

Ensuring that sentences are closely related to the seriousness of the criminal act is difficult in a system of justice that grants unbridled discretion to its criminal justice officials, particularly to those who determine the type and length of sentence. Consequently, the discretionary aspects of individualized justice have also come under attack from a variety of sources. The authors of *Struggle for Justice* claim that the core problem in the criminal justice system is "discretionary power" because it "serves only to blunt or twist the principles of justice and legality, for these are dependent upon the uniform application of rules and principles"

(1971: 125). Some members of the judiciary have been critical of their own discretionary powers. Judge Frankel (1973: 5), for example, has stated that "the almost wholly unchecked and sweeping powers given to judges in the fashioning of sentences are terrifying and intolerable for a society that professes devotion to the rule of law." Even the Chief Justice of the U.S. Supreme Court has noted the dangers in the discretionary powers given judges:

> Discretion in sentencing has been a double-edged sword. It permits the judge to accommodate unusual circumstances relative to each defendant. But this sometimes results in defendants who ought to be similarly treated receiving substantially disparate sentences [New York Times, 1977].

The Chief Justice called for new measures to help curb the sweeping discretion given to the courts.

Legal scholars have proposed a variety of means to reduce sentencing disparities. Some scholars, accepting the validity of the individualized justice model, have proposed what amount to piecemeal measures, including the formation of sentencing institutes and sentencing councils, requiring the judge to state the reasons for the sentencing decision, as well as appellate review of sentences (American Bar Association, 1967; National Advisory Commission, 1973a: 182; National Advisory Commission, 1973b; Frankel, 1973; Walsh, 1959: 250).

Others who challenge the philosophical premises of the rehabilitative model advocate more sweeping reforms. These reforms would abolish the indeterminate sentence and replace it with a system having more determinacy in sentencing, variously called determinate, presumptive, or flat-time sentencing (for an overview of such statutes, see Von Hirsch and Hanrahan, 1981). Two basic strategies of determinate sentencing have emerged to date. One approach abolishes the parole board and returns term-setting authority to the courts, as in the new determinate sentencing statutes of California, Maine, Illinois, and Indiana. The sentencing judge, aided by written standards of principles, selects a sentence from within a relatively narrow statutory range that determines how much time the prisoner spends in prison, minus possible reductions for "good time." The parole board is retained in the second approach, but the board is required to structure its discretion so that with the aid of sentencing guidelines, board members set terms from within a relatively narrow set of durational ranges dictated by the severity of the offense and a variety of criminal history and social background factors (see, for example, Oregon's new guidelines for setting prison terms). The aims are the same in both systems: to reduce the vast amount of discretion of persons imposing the sanctions, to make terms of imprisonment proportionate to the seriousness of the criminal conduct and, as the Twentieth Century Fund report states, to create "relative uniformity of sentences for persons of equivalent criminal records convicted of the same offense" (Dershowitz, 1976: 32).

It is important to note that persons of varying political and social philosophies have differently envisioned what the "justice" model was supposed to accomplish. "Liberals" hoped to reduce disparity, as well as lower the overall severity of criminal sanctions. At the same time, "law and order" advocates sought a way to control judges and parole board members who were "soft on crime." They wanted to reduce disparity by preventing the early release of dangerous criminals from prison and by preventing the granting of probation to various classes of offenders. While "justice demands that two individuals convicted of similar offenses, with similar backgrounds and criminal histories, should receive sentences that are roughly the same" (Wilkins et al., 1978: vii), there was much disagreement about how severe these uniform sanctions should be.

DISPARITY AND PRISON UNREST

The most publicized arguments for reducing sentencing disparity rest on philosophical grounds; scholars claim that a sentencing system should be based on "justice," that people facing the criminal sanction be treated equitably and fairly. These philosophical principles, however, should not overshadow the more pragmatic reason for promoting uniformity in sentencing—to reduce prison unrest. For decades correctional administrators have claimed that sentencing disparity is an important cause of misbehavior among prisoners. In fact, devising ways to reduce sentencing disparity in order to control prisoners is perhaps one of the oldest and most persistent themes in the correctional literature.

During the nineteenth century, most states had a "definite" sentencing system. For each felony, the legislature designated a moderate range of imprisonment from which the judge was to select a sentence. In California in 1865, for example, the statutory penalty for robbery was from one to ten years. The judge imposed a definite sentence from within the prescribed range, and that is how long the defendant would remain in prison, not counting possible time reductions for "good time," pardon, or commutation of sentence. Definite sentencing created problems because standards to guide the sentencing judge were nonexistent, and similarly situated offenders were often given substantially different sentences, depending on the county from which they were committed or on the predilections of the judges. Because inequalities in sentences caused problems in prison, correctional administrators sought alternatives to definite sentencing. As sentencing disparities were reduced, the reasoning went, prison unrest would subside.

To accomplish this end, many correctional administrators foresaw the practical advantages to parole and indeterminate sentencing. In its 1887 report to the legislature, for example, the California State Penological Commission recognized the problem of inequalities in sentencing and recommended adopting a system of parole that would provide a means to modify definite sentences:

> As we have shown there are great variances for sentences pronounced by different judges for the same offense. There is nothing that produces so much discontent and disaffection among prisoners as this inequality of sentence. . . . The parole system enables these great and often unjust inequalities to be corrected [p. 80].

This reasoning persisted through the 1940s. The federal prison system, for example, was susceptible to the problem of disparate sentences. The U.S. attorney general's report of 1938 stated that there were wide discrepancies in the sentencing of people who had committed "identical offenses involving similar states of facts." Disparity in sentencing, the report alleged, leads to a sense of injustice among prisoners and "creates a disciplinary problem inside the prison walls. . . . Marked differences in penalties for the same crime create a justifiable sense of injustice and disrespect" (Annual Report, 1939: 6-7). The attorney general in his 1938 report and the Judicial Conference of the Senior Circuit Court Judges in their reports of 1939 and 1940 recommended the adoption of the indeterminate sentence, in large part because it provided "a more adequate meeting of the disciplinary problems inside the penal institution, that is to say, overcoming the inevitable sense of injustice and resentment among prisoners caused by marked differences, that become known to them, in penalties imposed for the same offense" (Coleman, 1941: 8). Presumably a parole board, composed of only a handful of members and centrally administered, would more consistently set prison terms than a large number of judges situated throughout the country.

By the 1950s every jurisdiction in the country had some form of indeterminate sentence, but sentencing disparity was not eliminated—nor was prison unrest. Prisoners continued to compare the terms they received, believing that persons who committed essentially similar crimes under similar circumstances frequently faced substantially different periods of incarceration. Prisoners still made the same cries about "capricious" and "arbitrary" sentencing, only now the object of the allegations had changed. By the 1960s and the early 1970s, prisoners had a new focus for their resentment—parole boards and the indeterminate sentence. Disparity in prison terms continued under the indeterminate sentence because parole boards inherited two significant aspects of judicial sentencing authority: unbridled discretion and a lack of standards for the imposition of sanctions. These perceived disparities in prison terms, along with lax procedural protections, led to what Irwin (1970: 60) called a "sense of injustice" among prisoners such that their response "towards the perpetrators of the injustices . . . is presently . . . a growing resentment and anger."

Prison unrest reached crisis proportions at the end of the 1960s and the beginning of the 1970s, and the term-setting practices of parole boards received much of the blame. The Commission on Attica heard many complaints about the indeterminate sentence and the "arbitrary" decision-making practices of the parole board. "Far from instilling confidence in the Parole Board's sense of justice, the existing procedure merely confirms to inmates, including those receiving favorable decisions, that the system is indeed capricious and demeaning" (Official Report, 1972: 98). The commission concluded that "by 1971 conditional release and parole had become by far the greatest source of inmate anxiety and frustration" (p. 3).

The California Department of Corrections Task Force to Study Violence [in prisons] reached a similar conclusion in 1974. The report noted the increase in prison violence and unrest in the recent past and stated that "sentencing uncertainties are such a key factor in building misunderstanding and paranoid beliefs among inmates that change in this area is a most important precondition for reducing violence" (p. 35). The task force then made recommendations "with the objective of giving inmates more certainty in their future and reducing their sense of being victims of an erratic system" (p. 37). When a bill came before the legislature in California to enact a determinate sentencing law, designed in part to reduce sentencing disparities, many top correctional officials supported the bill on the assumption that increased determinacy and equity in sentencing would provide a major step toward quelling the turmoil that had existed in the prison system during the preceding decade.

CONCEPTUALIZING DISPARITY

The essence of disparity is *variation* from some norm or standard. The various conceptualizations found in the literature differ only as to the *nature* of the norm or standard from which the variation is measured. Most researchers gauge variation either from a norm of proportionality or from a statistical pattern of cases, but these alternate conceptualizations have created enormous confusion and must be explored in greater detail. Understanding how disparity is conceptualized is important for both theoretical and practical reasons. Conceptualizations guide the development of measurement techniques that in turn dictate the nature and extent of the cases identified as disparate.

Conceptualizing disparity as a variation from some norm of proportionality is a common theme in the literature. To some authors, disparity refers to the statutory penalties authorized by law that are disproportionate to the gravity of the offense; the penalties do not seem justified given the seriousness of the criminal conduct. Peter Low (1968: 29), for example, describes the "disparities" between penalties authorized by law and various forms of criminal conduct, concluding that "at the very least, it would seem that these facts should raise doubts about the extent to which presently authorized sentencing levels are necessary or justified." An article in the *University of Cincinnati Law Review* (1977), entitled "Disparate Sentencing Provisions of Ohio's Organized Crime Statute," provides another example. The author maintains that the statutory sentencing provisions of Ohio's new organized crime law are disparate because they provide for "equal culpability for the leader and a minor functionary of organized crime" (p. 590).

Allegations of disparity also surface when a norm of proportionality is violated in the imposition of a sanction, particularly an excessive sentence. A recent California case is illustrative. The defendant was convicted of one count of exhibitionism and, having one prior conviction for a similar offense, was sentenced to state prison for a term of one year to life. The offender had served five years in prison when the California Supreme Court found the sentence unconstitutional. Setting down a general standard, the court, in In re Lynch (1972), held that a sentence violates the constitutional prohibition against cruel and unusual punishment "if [the punishment] is so disproportionate to the crime for which it is inflicted that it shocks the conscience and offends fundamental notions of human dignity." How the court decides what sanctions "shock the conscience" and "offend fundamental notions of human dignity" is not clear. The decision rests not on a comparison of the sentences meted out to similarly situated offenders, but on a subjective evaluation of the seriousness of the offense, given current social and moral norms.

Researchers commonly find that sentences in different offense categories form statistical patterns and that some sentences vary, to a greater or lesser degree, from those patterns. In the alternative conceptualization of disparity, the statistical pattern formed by a large sample of cases is the reference point against which variation is measured. According to this reasoning, judging the disparity of cases is impossible without reference to some statistical pattern (Gottfredson, 1975: 56). Consider two persons convicted of mayhem, each committing a similar crime and having a similar prior record. The first defendant is sentenced to two years in prison and the second to fifteen years. There is an obvious discrepancy between these two sentences, but what can be said about disparity? Which one of the two is disparate? How much of it is disparate? Answering these questions suggests the need for a larger sample of cases for comparison. If all other persons convicted of mayhem received a sentence of two years, then the second defendant's sentence is disparate. If all others convicted of mayhem were sentenced to fifteen years, then the first defendant's sentence is disparate. If all others were sentenced to eight years, then both defendants' sentences are disparate.

Which of these competing conceptualizations of disparity one adopts is of primary importance, because each conceptualization will dictate the types of cases that are identified as disparate. Reid (1981: 447) cites an interesting example: One defendant was convicted of possession of marijuana and sentenced to six months in jail; a second defendant was found guilty of possession of an illegal weapon [gun] and sentenced to thirty days. These sentences strike Reid as "disparate" because the person who committed the most serious and potentially most dangerous offense received the less severe sanction. Reid's reference point is a subjective norm of proportionality. But suppose a researcher analyzed a large sample of cases in the jurisdiction in question and found that *all* persons convicted of possession of marijuana received a sentence of six months and that *all* persons convicted of illegal possession of a gun were given thirty days. Although the sentences are disproportionate to the seriousness of the offense, they are not disparate in the statistical sense because all offenders in each offense category are treated *uniformly*.

Consider another example. Suppose that in a particular jurisdiction the legislature (or a sentencing commission) designated a presumptive sentence of five years for robbery; by definition, the presumptive sentence is proportionate to the seriousness of the offense. The defendant in this example is charged with robbery, convicted by a jury, and given the presumptive sentence of five years. When this defendant then compares his sentence with the sentences of other prisoners, he or she finds that all other persons committing a robbery under similar circumstances and with a similar prior record were sentenced to three years in prison. In this situation, would the defendant's five-year sentence be "disparate"? If one's reference is a norm of proportionality, the answer is no. The judge, having sat through the trial and heard all the facts in the case, based the sentence on what the defendant deserved; that is, he imposed a sentence that was proportionate to the seriousness of the offense. Perhaps all the other cases were plea bargained and the sentence reduced accordingly, or perhaps all the other judges were simply lenient. But if one's measure of disparity is the proportionality of the sentence, then the lone defendant's five-year sentence might well be appropriate and the sentences of all the other robbers disparately low! If, however, one's reference point is the statistical pattern, then the five-year sentence would be considered disparate. To be labeled disparate, it does not matter that the sentence is just or proportionate, only that it is *different*.

DEFINING DISPARITY

Once a conceptual framework has been established, the next step is to formulate a specific definition of disparity. Unfortunately, more than six decades of research have failed to provide precise and generally accepted definitions of sentencing disparity. Of the more than 100 references (articles, books, and reports) that this author reviewed, a mere handful defined disparity, and only three set forth operational definitions (Diamond and Zeisel, 1975; Gottfredson, 1979a, 1979b). Of these few researchers who defined disparity at all, most used general definitions. A few illustrations will suffice. One author states that disparity means "discrepant sentences assigned for similar offenses and similar offenders" (Austin and Williams, 1977). Another authority says that there is disparity in punishment "when like individuals, committing like offenses, are treated differently" (Gaylin, 1974: 3). And yet another source claims that a sentence is disparate if "a substantial difference exists between the subject sentence and the sentences imposed on other offenders committing the same offense under similar circumstances" (Opinions, 1977: 143). These general definitions may sound acceptable, but they are not sufficient. The difficult task facing researchers and policymakers is to operationalize them.

Identifying and measuring disparity implies a process of comparison. To assess the similarities or differences among cases, common attributes must be compared. Comparison, in turn, necessitates classification. At issue is specifically how the cases are to be classified for comparison. Based on a review of the definitions found in the literature, it appears that there are three common dimensions that must be included in any analysis of disparity: the characteristics of the sanctions imposed, the details of the offense, and the attributes of the offender. To define disparity adequately, each of these three dimensions must be operationalized. Put differently, an operational definition of disparity must address the classification and comparison of variables within each of these three dimensions.

Classification and Comparison of Sanctions. A central problem to devising an operational definition is that disparity is a continuous, not a discrete variable. When researchers examine large numbers of judicial sentences (or parole board term sets), they typically find the formation of general statistical patterns. They also find variation from the established patterns; some of the variation is slight, some moderate, and some great. The difficulty is deciding where acceptable variation ends and disparity begins.

One possible way to draw the line between acceptable and unacceptable variation (i.e., to classify sanctions) is with absolute time. "How much time?" is the question. A researcher could arbitrarily decide that, all other things being equal, every sentence six months or more above or below the predicted sentence is disparate. But why six months? There are no objective or externally derived criteria for choosing six months instead of, say, six days, six weeks, or even six years.

Operationalizing the definition of disparity with absolute time presents other problems as well. Absolute time does not adequately allow consideration of the relative lengths of the sentences imposed. Consider the following cases: A defendant is convicted of robbery and is sentenced to 20 years in prison. A second defendant is convicted of robbery and, with the same degree of culpability and criminal background, receives a sentence of 20 years and six months. A difference of six months, considering the length of the sentences, probably would not shock the consciences of most people. Now compare the sentences of two pickpockets. The first is sentenced to six months in jail, while the second, having committed a similar crime under similar circumstances, receives a sentence of one year. In this situation, the difference between the two sentences is also six months. However, a six-month difference here means the second sentence is *twice* as long as the first. This discrepancy is much more likely to offend people's sense of justice.

As an alternative, disparity could be defined in relative terms, as a specific percentage or proportion above or below the central tendency or the predicted sentence. For example, any sentence 10 percent or more above or below the predicted sentence could be operationally defined as disparate. But why 10 percent instead of 5, 15, or 25 percent? However disparity is operationalized, the decision pinpointing where legitimate variation ends and disparity begins will necessarily be an arbitrary one.

Researchers face a different problem when they attempt to compare cases that have received various *combinations* of sanctions. Trial court judges often impose not one but several sanctions, in different combinations, on similarly situated offenders. This creates difficulties for comparison because disparity implies not only that *different* sanctions are imposed on similarly situated offenders, but that the sanctions are of a different *magnitude*. But assessing the degree of severity of different combinations is not easy. Which sanction is more severe—six months in jail, or three months in jail, two years on probation, and a $200 fine? Which sanction is more onerous for a child molester—two years in prison and three years on parole or three years in a mental institution as a sexual psychopath and registration as a sex offender? Researchers have repeatedly failed to understand the subtleties of the sanctioning process; they have consistently failed to develop techniques for weighing the relative severity of different combinations of sanctions. In short, they have failed to address the *quality* of the sanctions imposed. Until this is done, allegations of disparity will be less than compelling.

Classification and Comparison of Offenses. Disparity generally means that sentences of differing magnitude have been imposed on persons who committed the same or similar offense under similar circumstances. But what is the "same" or "similar" offense? How best to classify offenses for comparison is not at all obvious. The legal definition of most offenses is quite broad. Robbery, for instance, is commonly defined as the taking of property from another by force or fear of force. The fact situations within that legal category can, therefore, vary enormously. In one case the defendant may use fear of force to obtain the property, whereas in a second case the assailant used actual force. Are these two offenses the same? They are legally the same, as defined in the penal code. But the degree of harm done to the victim may have been substantially greater in the second case, and a judge or parole board would surely view the two cases differently.

In two other hypothetical cases of robbery, both of the defendants were armed with a pistol. In the first case the defendant brandished the gun, but in the second case the offender cocked it, pointed it at the victim, and said, "If you don't give me your money, I'll blow your head off." The defendant implicitly threatened the victim in the first case, whereas in the second case the defendant made an overt threat. Are these two cases the same? Should they be classified together for purposes of comparison? The point is that it is difficult to decide how fine the gradations should be in classifying cases for comparison. Grouping cases by legal definition makes sense superficially, but general definitions do not take into account the more subtle distinctions among crimes within any legal category—distinctions that are made by the people imposing the sentences. Finer gradations would be preferable, but it is difficult to determine just how fine they should be and what criteria should be used to distinguish among cases.

Another major dilemma in classifying offenses is whether to consider only the "official" offense (that crime for which the offender was found guilty) or to take into account the "real" or "underlying" offense or offenses. Limiting the classification and comparison to the official offense has distinct advantages. The task of coding cases is greatly simplified, since the researcher has merely to look up the conviction offense in an official document (e.g., the Register of Actions or the Order of Commitment). Of greater importance is the "fairness" of limiting the classification to the official offense. It is in keeping with the basic principles of American law not to attribute to a person unlawful acts for which he has not been convicted beyond a reasonable doubt in a court of law.

A good argument can also be made for "reading through" the official record to look at the "real" or "underlying" criminal activity. Prosecutors in different jurisdictions have different plea-bargaining policies that often result in distinct patterns of official conviction. Some prosecutors, for example, routinely strike the gun allegation in a charge of armed robbery, while other prosecutors do not. If researchers ignore the underlying criminal behavior, offenders who did the same thing would be placed in different categories and, consequently, would *not* be compared with each other. "Reading through" is a common practice among judges and parole board members, and since it is probably constitutional under certain conditions, it is important for the disparity researcher to take into consideration the actual sentencing criteria used by criminal justice officials (Schwartz, 1981).

Classification and Comparison of Offenders. Defined generally, disparity requires that "like individuals" or "similar offenders" be given different sentences for the same offense. How to classify "like" individuals or "similar" offenders is especially problematic, since the number of factors or variables that could conceivably be compared is practically endless. The characteristics of the offender could range from the number and type of prior convictions to the geographic location of the crime to his current employment status.

How to group "like" or "same" offenders depends to a great extent on one's underlying assumptions about the aims of the criminal sanction. The factors used to classify and compare offenders in a system embracing the rehabilitative ideal would be quite different from those used in a just deserts model of sentencing. Consider the case of two persons convicted of similar burglaries and having similar prior records. The first burglar is employed, married, and has strong family and social ties in the community. The second burglar is unemployed, has a poor employment history, is not married and, having recently moved into the area, has few established relationships. To a court or parole board, whose decisions are geared to the rehabilitation of the offender or the protection of the public, these two offenders are not the same, even though their offense and prior records may be identical. To adherents of a "justice" model of sentencing, these two offenders should be classified as the same and compared with each other in an analysis of disparity. Taking the *type* of sanction into account can cause even greater confusion. Perhaps the two offenders should not be classified as the "same" for the decision to grant or deny probation, but if they are sent to prison, they should be classified as the same for a length-of-stay determination.

Anyone who wants to show disparity in sentencing must demonstrate that the different sentences meted out to persons committing the same offense under similar circumstances cannot be justified by reference to some legally relevant variables, that is, to factors that have some rational relationship to the aims of the criminal law. This is a tall order to fill, since the aims of the criminal law are rarely clearly articulated. Holdings from a long line of appellate court cases, therefore, dictate that an almost endless variety of factors related to the offender can be taken into consideration in the sentencing decision. The U.S. Supreme Court, for example, has held that a judge in sentencing an offender is "largely unlimited either as to the kind of information he may consider, or the source from which it may come" (United States v. Tucker, 1972). Appellate courts in various jurisdictions have held that when imposing sentence, a judge may properly consider an offender's background and family life (United States v. Collado Betancourt, 1975), alleged prior criminal activity for which the offender was never convicted (Horowitz v. Henderson, 1975; United States v. Cifarelli, 1968), his or her sexual inclinations (United States v. Kohlberg, 1973; United States v. Duhart), religious predispositions (Frankel, 1973), impressions given on the witness stand (United States v. Cluchette, 1972), cooperativeness (United States v. Malcolm, 1970), and whether he or she made restitution to the victim (United States v. Landay, 1975). It is little wonder that researchers have such difficulty operationally defining "same" or "similar" offenders when so many offender characteristics can be legally taken into consideration in the sentencing decision.

CONCLUSION

Sentencing disparity has become a primary concern to legislators and criminal justice planners across the country. Although new laws are being passed and new programs implemented to reduce disparity in sentencing, policymakers have failed to appreciate the conceptual and methodological difficulties inherent in this task. Examples of the problems in designing and operating disparity reduction programs are vividly illustrated in the chapters in this book.

Many issues need resolution if the laws and programs aimed at reducing disparity will ever be truly effective. Conceivably, these issues could be addressed by the appellate courts. This, however, is unlikely since the courts have consistently demonstrated an unwillingness to intervene in trial court sentencing policies. As a practical matter, the issues raised in this book must be resolved politically. Legislatures must take a more active role in defining the proper goals of the criminal sanction. They must weigh, balance, and ultimately order the legitimate values of proportionality, uniformity, and individuality in sentencing.

NOTE

1. In this chapter the term "sentencing disparity" is defined broadly, referring to sanctions imposed both by trial courts *and* parole boards.

CASES

BURNS v. UNITED STATES (1932) 287 U.S. 216
HOROWITZ v. HENDERSON (1975) 514 F.2d 740
In re LYNCH (1972) 8 C3d 410, 424, 503 P2d 921

UNITED STATES v. CIFARELLI (1968) 401 F.2d 512
UNITED STATES v. COLLADO BETANCOURT (1975) 405 F.Supp. 1063
UNITED STATES v. CLUCHETTE (1972) 465 F.2d 749
UNITED STATES v. DUHART (1974) 496 F.2d 941
UNITED STATES v. KOHLBERG (1973) 472 F.2d 1189
UNITED STATES v. LANDAY (1975) 513 F.2d 306
UNITED STATES v. MALCOLM (1970) 432 F.2d 809
UNITED STATES v. TUCKER (1972) 404 U.S. 443
WILLIAMS v. NEW YORK (1949) 337 U.S. 241

REFERENCES

American Bar Association (1967) "Appellate review of sentences." Project on the Minimum Standards for Criminal Justice, pp. 1-12.

American Friends Service Committee (1971) Struggle for Justice: A Report on Crime and Punishment in America. New York: Hill & Wang.

American Law Institute (1962) Model Penal Code, Section 1.02.

Annual Report of the Attorney General of the United States (1939) Washington, DC: Government Printing Office.

AUSTIN, W. and T. A. WILLIAMS III (1977) "A survey of judges' responses to simulated legal cases: research note on sentencing disparity." Journal of Criminal Law and Criminology 68: 306-310.

BROCKWAY, Z. R. (1912) Fifty Years of Prison Service. New York: Charities Publication Committee.

BULLOCK, H. A. (1961) "Significance of the racial factor in the length of prison sentences." Journal of Criminal Law, Criminology and Police Science 52: 411-417.

California Department of Corrections (1974) "The task force to study violence—report and recommendations." Sacramento.

California State Penological Commission, Penology (1887) Report. Sacramento.

CANTOR, N. (1938-39) "A disposition tribunal." Journal of Criminal Law and Criminology 29: 51-61.

COLEMAN, W. C. (1941) "The indeterminate sentence: should it be made a part of the criminal procedure of the federal courts?" Federal Probation 5: 8.

DAVIS, G. F. (1956) "Variations in sentencing." Crime and Delinquency 2: 385.

DERSHOWITZ, A. (1976) Fair and Certain Punishment: Report on Criminal Sentencing. New York: McGraw-Hill.

DIAMOND, S. S. and H. ZEISEL (1975) "Sentencing councils: a study of sentencing disparity and its reduction." University of Chicago Law Review 43: 109-149.

EVERSON, G. (1919) "The human element in justice." American Institute of Criminal Law Journal (currently Journal of Criminal Law and Criminology) 10: 90-99.

FRANKEL, M. E. (1973) Criminal Sentences: Law Without Order. New York: Hill & Wang.

GAUDET, F. J. (1949) "The sentencing behavior of the judge," in V. C. Branham and S. V. Kutash (eds.) Encyclopedia of Criminology. New York: Philosophical Library. pp. 449-461.
――― (1946) "The differences between judges in the granting of sentences of probation." Temple Law Quarterly 19: 471-484.
GAYLIN, W. (1974) Partial Justice. New York: Alfred A. Knopf.
GIBSON, J. L. (1980) "Environmental constraints on the behavior of judges: a representational model of judicial decision making." Law and Society Review 14: 343-370.
GLUECK, S. (1927-28) "Principles of a rational penal code." Harvard Law Review 41: 469.
GOTTFREDSON, D. M. (1975) "Prosecution and sentencing decisions," in D. M. Gottfredson (ed.) Decision-making in the Criminal Justice System: Essays and Reviews. Rockville, MD: National Institute of Mental Health.
GOTTFREDSON, M. R. (1979a) "Parole board decisionmaking: a study of disparity reduction and the impact of institutional behavior." Journal of Criminal Law and Criminology 70: 77-88.
――― (1979b) "Parole guidelines and the reduction of sentencing disparity." Journal of Research in Crime and Delinquency 16: 218-231.
GREEN, E. (1964) "Inter- and intra-racial crime relative to sentencing." Journal of Criminal Law, Criminology and Police Science 55: 348-358.
HARRIES, K. D. and R. P. LURA (1974) "The geography of justice: sentencing variations in U.S. judicial districts." Judicature 57: 392-401.
HOGARTH, J. (1971) Sentencing as a Human Process. Toronto: University of Toronto Press.
HOOD, R. and R. SPARKS (1970) Key Issues in Criminology. New York: New World Library.
IRWIN, J. (1970) The Felon. Englewood Cliffs, NJ: Prentice-Hall.
Journal of Criminal Law and Criminology (1952) "The geography of justice." Vol. 43.
LANPHER, H. C. (1945) "Length of sentence and duration of detention of federal prisoners." Federal Probation 9: 13-14.
LOW, P. (1968) "Memorandum on sentencing structure for the federal criminal code." National Commission on Reform of the Federal Criminal Law. Section 3, Disparity.
MARTINSON, R. (1974) "What works? Questions and answers about prison reform." The Public Interest (Spring): 353-384.
McGUIRE, M. F. and A. HOLTZOFF (1940a) "The problem of sentence in criminal law." Boston University Law Review 20: 423-434.
――― (1940b) "The problem of sentencing in the criminal law." Federal Probation 4: 20-25.
MENNINGER, K. A. (1928) "Medicolegal proposals of the American Psychiatric Association." Journal of Criminal Law and Criminology 19: 376.
NAGEL, S. (1963) "Off-the-bench judicial attitudes," in G. Schubert (ed.) Judicial Decision-Making. New York: Free Press.
National Advisory Commission on Criminal Justice Standards and Goals (1973a) Corrections. Washington, DC: Government Printing Office.

——— (1973b) The Courts. Washington, DC: Government Printing Office.

New York Times (1977) Statement by Chief Justice Warren Burger, January 2.

Official Report of the New York State Special Commission on Attica (1972) Attica. New York: Bantam.

Opinions of the Attorney General (California) (1977) Volume 60. Sacramento.

PARTRIDGE, A. and W. E. ELDRIDGE (1974) "The second circuit sentencing study: a report to the judges of the second circuit." Washington, DC: Federal Judicial Center.

President's Commission on Law Enforcement and Administration of Justice (1967) Task Force Report, The Courts. Washington, DC: Government Printing Office.

REID, S. T. (1981) Crime and Criminology (3rd ed.) New York: Holt, Rinehart & Winston.

SCHWARTZ, L. B. (1981) "Options in constructing a sentencing system: sentencing guidelines under legislative or judicial hegemony." Virginia Law Review 67: 680-684.

SELLIN, T. (1935) "Race prejudice in the administration of justice." American Journal of Sociology 41: 212-217.

SEYMOUR, W. N., Jr. (1973) "1972 sentencing study for the southern district of New York." New York State Bar Journal 45: 163-171.

Texas Law Review (1967) "Texas sentencing practices: a statistical study." Vol. 45: 471-503.

THORNBERRY, T. P. (1979) "Sentencing disparities in the juvenile justice system." Journal of Criminal Law and Criminology 70: 164-171.

TIFFANY, L. P. et al. (1975) "A statistical analysis of sentencing in the federal courts: defendants convicted after trial, 1967-1968." Journal of Legal Studies 4: 369-390.

University of Cincinnati Law Review (1977) "The disparate sentencing provisions of Ohio's organized crime statute." Vol. 46: 583-590.

VON HIRSCH, A. (1976) Doing Justice. New York: Hill & Wang.

——— and HANRAHAN, K. J. (1981) "Determinate penalty systems in America: an overview." Crime and Delinquency 27: 289-316.

WALSH, L. E. (1959) "An expression of interest on the part of the Department of Justice, pilot institute on sentencing." Federal Rules Decisions 26.

Washington Law Review (1973) "Discretion in felony sentencing—a study of influencing factors." Vol. 84: 857-889.

WILKINS, L. T. et al. (1978) "Sentencing guidelines: structuring judicial discretion." Report on the Feasibility Study. Washington, DC: U.S. Department of Justice.

Chapter 2

CRIMINAL CODE REVISION AND
THE ISSUE OF DISPARITY

KATHLEEN J. HANRAHAN
ALEXANDER GREER

The sentencing of adult felons in the United States has undergone significant change in the past decade. Indeterminate sentencing, once considered an enlightened approach to dealing with convicted felons, has fallen into disfavor. State after state has reconsidered its sentencing laws and practices, and a fair number have revised them.

That actual change has occurred places the sentencing reform movement in a somewhat exclusive category. The history of criminal justice is littered with crises and calls for reform, but there have been few actual efforts to change in fundamental ways the identified source of the crisis. What set sentencing apart?

Indeterminate sentencing came under attack from most sides in the late 1960s and through the 1970s. The hallmark of indeterminacy is its emphasis on individualized justice: Criminal sentences are tailored to the

AUTHORS' NOTE: The information presented in this chapter was supported by grants 78-Ni-AX-0081/2 from the National Institute of Justice of the United States Department of Justice. Portions of this chapter are based on "A Taxonomy of Determinate Penalty Systems," a chapter written for the final report of the Strategies for Determinate Sentencing Project by Kathleen J. Hanrahan and Andrew von Hirsch. Points of view expressed are those of the authors and do not necessarily represent the official position or policy of the funding agency.

specific case at hand. The goal is the rehabilitation of the offender; sentences are designed to reduce the individual's propensity for further crime.

Criticisms of indeterminacy can be grouped into two broad categories. One addresses the choice of rehabilitation as the primary aim of the sentencing system. Critics first asked whether it was possible to rehabilitate and found little empirical support for earlier optimism (e.g., Lipton et al., 1975; Greenberg, 1977). They then asked whether sentencing decisions should be based on rehabilitative considerations—in effect, on whether it appears likely that the offender will continue to commit crimes—even if it were possible to make those judgments accurately. There is now general agreement that the goal of rehabilitation should be replaced. The debate as to what should replace it continues, but there is some consensus that dispositions are better based on matters such as the nature of the offense rather than guesses about rehabilitation (e.g., Von Hirsch, 1976; Fogel, 1975; Frankel, 1973).

The second type of criticism concerns the procedures used to determine sentence type and length. In order to rehabilitate, it had been assumed, decisionmakers had to be able to observe an offender's progress and needed the discretion to adjust the disposition accordingly. Indeterminacy, with its emphasis on individualized sentences, had vested extensive discretion in all officials of the sentencing process—judges, other court personnel, correction officials, and parole boards. Critics claimed, however, that the outcome of all this discretion was not individualized justice; it was generalized injustice (see Davis, 1971; American Friends, 1971; Frankel, 1973; Harris, 1975).

Perhaps the most striking effect attributed to widespread discretion is equally widespread disparity in criminal sentences. Disparity has been variously defined (Gottfredson and Wilkins, 1978; Barry and Greer, 1981), but at base it refers to differences in dispositions that cannot be explained by relevant characteristics of the offense or the offender.

Parity in sentencing—the idea that offenders convicted of similar crimes should receive roughly the same punishment—has universal appeal. It has been pointed out that even philosophically or politically diverse groups can agree that deviations from some sentencing norm are undesirable. This agreement, of course, contains seeds of future disagreement, namely, the implicit notions about the nature of the problem and its solutions. Those aligned at the conservative end of the continuum focus on deviations that result in leniency. Those at the liberal end of the scale tend to see only the unusually harsh penalties (Wilson, 1977).[1] But all can agree that a sentencing system that permits such disparity is in need of reform.

The proposals in the literature for reform of the sentencing process are varied. They range from relatively minor adjustments, such as appellate review of sentences, to wholesale redesign of the sentencing structure (see Von Hirsch, 1976; Fogel, 1975; Frankel, 1973; Harris, 1975; American Friends, 1971; Stanley, 1976). The latter proposals urge abolition of indeterminate sentencing and creation of determinate sentencing structures. While the models for determinacy vary, they have a common purpose: to reduce and structure the amount of discretion available to decisionmakers in the sentencing process.

The sentencing reforms that have been implemented are equally varied, but they too share a focus on reduced discretion. The concern with disparity that is so evident in the literature is also well represented in the new laws and sentencing rules themselves. In Alaska, for example, the new criminal code emphasizes "the elimination of unjustified disparity . . . and the attainment of reasonable uniformity in sentences."[2] In California the new sentencing legislation identifies the purpose of imprisonment as punishment and states:

> This purpose is best served by terms proportionate to the seriousness of the offense with provision for uniformity in the sentences of offenders committing the same offense under similar circumstances.[3]

Similar statements can be found in the enabling legislation for parole release guidelines of other jurisdictions and in the sentencing and parole rules themselves.[4]

Given this situation—that the new sentencing codes or practices are intended to increase or to help ensure more evenhandedness in sentencing[5]—what features do they contain that are intended to do so? This chapter will examine some of the new laws and administrative rules and describe in preliminary fashion how lawmakers have addressed the issue and what structures they have designed to control sentencing discretion.

There are several components of the legal structure surrounding sentencing that can affect the parity of dispositions. Clearly, the sentencing provisions themselves are central, but there are provisions that operate before and after sentencing that are relevant to disparity. In the sections that follow we will sketch out these features, discuss their role in controlling disparity, and describe the approaches taken in some states to deal with their influences on disparity.

SOURCES OF INFORMATION

Much of the information on state sentencing practices is drawn from a national survey of sentencing and parole reform conducted during 1979 and 1980. The survey was part of a larger study designed to examine determinate sentencing, and thus it focused on those sentencing reforms that were intended to result in more determinate sentencing practices.

The definition of determinacy developed for the study was intentionally inclusive. The definition itself is explained at length elsewhere (see Final Report, forthcoming: Ch. 1); here we need repeat only the central themes. Our approach was to identify the central features of indeterminacy and then to inquire how determinate sentencing schemes proposed to modify those features.

Indeterminate sentencing has two principal characteristics. First, actual length of sentence is decided well into the sentence; imprisoned offenders ordinarily do not know the duration of the sentence until very late in the term. Second and more fundamentally, no rules or standards guide the sentencing decision; courts and parole boards have nearly total discretion in imposing sentences. M. Kay Harris (1975: 297) describes the traditional parole decisionmaking process as follows:

> The overall picture . . . [has been] one of systems unguided by rules, policy statements, or explicit decision-making criteria, unbounded by requirements for statements of findings or reasons, . . . devoid of procedural safeguards [and] unchecked by administrative review.

Accordingly, the definition of determinacy used throughout this study identified two central features: (1) explicit and reasonably detailed standards designed to govern imposition of felony sentences; and (2) where the standards prescribe imprisonment, an early decision about duration of the term. Both features are necessary. In this chapter, however, we will be concerned primarily with the first feature—the standards—and how well they control sentencing discretion.

Before turning to the results of the survey, it is important to point out what this definition of determinacy does *not* require. It does not presuppose any particular format for the sentencing standards; the standards can be presented in words, charts, or grids—any format—as long as they are reasonably specific. The definition is also silent with respect to the agency that develops the standards and the agency that applies them. Any agency—the legislature, the judiciary, a new body such as a sentencing commission, the parole board, or some combination of agencies—may design the standards. Similarly, the rules may be applied in individual cases by the courts or by the parole board.

Thus, under this definition, the standards that were developed by the Oregon Advisory Commission on Prison Terms and Parole Standards to govern length of imprisonment, and that are applied by the parole board shortly after the prisoner is admitted, qualify as determinate.[6] Conversely, the sentencing legislation passed in Maine[7] and widely heralded as determinate sentencing, does not. Maine's new law failed to provide any standards to govern the sentencing decision. Instead, the law established traditional statutory maximum terms for each felony class and permits the court to select any term within that broad range.

In each state we contacted the following offices, requested information on any proposed or enacted sentencing reform, and specifically inquired about presumptive or determinate sentencing, sentencing guidelines, sentencing commissions, and parole guidelines: the legislative research office, the office of the administrator of the courts, the chief justice, and the parole board. This information was augmented in two ways. The first was an ongoing literature search. The second was contact with individuals involved either in a particular state's reform or with other studies of sentencing change.

In all, 20 jurisdictions reported sentencing reform that either met our definitional requirements to some degree or were clearly intended to increase determinacy.[8] Several additional states reported that sentencing reform was being studied or receiving serious consideration.[9]

The approaches taken by legislators and other rule-makers in these jurisidictions to control discretion and reduce disparity will be described throughout this chapter. Two qualifications are in order. The first is an obvious point: Sentencing laws and rules evolve over time. What we are describing in most instances is the "original" reform; most have undergone subsequent revision. Second, and more importantly, we are looking at the structure or design of the new sentencing codes, not their actual operation. We are examining statutes and rules as they are written. Actual sentencing practices depend on more than the written law. The interpretation of officials in the sentencing system, both formal and informal, levels of funding, local traditions, political realities, and a host of other factors all influence the operation of the system.

STATEMENT OF RATIONALE

The portions of the new codes or rules that are designed to control discretion and reduce disparity are found in the sentencing provisions themselves. But criminal codes function as a whole, and there are antecedent provisions—those that establish the larger structural contours of the sentencing system—that bear on the success of the sentencing model for reducing disparity. Chief among them is the decision about the aim or aims of the system.

This selection of penal goals does not much concern the mechanics of sentencing, the definitional elements of offenses, or the other detailed prescriptions for operating the criminal law. The choice of penal philosophies is, instead, a policy decision; it concerns what the code is intended to accomplish through its sentencing rules.

Traditionally, four aims of sentencing have been recognized: deterrence, incapacitation, rehabilitation, and desert.[10] Rehabilitation, as mentioned earlier, is the goal most closely associated with indeterminate sentencing, and it has been strongly criticized. Proponents of determinate sentencing tend to emphasize penal philosophies that focus on the offense rather than the offender.

This tendency in the literature for particular penal philosophies to be associated with particular sentencing structures is more than historical accident but less than causally determined. While some aims (e.g., desert) seem more consistent than others with carefully defined rules and standards (because of the nature and availability of relevant information; see Von Hirsch and Hanrahan, 1979: ch. 4), it is not the case that determinacy or more general efforts to structure discretion require or preclude any particular sentencing philosophy. Once a decision to structure the sentencing decision is reached, however, the choice of goals matters a great deal.

A clear, explicit statement of the aim or aims of the system should precede its design. Where there is more than one aim, there should be a rank ordering or some indication of priority. This is necessary because the traditional goals of sentencing are in potential conflict; the best deterrent, for example, may be disproportionate to the seriousness of the offense. Where there is no agreed-upon balance of objectives, there is bound to be confusion in the design of the system.

Disparity, we have noted, is defined as differences in criminal sentences that cannot be accounted for by relevant offense or offender characteristics. But what factors are relevant to the sentencing process—the likelihood that the offender will repeat the offense? the seriousness of the crime? gender? addiction? prior record? When no goal is established for the sentencing system, any characteristic within fairly broad constitutional and ethical limits can be used. The choice of penal philosophies provides guidance here. It focuses attention on relevant categories of factors and excludes others. The aim establishes the boundaries of inquiry.

Given all the debate about the purposes of sentencing and the pivotal role of the decision about aims, how have the new sentencing systems addressed the issue? Some have explicitly stated the purposes of the new sentencing rules. The California determinate sentencing law, for example, states: "The purpose of imprisonment for crime is punishment."[11] The enabling legislation for the Oregon parole guidelines also contains a statement of purpose; it directs that the parole standards be designed to achieve the following objectives:

(a) Punishment which is commensurate with the seriousness of the prisoner's criminal conduct; and (b) to the extent not inconsistent with paragraph (a) . . . the deterrence of criminal conduct and the protection of the public from further crimes by the defendant.[12]

Explicit choices have been made in some other jurisdictions as well—sometimes in the statutes, sometimes in the rules created by a parole board or sentencing commission. There is variety in the aims selected; often, as in Oregon and California, they look primarily to the offense, but some, like Georgia's parole statute, stress incapacitation.[13]

In some of the jurisdictions that reported sentencing reforms, the new laws or rules do not include a statement of aim. There is simply no statement in the statutes or rules about the purposes the new provisions are to achieve. Elsewhere, designers of the new code have failed to make a choice; all the traditional aims are listed.[14]

The lawmakers' failure to make a choice—or at the very least, to state a choice—is understandable. The aims of felony sentencing are controversial, emotionally charged issues. Few hard and fast data can be brought to bear on these questions. Further, these decisions can have political consequences for those involved (see Von Hirsch and Hanrahan, 1979: ch. 9). Unfortunately, as we shall see, there are also practical consequences for the sentencing system.

THE SENTENCING PROVISIONS

A central assumption in the sentencing literature is that unregulated discretion is the principal cause of disparity—that the leeway granted courts and parole boards under indeterminate sentencing systems could only result in disparate decisions. The move toward determinacy is in large part simply a move toward more specificity in sentencing provisions.

The newly enacted sentencing provisions attest to the variety of approaches to structuring discretion and the complexity of the task. As noted earlier, any of a number of agencies can develop the standards characteristic of determinate sentencing schemes—the legislature, the judiciary, a specialized body like a sentencing commission, some combination of agencies, or even a parole board. In practice, only a few jurisdictions have selected a sentencing commission or combination approach; legislatively prescribed standards and parole guidelines are the more common approaches.

There is some variation in the scope of the standards, but here too some common approaches emerge. There are essentially three aspects of the sentencing decision: (1) whether or not to incarcerate the offender; (2) the severity of nonincarcerative dispositions if the decision is other than incarceration; and (3) the duration of confinement if the decision is to incarcerate. Disparity can occur at any of these decision points; control of disparity would require that the sentencing provisions regulate each of these decisions. In practice, such comprehensive regulation is rare.

The sentencing reforms enacted in the majority of states concern only duration of imprisonment. Obviously, this is true of parole guidelines; parole boards typically have no jurisdiction over the decision to incarcerate or the fate of nonincarcerated felons. It is also true of nearly all the legislatively prescribed sentencing standards. Nonincarcerative sentences have largely been ignored. And, although disparity is most evident and serious when some offenders receive probation while other similarly situated offenders are imprisoned, there have been few attempts to regulate systematically the decision to incarcerate.[15]

The sentencing guidelines developed by the Minnesota Sentencing Commission are one exception (Minnesota, 1980). There, as directed by the enabling legislation, the commission has developed standards to govern both the decision to imprison and the duration of imprisonment. The commission's guidelines follow a conventional matrix format: one axis of the sentencing grid is an offense seriousness score, the other a criminal history score. The cells formed at the intersection of these scores contain a presumptive term. The matrix differs from most by also including a roughly diagonal line separating imprisonment cells from those that prescribe a disposition other than imprisonment. A similar grid has been developed in Utah, and one has been proposed in Pennsylvania.[16]

The remainder of this section will examine the standards that govern duration of imprisonment. There are real differences in the design and format of the standards. One of the more significant elements, in terms of controlling disparity, is the number of distinct categories of offense or offender that the standards or rules recognize for purposes of punishment. Simply stated, we are referring to the number of felony classes or guideline cells.

There is, of course, no magic number of categories (nor is there any reason to prefer a particular format). It is an obvious point, however, that a sentencing system that seeks to treat similar offenders similarly needs enough classes or cells to create categories that are reasonably homogeneous on relevant factors, be they offense seriousness (the most common) or some other factor. If the standards do not make distinctions that are fine enough to suit their purposes, disparity will result. It is, in fact, built into such a system.

Differences in format aside, the standards in use have certain central features in common. All prescribe a term or a range of terms for categories of offense or offender. In Colorado, for example, the code that was ultimately enacted prescribes a range of 2-4 years for a class 4 felony such as robbery.[17] Similarly, the Minnesota guidelines prescribe a range of 29-31 months for offenders with average criminal history scores (i.e., three points) who have been convicted of a similar offense (Minnesota, 1980). The terminology varies; we will refer to the terms prescribed for the ordinary case as the presumptive disposition. All standards permit decisionmakers to vary from the presumptive term if aggravating or mitigating circumstances are present. And some of the new sentencing schemes permit the imposition of separate additional terms if certain factors are present in the offense.

These three features—presumptive terms, provisions for aggravating and mitigating circumstances, and additional penalty provisions—are the central features of the new codes and rules. They are not, however, the only provisions directly affecting prison dispositions. Sentencing authority is more diffuse; it is shared to some degree with corrections officials and with the agency that administers the parole supervision system. Accordingly, we will also examine the provisions that govern the exercise of these portions of sentencing authority.

PRESUMPTIVE DISPOSITIONS

The standards governing duration of prison terms provide either a specific term or a range of terms within which the decisionmaker selects a specific sentence in the individual case. Specific terms have been created in several of the systems where the legislature prescribed the new sentencing rules—Alaska, California, Indiana, New Mexico, and North Carolina. Specific terms are less common in guideline systems, but two parole boards—Georgia and Oklahoma—have reported the use of specific presumptive terms. The sentencing standards developed elsewhere provide ranges of terms.

The degree to which the ranges reintroduce discretion depends on the width of the ranges. If the new rules are judged by how likely they are to structure discretion, there are some that most observers would agree, even in the absence of an agreed upon standard, will do little to guide discretion or limit the options available to a sentencer. The initial guidelines developed in Oklahoma, for example, merely describe prior practice and consequently provide very broad ranges.[18] Other standards have narrower ranges. The Minnesota guidelines, for example, prescribe very narrow presumptive ranges for the less serious offense categories; the ranges become somewhat broader for the more serious offenses (Minnesota, 1980).

The degree of discretion introduced by using ranges can be limited by rules designed to govern the selection of a term within the range. The Minnesota sentencing guidelines indicate that the midpoint of the range is ordinarily the preferred disposition (Minnesota, 1980). In Oregon, there was some discussion about creating a preferred point within the parole guideline ranges, but no formal action has been taken (Final Report, forthcoming). The majority of jurisdictions that use ranges do not provide any guidance on the matter and thereby fail to structure decisionmakers' discretion.

AGGRAVATING AND MITIGATING CIRCUMSTANCES

The standards in every jurisdiction permit the decisionmaker to vary from the presumptive disposition in a particular case if aggravating or mitigating circumstances are found. In order to determine how much discretion is introduced by provisions of this type, two questions need to be asked: How precise or vague are the rules governing variation from the presumptive term, and how great a deviation from the presumptive term is permitted?

The degree to which the rules clearly identify relevant aggravating and mitigating circumstances has obvious consequences for the control of disparity. Because there are so many possible aggravating and mitigating factors (especially in those jurisdictions that fail to state explicitly the aim of the sentencing system), concern with disparity requires at least an indication of categories of factors or a listing of illustrative factors. Most of the new codes do contain such a list, but a few do not. In New Mexico, for example, the new law provides that the court may depart from the presumptive term "upon a finding . . . of any mitigating or aggravating circumstances surrounding the offense or concerning the offender."[19]

Where there are lists of factors, their specificity is often uneven. Some of the commonly included factors are straightforward and require little explanation: weapon use, for example, or multiple victims. Others require some judgment on the part of the sentencer: unusually sophisticated manner of commission of the offense, for example, or property loss that is more or less than is customary for the offense.[20] The criteria for making these judgments are usually not supplied. Thus, decisionmakers are left to interpret the factors as they see fit.

Few jurisdictions intend the lists to be exhaustive. Usually, nonlisted factors can be used if the "interests of justice" would be served. Occasionally, though, an effort is made to limit the use of nonlisted factors. In Minnesota, for example, the enabling legislation specifically precludes consideration of certain factors such as race, gender, or employment history.[21] Alaska has gone even further. There, if the sentencing judge finds that failure to consider an unlisted factor would result in "manifest injustice," the case may be referred to a three-judge panel for sentencing.[22]

The standards in these two states are exceptions, however. Most jurisdictions' rules leave the application of aggravating and mitigating factors largely to the discretion of the decisionmaker. Further, the levels of proof required to establish the factual existence of a factor are among the least restrictive: a preponderance of evidence, competent evidence, clear and convincing evidence, or a requirement that the factor be "based upon documentation."[23]

The consequence for disparity of lax definition and factual proof requirements depends on the amount of time that can be added or subtracted from the presumptive term. In many jurisdictions, the amount of time at stake is substantial.

As is the case with every feature of the new sentencing standards, the provisions for variation from the term differ from system to system. One distinction is especially important, however. In some states decisionmakers may set a term outside the presumptive range if aggravating or mitigating circumstances are present. In other jurisdictions, the rules limit the amount of variation.

The former arrangement—that of permitting a decision outside the normally prescribed terms—is common in parole guideline systems and was adopted for the Minnesota sentencing guidelines. It generally permits a decisionmaker to impose *any* disposition within the statutory or judicial maximum and minimum term. Some standards attempt to limit the frequency of departures from the guidelines by requiring or permitting a review of decisions outside the terms. Minnesota's rules go still further; they state that the presumptive sentences are "presumed to be appropriate for every case" and direct the court to use those terms unless the case "involves substantial and compelling circumstances" (Minnesota, 1980)—suggesting strongly that decisions outside the guidelines are to be imposed sparingly.

The other common approach involves provisions that define permissible amounts of variation from the presumptive terms. The Oregon parole rules, for example, provide a graduated approach. Ordinarily, the term-setting decision is made by a panel of two board members, and the standards specify the permissible amount of variation for aggravating and mitigating circumstances. The panel may recommend a greater departure from the presumptive term and refer the case to the full board (three members) for decision. The rules permit the full board more leeway—approximately twice that allowed the panel. The rules authorize still greater departure if four of the five board members concur.[24] The net result is a wide range of dispositions.

Other states permit similarly wide variation. The New Mexico statute permits variation of up to one-third of the presumptive term. Alaska's provisions effectively create a range bounded by the maximum term for the felony class, with a minimum created by excusing all or one-half of the presumptive term. The range for a class B felony (e.g., first degree burglary) thus becomes zero to ten years with a four-year presumptive term. Similarly wide leeway for varying the term is found in the Indiana and Oklahoma standards.[25]

Provisions for aggravation and mitigation have the potential to reintroduce substantial amounts of discretion, and thus have potential consequences for disparity. By and large, the provisions now in effect have not been drafted with the requisite care. Too often, the definitions of factors are imprecise, levels of proof are low, and the amount of time at issue is substantial. Whether disparate decisions result depends on how these provisions are applied, but in many jurisdictions there is little in the rules to ensure evenhanded application.

ADDITIONAL PENALTY PROVISIONS

Some of the new sentencing systems have provisions that increase the presumptive term by a specific amount if certain facts are found true. Provisions of this type are distinct from those governing the use of aggravating factors, but they raise similar issues: How well regulated is the imposition of terms and how much do such provisions affect the disposition?

Their effect on sentence—in answer to the second question—is generally substantial. In California, for example, there are enhancement provisions that permit the imposition of an additional one-, two-, or three-year term to the normal disposition if the offense involved arming, weapon use, infliction of great bodily injury, excessive property damage, or prior prison terms.[26] Elsewhere, the additional penalties are more severe.

New Mexico's additional penalty provisions, also called enhancements, range from one to ten years and govern habitual offenders and offenses involving deadly weapons or elderly victims.[27] In Illinois, the new code permits the imposition of "extended terms" where a second felony is involved or where the offense is exceptionally brutal. The extended term ranges are roughly double the presumptive term ranges.[28] North Carolina requires an additional term of 14 years for offenders convicted of repeat felonies involving deadly weapons.[29] Finally, Indiana's new code provides for an additional 30 years for defendants with two prior felony convictions.[30]

The potential severity of these terms makes the standards governing their imposition crucial. With the few exceptions where the imposition of these terms is mandatory, the statutes and rules provide decisionmakers with little guidance in imposing these terms. In California, for example, imposition of the enhancement is discretionary; the court may strike the additional penalty if it sees fit. Similarly, the decision to impose extended terms in Illinois appears discretionary. In Indiana, a recent amendment permits the court to suspend up to 25 years of the 30-year term if the defendant has had a 10-year crime-free period before the instant offense.[31]

So far we have been talking about those exceptional provisions of the new codes that permit a decisionmaker to increase terms. There is one very traditional feature of penal codes that has a bearing on sentence length: the decision to impose consecutive or concurrent terms. Many defendants are convicted of or plead to more than one offense, and this decision, even under more traditional systems, has serious consequences for duration of term.

With very few exceptions (and once again, Minnesota is among them; Minnesota, 1980), this decision has been left unregulated in the new sentencing systems.[32] The statutes or rules commonly permit the imposition of consecutive or concurrent terms at the discretion of the court. Occasionally there are some rules for calculating duration of sentence if consecutive terms are imposed,[33] but there are no rules, standards, or even presumptions to guide the court when making this decision. The consequences for disparity are obvious.

INSTITUTIONAL MISCONDUCT AND SENTENCE LENGTH

Under these new sentencing schemes, the term set by the court or the parole board largely determines the actual duration of imprisonment. However, every jurisdiction has some provision for modifying the length of the prison term on account of prisoner conduct. The most straightforward are good time credits. Typically, prisoners who refrain from rule infractions earn a reduction of their term by some fraction.[34] In jurisdictions where the duration of imprisonment is established according to parole standards, comparable provisions permit the board to extend the term by tacking on time to the presumptive release date.

The significance of parole procedures is immediately apparent: the penalty for misconduct is additional time in prison. The role of good time credits is often obscured by their traditional (and more indirect) role. Under indeterminate sentencing systems, good time credits are usually deducted from the maximum term, or less frequently, from a minimum term. But actual release (and thus length of sentence) is determined by the parole decision. Under determinate sentencing systems, good time affects release directly. Once the presumptive term has been set, it is the accumulation and/or forfeiture of good time credits that determines the actual date of release.

The amount of time at stake is often substantial. Good time credits normally reduce the court-established term by one-third, one-half, or less frequently, one-fourth. Parole rules are less specific about the time available to the board, but it too is substantial. Once again, the effects of disparate decisionmaking can be pronounced. But concern with disparity is less evident here than with the more central features of the new sentencing systems.

Of the new codes surveyed, only three—California, Colorado, and Minnesota—include vesting provisions.[35] Under these provisions some portion of previously earned good time credits accrues permanently and the credits are not subject to forfeiture for infractions committed there- after. Colorado's determinate sentencing law, for example, provides that prisoners may earn roughly one day of credit (or sentence remission) for each day served. Credits vest quarterly; no more than 45 days good time may be forfeited during any one quarter.[36] In the absence of vesting provisions (that is, in most jurisdictions), all earned credits are at least theoretically available for forfeiture.

In some of these states there are statutory restrictions on the operation of good time, such as limiting good time forfeiture to "serious" infrac- tions. Even such minimal restrictions are, however, unusual. More often the statutes merely set a rate at which good time may be earned and provide that any or all credits may be forfeited for any infraction of the rules. Many statutes also permit the restoration of previously revoked credits at the discretion of correction officials.

The Supreme Court reviewed good time forfeiture proceedings and established minimum procedural and evidentiary requirements (Wolff v. McDonnell, 1974). The protections afforded by the ruling are marginal, particularly so today, because of the increased significance of these credits in determinate sentencing systems. By and large, few states have attempted to structure the discretion available to officials of departments of correc- tions. The result is that these officials have control over a substantial portion of the term of imprisonment.

In those jurisdictions where the duration of confinement is governed by parole release standards, extensions of terms for misconduct are no more likely to be governed by carefully articulated standards. Some parole boards—those of New York and Oklahoma, for example—reported no rules for extending terms. Instead, institutional infractions can lead to parole denial; the prisoner is then rescheduled for a hearing and a new date is set. Elsewhere, boards have developed some rudimentary rules, such as relying on department of corrections findings that an infraction occurred and setting extensions on a case-by-case basis without the aid of rules.[37]

There are, thankfully, two exceptions to this bleak review of parole rules. The parole standards developed by the Oregon and the federal parole boards include efforts to structure this decision. The federal rules establish a schedule of penalties for infractions. The board, however, relies on the factual findings of the department of correction's disciplinary committee; there is no independent determination of guilt or of the seriousness of the infraction. The parole rules developed in Oregon also contain a schedule of penalties for infraction, albeit a less precise schedule, and the board is required to hold a hearing to determine independently the seriousness of the infraction.[38] While there are shortcomings in each approach, these measures at least begin to respond to the issues raised by extending terms because of infractions.

PAROLE SUPERVISION

Every jurisdiction that revised its sentencing or parole practices retained postrelease supervision and with it the potential for revocation and reimprisonment. Regardless of the stated intention of the drafters of the code for continuing parole supervision (e.g., reintegration of the offender or provision of services), there can be no doubt that parole supervision is part of the criminal penalty. As such, it increases the duration of the sentence as a whole and, if parole is revoked, the duration of imprisonment as well. Therefore, we need to examine this final feature of the criminal penalty to see to what extent the provisions attend to the issue of disparity.

There are three features of parole supervision that require regulation: the duration (and conditions) of supervision; the decision to revoke parole; and the duration of reimprisonment at revocation. With respect to length of supervision and reimprisonment at revocation, a few jurisdictions sought to limit these durations. The original determinate sentencing law in California provided one-year supervision terms for most offenders and limited the penalty at revocation to six months; later, those terms were increased.[39] In Colorado, the new law also limited supervision to one year for most offenders and revocation to six months.[40] In North Carolina, supervision is limited even further: The duration of supervision and any penalty at revocation cannot exceed ninety days.[41]

Elsewhere, there is little evidence that attention was given to the issue of duration of supervision. Nor is there evidence of much concern with procedural issues. The decisionmaking that surrounds supervision, almost without exception, remains discretionary. Failure to attend to these issues creates the potential for more disparity. Actual practice will reveal the extent to which these provisions contribute to the problem.

POSTSENTENCING PROVISIONS

The degree to which sentencing standards can alleviate disparity depends ultimately on both the quality of the standards and the extent to which they are actually implemented. Much of this chapter has concerned the first issue. Implementation is equally important, but information about it, as we discuss in the next section, is still largely lacking. What we intend to examine here are those provisions designed to monitor use of the standards.

Very broadly, a monitoring system has two functions. From the viewpoint of the defendant, more significant is the provision for sentencing review—overseeing the application of the standards to individual cases. From a system perspective, equally important is some mechanism for reviewing and fine-tuning the standards over time.

The possibility of misapplication of the standards in individual cases is most conspicuous when the sentencing decision departs from the ordinary—when additional penalties are imposed, for example, or when a decision outside the guidelines is made. Other errors—those where the exceptional provisions should have been invoked but were not—are less easily detected (Zimmerman, 1981).

Routine review provisions—appellate review of sentences, internal review of parole decisions—are useful and are becoming more common.[42] Review provisions that are dependent on the imposition of out-of-the-ordinary sentences (e.g., decisions set outside guideline ranges) are less useful because they can identify only the first type of error. A better approach is to make sentencing review possible in all cases.

This approach raises an issue that has long plagued proponents of sentencing review—whether the state should be authorized to initiate review proceedings. It has been argued that prosecutorial appeal of sentences is unconstitutional, and that it too drastically increases the power of the prosecutor and leaves defendants open to the vindictive exercise of that power (see Dunsky, 1978).

Many of the arguments against giving the state the authority to appeal were made with indeterminate sentencing in mind. Under more determinate schemes, the objections are less compelling. As a practical matter, appeal of a sentence by the state is likely to result only in increased penalties, and the abuse of authority would be serious. In a sentencing system in which the reduction of disparity is a stated goal, however, too lenient dispositions as well as excessive sentences threaten the success of the system.

The California determinate sentencing law contains a provision that sidesteps this issue while providing the benefits of comprehensive review. The law establishes an administrative review of sentencing decisions that does not require the motion of either the defendant or the state:

> In all cases the Community Release Board shall, not later than one
> year after the commencement of the term of imprisonment, review

the sentence and shall by motion recommend that the court recall the sentence and commitment previously ordered and resentence the defendant . . . if the Board determines the sentence is disaprate.[43]

The scope of review is comprehensive; the statute specifically directs the Community Release Board to examine the decision to imprison as well as the duration of imprisonment.

This review provision has the obvious advantage of being automatic. All sentences are reviewed, and neither the state nor the defendant need take any action. The principal shortcoming is the lack of enforcement authority; the Community Release Board may merely "recommend," not require, that the sentencing court recall the case for resentencing. The court in its discretion decides whether or not to resentence.

Defendants in California are not without recourse. The new code includes the traditional appellate review provisions allowing defendants to appeal a sentence. Less clear from the statute is prosecutorial authority to appeal, but recent case law suggests that the state has that right.[44]

The California determinate sentencing law, by providing both automatic review and traditional appellate review, has the most comprehensive approach to sentencing review. As discussed elsewhere in this text, however, California's approach is far from problem-free (see chs. 6 and 8, this volume). The principal difficulty has been creating a workable definition of disparity. That California is experiencing difficulties suggests how formidable the task of ensuring evenhanded application of the sentencing standards becomes in jurisdictions where review provisions exist in only rudimentary form.

The second type of monitoring activity is addressed to the standards themselves, to the adjustment and revision of the sentencing rules in light of accumulating experience with their application and with changes in the environment. This task is apt to be less cumbersome where the standards are applied by a small group of decisionmakers in frequent contact with the standard drafters (as is typically the case with parole release standards) or where the standard-setting body is a specialized agency (as is the case with sentencing commissions or most parole boards). In fact, monitoring procedures are relatively common among sentencing commissions and parole guidelines (see Von Hirsch and Hanrahan, 1979: ch. 9).

Legislatures are less well suited to this task. The responsibility for implementing legislatively prescribed standards is held by a judiciary whose members are geographically dispersed. Channels for alerting the legislature to problems with the standards tend to be only poorly developed. A few legislatures apparently recognized the need for ongoing review of the standards and created special committees to oversee the system or delegated that responsibility to existing bodies. In Illinois, for example, the legislature created a Criminal Sentencing Commission with fairly broad oversight authority. Similar provisions can be found in a few other states.[45] It remains to be seen whether these arrangements are adequate to the task.

CONCLUSION

Throughout this discussion we have been looking at the new rules and statutes as they are written. We noted earlier that the actual operation of these systems is bound to be very different from the written laws. To ask how well these new systems actually limit discretion or reduce disparity is a question of a different order, one that can be answered only after empirical study of the new systems.

Some studies of this type have been undertaken (e.g., Final Report, forthcoming and Sparks et al., n.d.), but they are recent and few. In the absence of empirical information, there has been speculation on the likely outcome of sentencing reform. Quite a bit is pessimistic—that system inertia and pressures to operate "business as usual" will reduce the impact of the reform, and that prosecutors in particular will undermine the reform effort (see Altschuler, 1978). Others are cautiously optimistic and point to the variation in the approaches that have been taken to increase determinacy (Von Hirsch and Hanrahan, 1981). As members of the second category, we will conclude this chapter with some observations or speculation about the likely impact of determinate sentencing reforms on discretion.

Returning again to the laws as they have been written, it is obvious that there is tremendous variation in the quality of the standards produced to date. We have outlined the key features that the new codes or rules should address if sentencing decisions are to be made more equitable. The new codes differ in how many of these areas have been addressed and in how well the rules do so.

Our review of approaches to determinate sentencing suggests some factors that might help explain the variation. It seems to matter which agency develops the standards. Certainly any agency can serve as the standard-setter, but some are better suited to the task than others.

Legislatures, it has been argued,[46] are particularly ill equipped for the task of defining sufficiently detailed rules and establishing penalty levels.

Legislatures are inexperienced in establishing actual sentence rules and lengths, having left that previously to courts and parole boards. Their work, moreover, takes place in a highly political environment where sentencing is but one of many pressing issues. Smaller, more insulated bodies, such as sentencing commissions and parole boards, seem better located and better suited through experience to the task. They have or can acquire experience with drafting detailed penalty standards. And, as noted earlier, smaller, more specialized bodies can more readily monitor and refine the sentencing standards. With some exceptions, the survey findings lend support to these notions.

There is a second, related criterion for judging the new rules and standards: comprehensiveness. We have taken a broad view of sentencing that includes the decisions of corrections personnel as well as those of judges and prosecutors. It matters, in this view, whether sufficient attention has been given to the decisionmaking systems of good time and parole supervision. In practice, only the legislature has authority over all the components of the sentencing system.[47] This is not to say the legislature should set the standards. It is to suggest, rather, that the legislature can be used to establish the framework and to delegate authority for the reform. This is the approach taken in states where there has been more success with the sentencing reform.[48]

The success of any of these systems will depend on implementation. It is clear that the quality of the standards will affect their use. It is also likely to matter whether those who will apply the standards have had a hand in their creation and to what degree this group is centralized.

Involving the decisionmakers in the standard drafting process should help insure that the standards reflect the realities of sentencing and the problems faced by decisionmakers. There is also a tendency for those who contribute to a set of rules to express their stake in those rules by compliance. Centralization of decisionmakers—or the opportunity for fairly regular contact—makes it more likely that ambiguities and gaps in the standards will be recognized and remedied.

Empirical studies will discover which organizational, political, and social factors contribute to the success of sentencing reform and, importantly, how those factors interact. Whether and the degree to which the determinate sentencing movement reduces disparity is a question that will require a lengthy period of study in a variety of jurisdictions. The issues are complex, and knowledge gained in one jurisdiction will not be directly applicable to the next. Evaluations of the new sentencing approaches are now being conducted. It is our hope that the findings will inform the process of change.

NOTES

1. See also the discussion of convergences of opinion among groups involved in California's law reform in Messinger and Johnson (1978).
2. Alaska Statutes, Title 12, Section 12.55.005.
3. California Penal Code, Section 1170 (a)(1).
4. See, for example, Florida Administrative Code, chs. 23-19.
5. We do not mean to suggest that concern with unregulated discretion and the resulting disparity are the only factors that account for the recent changes in sentencing. When more is known, doubtless we will learn that factors such as fear of crime, widespread disillusionment with social programs, economic conditions, and other matters were partly responsible. But the evidence now available suggests that concern with fairness, with reducing inequity in dispositions, has played a part.
6. Oregon Revised Statues, ch. 144 and Oregon Administrative Rules, ch. 254; and see Chapter 4, this volume, for an overview.
7. Maine Revised Statutes, Title 17-A, chs. 47-53.
8. Alaska, Arizona, California, Colorado, Connecticut, Illinois, Indiana, Maine, New Jersey, New Mexico, North Carolina (legislative approaches); Florida, Georgia, New York, Oklahoma, Oregon, Washington (the federal parole system); Minnesota, Pennsylvania (sentencing commission standards); and Utah (standards developed through the joint efforts of the parole board, judiciary, and the department of corrections). A description of these systems is contained in the appendix to the Final Report (forthcoming).
9. For example, Hawaii, Kansas, Montana, Nebraska, Washington, and Wyoming reported that sentencing reform was being studied. Still other states were developing sentencing guidelines. For a description, see Sparks et al. (n.d.).
10. There is a vast literature in this area; for an overview see Stanley (1976: ch. 2).
11. California Penal Code, Section 1170(a)(1).
12. Oregon Revised Statutes, Sections 144.780(2)(a),(b)(A),(B).
13. Georgia Statutes, Section 77-512.
14. See, for example, North Carolina Statutes, Section 15A-1340.3.
15. We should note that nearly all jurisdictions have some mandatory imprisonment provisions. Typically they require a prison sentence for specific and serious offenses such as murder, or for certain categories of offenders such as repeat felons. Provisions of this type do limit the number and type of cases in which there is a decision about imprisonment to be made, but they provide no guidance on how the discretion to imprison should be exercised in cases where there is a decision to be made.
16. Utah Guidelines (unpublished, on file at Rutgers University, School of Criminal Justice); the proposed Pennsylvania guidelines were published in the Pennsylvania Bulletin, January 24, 1981. The proposed guidelines were not adopted by the legislature; they have since been revised. The revised guidelines—which are expected to be adopted—no longer contain standards governing the decision to imprison (see Kramer et al., 1982).
17. Colorado Revised Statutes, Section 18-1-409.5.
18. Oklahoma Parole Guidelines (unpublished, copy on file at Rutgers University, School of Criminal Justice).

19. New Mexico Statutes, Section 31-18-15.

20. For an example of lists of aggravating and mitigation factors, see Indiana Penal Code, Section 1005-3-3.1.

21. See Minnesota Statutes, ch. 244, Appendix Section II(D).

22. Alaska Statutes, Section 12.55.165.

23. See, for example, Oregon Administrative Rules, 254-30-033; Alaska Statutes, Section 12.55.155; and Florida Statutes, Section 947.172(2).

24. Oregon Administrative Rules, 254-30-033.

25. Alaska Revised Statutes, Section 12.55.125; Indiana Penal Code, Section 35-50-2-3 to -7.

26. California Penal Code, Section 12022, 12022.5, 12022.6, 12022.7, and 667.5.

27. New Mexico Statutes, Section 31-18-16 through 31-18-19.

28. Illinois Statutes, Section 1005-5-3.2B.

29. North Carolina Statutes, Section 15A-1340.5.

30. Indiana Penal Code, Section 35-50-2-8.

31. Indiana Penal Code, Section 35-50-2-8, as amended by S.B. 277 (1980).

32. Pennsylvania's 1981 proposed guidelines contained detailed rules; the 1982 version of the guidelines does not (see Kramer et al., 1982).

33. See, for example, California Penal Code, Section 1170.1(a); or Oregon Administrative Rules, 254-30-032(7).

34. We are discussing credits awarded for good conduct. Some jurisdictions award additional credit for program participation, e.g., Colorado Revised Statutes, Section 17-22.5-102; or California Penal Code, Section 2931(c). In general, these credits involve less time and are more likely to be vested.

We are also discussing only those measures that affect the quantity of time served. Forst (forthcoming) has pointed out that corrections officials also have at their disposal disciplinary measures that affect the quality of time served, e.g., assignment or transfer to particular institutions, security classification within an institution, or program eligibility.

35. California Penal Code, Section 2932(a); Colorado Revised Statutes, Section 17-22.5-101; Minnesota Statutes, Section 244.04.

36. Colorado Revised Statutes, Section 17-22.5-101.

37. See, for example, the rules developed by the Florida Parole Commission, Florida Administrative Rules, 23-16.01(17).

38. 28 C.F.R., Section 2.34; Oregon Administrative Rules 254-30-055.

39. California Penal Code, Section 3000(a)(b);

40. Colorado Revised Statutes, Section 18-1-105.

41. North Carolina Statutes, Section 15A-1380.2.

42. See, for example, Alaska Statutes, Section 12.55.088; California Penal Code, Section 1237; or Minnesota Statutes, Section 254; and see the discussion in Chapter 9, this volume.

43. California Penal Code, Section 1237.

44. Under Section 1238(a)(6) of the California Penal Code, the state can appeal "a finding reducing . . . the punishment imposed." The decision in *People v. Broady* (1953) held that there was no appeal of sentences by the state. However, in 1980 it was held that the court's failure to enhance a sentence because of the defendant's prior record was contrary to the mandate of the legislature, and therefore the state was allowed to appeal under Section 1238(a)(6) of the code.

45. See Chapters 6 and 8, this volume.

45. Illinois Statutes, Section 1005-5-4.2; and see California Penal Code, Section 1170.4.

46. Much of this discussion is taken from Von Hirsch and Hanrahan (1979: ch. 9); see also Singer (1979: ch. 4).

47. More practically still, the legislature determines appropriations; the success of these efforts depends in part on adequate funding.

48. We are speaking here of states like Oregon and Minnesota. The experience in Pennsylvania, described in the paper by Kramer et al., demonstrates that this approach does not guarantee success.

CASES

PEOPLE v. BROADY (1953) 262 P.2d 669, 170 C.A.2d 901
WOLFF v. McDONNELL (1974) 418 U.S. 539

REFERENCES

ALSCHULER, A. W. (1978) "Sentencing reform and prosecutorial power: a critique of recent proposals for 'fixed' and 'presumptive sentencing.'" University of Pennsylvania Law Review 126(2): 550-577.

American Friends Service Committee (1971) Struggle for Justice: A Report on Crime and Punishment in America. New York: Hill & Wang.

BARRY, D. M. and A. GREER (1981) "Sentencing versus prosecutorial discretion: the application of a new disparity measure." Journal of Research in Crime and Delinquency 18(2): 254-272.

DAVIS, K. C. (1971) Discretionary Justice: A Preliminary Inquiry. Chicago: University of Illinois Press.

DUNSKY, G. P. (1978) "The constitutionality of increasing sentences on appellate review." Journal of Criminal Law and Criminology 69(1): 19-39.

Final Report of the Project on Strategies for Determinate Sentencing (forthcoming) Washington, DC: National Institute of Justice.

FOGEL, D. (1975) We Are the Living Proof: The Justice Model for Corrections. Cincinnati: W. H. Anderson.

FORST, M. L. (forthcoming) "Effects of determinate sentencing on prison disciplinary procedures and inmate misconduct," in the Final Report of the Project on Strategies for Determinate Sentencing. Washington, DC: National Institute of Justice.

FRANKEL, M. (1973) Criminal Sentences: Law Without Order. New York: Hill & Wang.

GOTTFREDSON, D. M. and L. T. WILKINS (1978) "Parole guidelines and the evolution of paroling policy," in D. M. Gottfredson et al. (eds.) Classification for

Parole Decision Policy. Washington, DC: National Institute of Law Enforcement and Criminal Justice.

GREENBERG, D. F. (1971) "The correctional effects of corrections: a survey of evaluations," in D. F. Greenberg (ed.) Corrections and Punishment. Beverly Hills, CA: Sage.

HARRIS, M. K. (1975) "Disquisition on the need for a new model of criminal sanctioning systems." West Virginia Law Review 77(2): 263-326.

KRAMER, J. H., J. P. McCLOSKEY, and N. J. KURTZ (1982) "Sentencing reform: the Pennsylvania Commission on Sentencing." Presented at the annual meetings of the Academy of Criminal Justice Sciences, Louisville, Kentucky.

LIPTON, D., R. MARTINSON, and J. WILKS (1975) The Effectiveness of Correctional Treatment: A Survey of Treatment Evaluation Studies. New York: Praeger.

MESSINGER, S. L. and P. E. JOHNSON (1978) "California's determinate sentencing statute: history and issues," in Determinate Sentencing: Reform or Regression? Proceedings of the Special Conference on Determinate Sentencing, June 2-3. Washington, DC: Government Printing Office.

Minnesota Sentencing Guidelines (1980) Report to the Legislature. St. Paul.

SINGER, R. G. (1979) Just Deserts: Sentencing Based on Equality and Desert. Cambridge, MA: Ballinger.

SPARKS, R. F., B. A. STECHER, J. S. ALBANESE, P. L. SHELLY, and D. M. BARRY (n.d.) "Stumbling toward justice: some overlooked research and policy questions about statewide sentencing guidelines." Final Report of the Evaluation of Statewide Sentencing Guidelines Project. Washington, DC: National Institute of Justice.

STANLEY, D. T. (1976) Prisoners Among Us. Washington, DC: The Brookings Institution.

VON HIRSCH, A. (1976) Doing Justice: The Choice of Punishments. New York: Hill & Wang.

——— and K. HANRAHAN (1981) "Determinate penalty systems in America: an overview." Crime and Delinquency 17(3): 289-316.

——— (1979) The Question of Parole: Retention, Reform or Abolition? Cambridge, MA: Ballinger.

WILSON, J. Q. (1977) "The political feasibility of punishment," pp. 112-114 in J. B. Cederblom and W. L. Blizek (eds.) Justice and Punishment. Cambridge, MA: Ballinger.

ZIMMERMAN, S. E. (1981) "Developing sentencing guidelines," pp. 71-72 in S. E. Zimmerman and H. D. Miller (eds.) Corrections at the Crossroads: Designing Policy. Beverly Hills, CA: Sage.

Chapter 3

THE POLITICS OF SENTENCING REFORM

LAWRENCE F. TRAVIS III

In 1976 the state of Maine implemented a new sentencing structure wherein the trial judge was empowered to establish a sentence of incarceration at any length not to exceed legislatively set maximum terms.[1] This sentence was to be definite in that discretionary parole release was abolished, as was parole supervision. In the next five years, several other states also changed their sentencing structures in an attempt to achieve more determinacy in criminal penalties (Travis and O'Leary, 1979).

These actions by state legislatures and parole authorities led some observers to identify a national movement toward determinate sentencing. This movement attracted support from diverse and sometimes traditionally antagonistic groups. These advocates of sentencing reform agreed that existing sentencing structures should be overhauled, and they worked together to attain more certainty in criminal sentences. The solidarity of reform advocates was not deeply rooted in philosophy, but rather based on a perceived need for change. The reasons for change and the expectations of reform held by various groups of advocates were not well delineated and discussed.

Thus, while a national movement for sentencing reform could be identified in the middle of the 1970s, reforms adopted in several states were markedly different from one another. One reason for these different outcomes of a national movement is the relative success of "liberal" or "conservative" advocates in specific states (Reckless and Allen, 1979).[2] The growing national movement made reform inevitable in some states, but the specific nature of the reforms in any given state was dependent upon the political acumen of groups seeking changes in criminal sentencing.

It has often been repeated that "politics makes strange bedfellows." This axiom is a particularly accurate depiction of recent reforms in criminal sentencing in several states. Newman (1978: 357) has noted that "critics of parole tend to come from both ends of a liberal-conservative spectrum, and often their arguments are diametrically opposed." In many states the impetus to reform sentencing and parole structures has come from a collation of liberals and conservatives rather than the middle of the political continuum.

With regard to the adoption of a new sentencing structure in Indiana, Clear et al. (1978: 429) reported the emergence of diverse expectations of reform: "In the eyes of one interest group or another, the new Indiana Penal Code is variously expected to increase deterrence, increase humaneness, decrease discrimination, increase prison populations, make penalties more appropriate to the offense, equalize penalties, reduce arbitrariness, increase public protection, increase system efficiency, reduce harshness and reduce leniency."

This chapter will trace the development of disparity in criminal sentencing as a political issue, the emergence of a national reform movement, and the processes of changing a state's sentencing structure and procedures. This discussion will illustrate several difficulties with achieving such basic reform in the justice process and conclude with some observations for would-be reformers.

SENTENCING DISPARITY AS A REFORM ISSUE

In his keynote address to a conference on determinate sentencing held in June 1977, Norval Morris (1978: 2) asked the participants:

Why the sudden interest in sentencing reform? Why the bills, books, papers, conferences and seminars? Is it because we have at last recognized that unjust disparity characterizes the anarchy of unguided, unreviewed judicial sentencing? Surely not. Twenty-five years ago when I first approached the literature on sentencing, that point was clear; that sentencing was a lottery. Of course, recent studies have driven the point home, but we have known about unjust disparity for a long while.

Indeed, the issue of disparity in criminal sentencing was widely known and well documented prior to the rise of a national reform movement.

Two of the most commonly cited illustrations of sentencing disparity come from the Pilot Institute on Sentencing (1966: 231) and from the Highland Park Institute on Sentencing (Remington and Newman, 1962) in the late 1950s and early 1960s. Dawson's (1969) study of sentencing further indicated the importance of factors unrelated to offense severity or criminal record on sentence determination.

One of the stated aims of both the Model Penal Code and the Model Sentencing Act was the regulation of judicial sentencing discretion in order to equalize sentencing dispositions for similar offenders. Appellate courts also engaged in sentencing review, often struggling with legal, but inequitable, dispositions. The involvement of appellate courts in sentence review mirrored the growing activism of courts in other areas previously characterized by the "hands off" doctrine. Several jurisdictions have experimented with sentencing councils where the sentencing judge consults with two or more of his fellow judges before imposing a sentence. These councils operate to reduce sentencing disparity (Newman, 1978: 254). The idea of sentencing councils was endorsed by the National Advisory Commission on Criminal Justice Standards and Goals (1973: 182-183).

Concern over disparate sentences was evident and mounting throughout the two decades preceding the abolition of indeterminate sentencing in Maine and similar actions in other states. With respect to these developments, Morris (1978: 2-3) answered his own question about the "sudden interest" and activity in sentencing disparity. He suggested several explanations but concluded that none was sufficient to understand the rapid growth of the sentencing reform movement.

The lack of a ready explanation does not lessen the importance of the original question. Why the sudden interest? Morris himself noted that the interest was not sudden but had existed for at least 25 years. It is not a question of interest, but one of action which predominates. After years of awareness of the problems with criminal sentencing, years interspersed with periodic calls for reform, the interesting question is how sentencing reform became a priority for public policy decisionmaking in the middle 1970s.

To some degree, the "books, papers, conferences and seminars" on the issue of sentencing reform represented a reaction to legislative proposals. Such legislative actions added impetus to scholarly efforts and in turn were further stimulated by them. The tautological nature of this process, however, renders it an unsatisfactory explanation of the rise to prominence of sentencing reform as an issue of public policy. Rather, the centripetal force of this cycle of proposals leading to treatises leading in turn to more proposals reflects the ascendancy of sentencing reform as an issue for public debate and decision.

The key to actual reform proposals and the legislative, judicial, and administrative implementation of sentencing reforms is to be found in the emergence of sentencing reform as a public policy question in the political arena. Hence, the answer to Morris's original question is found in the development of sentencing disparity as a political issue. It was this development of political support for sentencing revisions that demonstrates the "strange bedfellows" axiom. Perhaps most significant was the development of liberal political support for sentencing reform through existing channels. The formation of loose coalitions among liberal and conservative interest groups provided the needed leverage to see changes enacted.

Smith (1973: 279) has noted that liberal and radical groups are often unwilling or unable to engage in "establishment politics." He wrote:

> Most leftist groups in America have been unwilling or unable to participate this way in establishment politics. They express outrage at the inhumanity and repression of the criminal justice system, but refuse to become involved in correctional politics as a way of dealing with these problems. Instead they engage in armchair discussions of revolution and "increasing political consciousness." . . . The impotence of the American left is not so much a matter of its intrinsic weakness as rather its pervasive unwillingness to unite and gain political power through established channels.

The conservative opposition to discretionary sentencing is traditional and has continued for as long as the indeterminate sentence has existed. The growth of a liberal interest group concerned with increasing equity in criminal sentencing spawned the national movement and supplied support and impetus to reform efforts in specific jurisdictions. "Sentencing reform legislation has commonly been introduced by legislators in response to the criticism of discretionary sentencing generated by justice model proponents" (Greenberg and Humphries, 1980: 223). This "justice model" is a label that has been applied to a wide variety of sentencing reform proposals and forms the philosophical basis of most liberal opinion about sentencing disparity.

THE DEVELOPMENT OF THE JUSTICE MODEL

Between 1970 and 1976, several important works detailing the problems inherent in criminal sentencing and corrections were published. These works were important not simply because of the logical consistency of the arguments, nor because they questioned theretofore unquestioned "truths," but because in some degree they molded public (or political) opinion and laid the groundwork for concrete action. The authors of these documents analyzed then current practice, comparing it to a perceived better state and proposed courses of action to follow in reaching their objectives. These works are the ideological sources of the sentencing reform movement; in Rothman's words, they represent the "conscience" of contemporary reforms.

Struggle For Justice (American Friends, 1971) presented a wide-ranging justice reform strategy. The report attacked the rehabilitative model of corrections, contending that it was ideologically faulty, repressive, and discriminatory. It stated that an unavoidable, perhaps even intended effect of the discretionary power given sentencing and correctional authorities under the rehabilitative ideal was the suppression of political and social minorities (1971: 140-142), and that the acceptance of the treatment ideal was the unreasonable act of an ethnocentric and naive power elite (1971: 46-47).

This action relieved white, middle-class America of guilt and anxiety by entrusting the crime problem to experts. The results of the rehabilitative ideal, however, were identified as institutionalized prejudice and discrimination, increased severity of criminal penalties, overregulation of private behavior by criminal law, and an attempt at "cultural indoctrination" through correctional treatment. The Friends contended for those reasons: "Therefore, discretion is at the core of the problem" (1971: 124).

The solution of the problem was to be found in the systemwide elimination of discretion through the repeal of vaguely worded laws, decriminalization of victimless crimes, police accountability, abolition of money bail and plea bargaining, reduced use of incarceration, and voluntary correctional treatment. When incarceration is required, sentences would be short, fixed by law, and all discretion in sentencing would be eliminated, including parole.

In early 1974, the Citizen's Inquiry on Parole and Criminal Justice published a *Report on New York Parole*.[3] This report was quite similar to that of the American Friends, but while the Friends relied heavily on the California experience, the inquiry confined itself to the justice system in New York. In short, the report criticized parole and indeterminate sentencing as based on a faulty theory, unnecessarily abusive, unfair, cruel, and a camouflage for other actors in the justice system. They too identified the root of the problem in the broad discretionary power of sentencing and parole authorities.

As a long-range goal, the inquiry sought the abolition of parole and indeterminate sentencing. Like the Friends, its members recognized a need to attain massive reforms in the justice process and in American society.[4] First, it would be necessary to reduce reliance on incarceration as a sanction for criminal conduct and to restrict the maximum length of those prison terms which were imposed. The discretion of the police, prosecutors, and correctional officers needed to be controlled and broader social changes initiated to achieve a more just society.

The efforts of the Friends and the Citizen's Inquiry, as well as the works of Davis (1969), Allen (1964), Kittrie (1967), Martinson (1975), Dawson (1969) and others served to identify problems and focus attention on the need for change. Later writers suggested specific types of sentencing reforms. Their works can be dichotomized into those advocating the retention of structured discretion and those advocating confinement of discretion through the curtailment of judicial and parole powers by the imposition of legislative limits (see Davis, 1969).

Structuring Discretion

A major development in parole reform occurred in the spring of 1970. The U.S. Board of Parole and the Research Center of the National Council on Crime and Delinquency were awarded a three-year grant by the National Institute of Law Enforcement and Criminal Justice to study parole decisionmaking (Gottfredson et al., 1974). The product of that study was a new technology for structuring discretion. This technology has had a significant impact on the recent reforms of parole and sentencing in several jurisdictions.

Prior to the Parole Decision-Making Project, what structure was given to the exercise of parole discretion was limited to general legislative prescriptions, such as:

> A prisoner shall be placed on parole only when arrangements have been made for his proper employment or for his maintenance and care, and when the Board believes that he is able and willing to fulfill the obligations of a law abiding citizen.[5]

The Model Penal Code (American Law Institute, 1962), the Model Sentencing Act (National Council on Crime and Delinquency, 1963), and several national bodies have also suggested criteria or guidelines for structuring parole authority decisionmaking. These too tended to list the factors a parole board should consider in making a parole decision but did not give directions regarding how to weigh the factors against each other, nor the specific elements within each type of criteria the board should address.

The Parole Decision-Making Project studied the actual practice of the U.S. Board of Parole and discovered that although the members of the board stated that decisions were made on a case-by-case basis, sentencing patterns in decisionmaking could be detected. Three factors, or focal concerns, of the board were identified: severity of commitment offense, risk of recidivism, and the institutional conduct of the prisoner (Gottfredson et al., 1978: 5-8). These three factors "explained" much of the variation in parole decisions. In short, the U.S. Board of Parole was operating with an unstated, implicit policy regarding the grant of parole release.

The board and the project staff sought to make this implicit policy explicit. The institutional conduct of the prisoners was less "explanatory" than the offense severity or risk factors and was dropped from the model they developed. This model was a matrix or chart on which the degree of risk posed by a prisoner and the severity of his or her offense(s) could be plotted. The intersection of these two dimensions identified a range of time covering the terms served by the majority of similarly situated offenders. This range of time was then presumed also to cover the term to be imposed. That is, for a particular combination of risk and offense severity characteristics, a range of 20-24 months might be appropriate. A prisoner having these characteristics was presumed to serve between 20 and 24 months incarcerated prior to parole release. A term longer or shorter than that range could be imposed, but only if a decisionmaker justified the variation with explicit, written reasons. Initially, these ranges included about 63 percent of all terms established by the board of parole (Gottfredson et al., 1978: 12). That figure has now reached almost 80 percent (Gottfredson et al., 1978; Hoffman, 1975).

This matrix system can be considered to be a statistically established "common law."[6] Ranges are based on past practices of the parole authority and as such have precedental value in establishing current terms. The factors on which the board relied in arriving at a particular range were published in the Federal Rules Digest, as were the ranges.[7] Thus, the policy of the board and its decisionmaking criteria were public knowledge and open to challenge. Deviations from the ranges were, by this action, openly identified as deviations from normal practice, and the requirement for written reasons provided a basis on which decisions could be appealed.

The parole-decision matrix demonstrated first that an implicit policy existed in a parole board and that that policy could be made explicit; and second, that it was possible to structure the exercise of parole discretion in such a manner as to control the power of the parole board. Finally, it established the criteria used by the U.S. Board as well as the weights given to various factors by the board.

Parole, of course, is only one part of the equation of sentencing. Judicial and legislative authority also defines the nature of criminal penalties. The argument has been raised that the proper place to begin to structure sentencing discretion is with the judge, not the paroling authority. In fact, taken further, if the sentencing discretion of the judge is adequately structured, there would be no need for a paroling authority. Former Judge Marvin E. Frankel (1973) has argued that the discretion of sentencing judges must be structured. He decries what he has termed "lawless" sentencing practices in America and has suggested that guidelines for judicial sentencing be developed and implemented. These guidelines would then structure judicial sentencing decisions, and he would further add a presumption of a definite sentence.

Frankel proposed a sentencing commission to be created by the legislature and empowered to study sentencing, corrections, and parole. The legislature would also be required to define goals of criminal sentences and create a system to review criminal sentences. These reforms would unify criminal sentencing and create an equitable allocation of punishments.

The sentencing commission would develop a method of scoring criminal offenders in a manner that would suggest an appropriate penalty, much like the U.S. Parole Commission's matrix. This commission would propose legislation and enact administrative rules for sentencing. These rules would be checked by the Congress and the courts. The commission would then be empowered to control criminal sentencing, subject to review by the legislature and the courts.

While both Frankel's proposal and the decisionmaking matrix were directed at the federal system, either could be or has been applied in a state system. Under both of these systems, it is possible that a great deal of discretionary authority would remain in the hands of those setting criminal penalties, but this authority is structured on objective, published criteria and open to criticism. These systems would limit abuses of discretion, but the potential for abuse remains.

The potentially arbitrary imposition of penalties that is a part of any discretionary sentencing system is the price tag attached to a flexible system of punishment. In order to preserve the authority to deviate from the norm in abnormal cases and to respond quickly to emergencies or changes in public opinion and the like, those advocating the structuring of discretion must accept the possibility of abuse as a reasonable cost. But any abuses of discretion are reviewable by the courts, and the requirement for written reasons and the existence of a norm against which to measure a particular exception would enhance those procedural safeguards which now attend offenders who seek a review of their sentences. Moreover, the cost of rigidity in sentencing which the abolition of discretion would involve is viewed as too high a price to pay for certainty (Gottfredson et al., 1978: 2-3).

Confining Discretion

By far the most numerous of the recent sentencing and parole reform proposals can be classified as measures that seek to confine or limit discretion. Variously termed as determinate, definite, or presumptive sentencing schemes, these models eliminate or sharply curtail the authority of sentencers to impose different sanctions on essentially similar offenders. They primarily depend on legislative action that would establish narrow limits on the authority of sentencing judges to impose penalties, and most would involve the abolition of the traditional parole board.

Richard McGee (1974) has urged the abandonment of the indeterminate sentence, the abolition of parole, and the establishment of due process protection in judicial sentencing, including a systematic review of sentences. His model would allow the sentencing judge some discretion in setting a prison term within the statutory minimum and maximum terms for the particular offense. All offenses would be classified into degrees ranging from first to fifth degree felonies. The ranges within which the sentencing judge would impose a definite term are quite broad: fifth degree felonies carry a term from 3 months to 3 years; fourth degree, 6 months to 5 years; third degree, 1-12 years; second degree, 18 months to 20 years, and first degree, 7 years to life, or the death penalty, if allowed.

David Fogel (1976: 249-256) has presented a similar plan, in that penalties were tied to felony classification and further modified by a different set of enhanced terms for those offenders adjudged dangerous or repeat offenders. The average offender would receive definite terms on the basis of the seriousness of the offense. These terms could be altered by the judge by a specified amount for findings of aggravating or mitigating circumstances.

The sentencing judge would impose the presumptive term if no finding were made of aggravation or mitigation. Thus, a Class I felon would receive a term of 8 years. A finding that the offender was dangerous or a repeat offender would carry the presumptive term of 15 years. This enhanced term could be set anywhere between 15 and 18 years upon a finding of aggravation—for example, 17 years. The "average" penalty for a class 1 felon could be altered upward or downward by two years for aggravating or mitigating factors. Thus, the judge would set a definite term between 6 and 10 years, say 7 years. These terms would be reduced by "good time" earned by the inmate at the rate of one day off for every day served without misconduct.

Another form of "presumptive" sentence has been proposed by Andrew von Hirsch (1976) in *Doing Justice,* the report of the Committee for the Study of Incarceration. That model would create a matrix, such as the decisionmaking matrix, scaling offense and prior record. Depending upon where the two axes intersect, a penalty would be imposed that would be uniform for all offenders in that category. Here too the sentencing judge would be allowed to vary the term within specified limits, depending on aggravating or mitigating circumstances.

Similarly, the Twentieth Century Fund's Task Force on Criminal Sentences (1976) report, *Fair and Certain Punishment,* would scale penalties according to the severity of the offense and obligate the judge to impose the presumptive term. The judge would be allowed to vary from this term by a certain percentage of the presumptive sentence for aggravating and mitigating circumstances. Unlike von Hirsch or Fogel, the task force would retain a parole board but limit its authority to reduce prison terms by a small range, no more than 15 percent.[8]

David Stanley (1976: 185) has advocated a system in which prison terms would be imposed by the judge alone. These terms could initially be established at the median time served by offenders convicted of the particular offense in the past. While he would abolish parole boards and parole release, he would allow "modest variations" in the terms set by the judge for aggravating and mitigating factors (Stanley, 1976).

Constance Motley (1973) has proposed a definite sentence plan in which the sentence imposed would be determined by the seriousness of the crime and the number of previous convictions of the offender. She would retain a parole authority to authorize release in certain cases for "compelling humanitarian reasons."

In each of these proposals, the legislature would take a commanding role in the sentencing process by clearly defining the limits on judicial discretion in the imposition of prison terms. Most abolish parole release or relegate it to a very minor role. All seek to bring certainty and fairness to the sentencing process.

GOALS OF CONTEMPORARY SENTENCING REFORMERS

The goals of those advocating more certainty in criminal sentencing, like those of the entire American justice process, can be dichotomized into two competing, and often conflicting, values. On the one hand, the purpose of sentencing is to control crime for societal protection. Offenders must be punished and incapacitated, while would-be offenders should be deterred. On the other hand, the justice system must protect the rights and liberties of individuals. Offenders must be treated fairly.

Reckless and Allen (1979: 133) distinguish between liberals and conservatives on this basis. Liberals, they write, "are more concerned with and traditionally emphasize the amount of fairness in the criminal justice process," while conservatives "tend to be much more optimistic about the potential capacity of the system and see promise for reversing crime trends through such approaches as 'swift and certain trials,' less regard for rules of procedure, mandatory sentences, and stiffer sentences" (1979: 144).

This dichotomized approach to the analysis of the justice system and its components has a rather long tradition. Packer (1968) used two ideal types in *The Limits of the Criminal Saction* to analyze the justice process. He compared the due process (liberal) and crime control (conservative) models. O'Leary and Duffee (1972) used a similar dichotomy between "concern for the offender" (liberal) and "concern for the community" (conservative) to classify correctional policies. Similarly, Wilson (1968: 281-282) has characterized law enforcement policies as "bureaucratic" (liberal) and "professional" (conservative). In fact, of course, such "ideal types" are almost never encountered in operating agencies.[9]

Rather, it is more likely that an existing justice system or agency will fall somewhere between the two extremes. The value of such models rests on their utility in highlighting the relevant issues through providing a basis for comparison. The danger in using "ideal types" is that they have normative overtones leading the analyst into discussions of "should" as opposed to "would." As Packer (1968: 153) has noted:

> There is a risk in an enterprise of this sort that is latent in any attempt to polarize. It is, simply, that values are too various to be pinned down to yes-or-no answers. The models are distortions of reality. And, since they are normative in character, there is a danger of seeing one or the other as Good or Bad.

Remembering these two qualifications—that the ideal type is unlikely to be found in practice, and that for pupuses of description, one must avoid the normative aspects of such models—the discussion of sentencing reform proposals can proceed.

Sentencing policy can be considered a zero-sum game between concerns for efficiency or societal protection and concerns for individual rights. Conceptually, it is possible to speak in terms of a "whole" of sentencing policy. That whole policy represents 100 percent of the concerns evident in sentence determinations and must be divided up between an emphasis on societal protection and individual rights. It is conceivable that 100 percent of the policy be devoted to either of these concerns, or that the policy be evenly divided between the two.

In practice, sentencing policy is at least partially dependent upon external factors such as the cost of sentencing. That is, even if the policy would support life imprisonment for all offenders, the cost of such a policy would be intolerable, and thus it is not a viable option. Additionally, the amount or extent of sentencing policy that is variable is limited by constitutional requirements and the nature of criminal law as, implicitly at least, a tool to promote social order and societal protection. In this sense, then, the real outer limits are not 100 percent, but rather some lower order determinate of sentencing practice.

A SOCIAL PROTECTION MODEL

The social protection model of sentencing policy is most congruent with Packer's crime control model. The objective is swift, simple crime prevention. The underlying rationale for this policy is one of criminal law as a general deterrent and incapacitation in the imposition of specific sanctions. Uniformly harsh sanctions are seen as a means of achieving both ends. Any facilities for reducing or avoiding those sanctions pose a threat to the overall effectiveness of the sentencing process, and therefore discretion is to be reserved to the legislature that establishes criminal penalties with particular reference to their deterrent value.

Sentences will be severe and mandatory as established by the legislature. Yet such laws are desirable because they are not easily subject to challenge and they reserve sentencing power to the legislature.

> The aim of these laws is to preclude early, "lenient" release of . . . offenders because . . . [their] crimes are seen as particularly dangerous or harmful. In many instances, the hope is that such stiff penalties will deter offenders or at least separate from society persons seen as dangerous [Travis and O'Leary, 1979: 36].

Uniform, mandatory sanctions not only insure the imposition of legislatively intended sanctions, thereby reaffirming the laws, but also reduce the sentencing process to a formality, speeding it and reducing inefficiency. There is no need for a sentencing hearing, for once guilt is established, sentencing has been accomplished. These sanctions also negate the possibility of leniency that would undermine the deterrent effect of the law.

The individual rights model of sentencing policy is congruent with Packer's due process model. The objective is fair, equitable punishment of offenses. The underlying rationale for this policy is one of criminal law as a general deterrent and equity in the imposition of criminal sanctions. Certainty and restraint in criminal punishment are seen as the means of achieving both ends. Uniformity in procedures and parity in outcome are necessary to this goal, and therefore limited discretion is delegated to nonlegislative decisionmakers.

In this sentencing system, the legislature would perform two basic functions. In the area of substantive law, the legislature would narrow and structure the discretionary power of sentencing decisionmakers through the articulation of criteria on which sentencing decisions should be based and a reduction in the scope of criminal sentences. In procedural matters, the legislature would create the mechanisms for sentencing hearings and sentence review proceedings. The "heart" of sentencing under an individual rights model is fair sentencing.

Fair sentencing is achieved through standardized procedures and criteria applied uniformly to each case. It does not, however, require blind uniformity, which is anathema to just sentencing.

There is scope for legitimate and necessary moral variations in sentencing practice. The goal is equity in sentencing practices as realized by achieving consistency over time and over an entire court [sentencing] system [Kress et al., 1976: 220].

Actual sanctions imposed under an individual rights model of sentencing would be less drastic than those now employed. The privacy of the individual precludes unnecessarily intrusive sanctions. The principle of the least drastic alternative would predominate, encouraging the use of non-incarcerative sanctions and, failing these, incarcerative penalties of very limited duration. Probation sentences, fines, and restitution would be preferred to imprisonment, and sentencing dispositions would exist *as* punishments and not *for* punishment.[10]

Models of Sentencing Policy and Current Sentencing Reforms

The majority of proposed sentencing reforms presented earlier involve attempts to balance the two emphases of societal protection and individual liberty. If anything, they tend to advocate measures that enhance the protection of individual rights at sentencing.[11] The existence of criminal punishments is supported for societal protection, but the cause of social protection is strictly restrained by requirements of fairness in dealing with individual offenders.

These proposals, however, must be operationalized in working sentencing systems, and it is in this setting that they face their greatest challenge. Particularly those models that would confine sentencing discretion (and therefore require legislative action) depend upon an acceptance of the philosophical positions held by their authors, who support controlling discretion for the purpose of protecting the rights of the offender. There are no guarantees that this will happen in practice.[12] On the contrary, it is more likely that legislatures seeking to confine sentencing discretion will do so to enhance societal protection at the expense of individual rights.

Contemporary sentence reforms have taken the legislative and administrative approaches, as well as intermediate types. They have been variously supported as means of enhancing both crime control and individual rights, and have been supported in some jurisdictions by groups whose counterparts have opposed similar changes in other places. No two reforms adopted in different jurisdictions have been identical, although each has been motivated in large part by a desire to reduce broad discretion in the sentencing process.

The remainder of this chapter will briefly describe the reform processes in two states and attempt to describe the manner in which forces in each state have operated to shape the specific type of sentencing system adopted.

THE SENTENCING REFORM PROCESS IN CALIFORNIA

On August 31, 1976 the Uniform Determinate Sentencing Act of 1976 was passed into law in California.[13] The creation of presumptive sentencing in California represented a major policy change in the state until that time, since that state, perhaps more than any other, was identified with the indeterminate sentence and correctional rehabilitation. Several groups, individuals, and events shaped the development of this new law.

Historical Background of the Movement

In 1917 California adopted a radical form of indeterminate sentence. This law empowered the Board of Prison Directors to actually set the term of confinement at any point prior to the expiration of the maximum sentence.[14] Over the next two decades, the Board of Prison Directors was granted the power to extend terms established earlier, and a Board of Prison Terms and Paroles was established. For over a decade, the Board of Prison Terms and Paroles held the power to grant release, and the Board of Prison Directors held the power to award good time. The two boards were in conflict over control of prison terms.

In 1944 legislation was proposed that led to the California system as it existed before passage of the Uniform Determinate Sentence Act. This law created a separate department of corrections headed by a director who oversaw the operations of the prison system. An Adult Authority was created to make parole decisions and administer parole supervision. Good time was abolished in 1947 because it was inconsistent with an indeterminate sentence system.

Throughout its history in California, the power to parole was exercised, at first openly, later less directly, to control institutional populations and discipline.[15] The early legislation on parole recognized its function to control inmate behavior and population problems. In later years, governors instructed the Adult Authority to reduce prison populations or to reduce releases.[16] For these and other reasons, the Adult Authority and Department of Corrections experienced conflicts over the course of their stormy coexistence.

In the 1960s and early 1970s, several events took place that directly established a basis for reform in the California system. Prison disturbances and an increase in assaultive violence by prison inmates against each other became a concern statewide. The prison population began to swell after a directive by Governor Reagan to slow the parole release process, and two reports were published that were very critical of the California sentencing and correctional processes. These were the *Struggle for Justice* and the *Kelgord Report* (National Council on Crime and Delinquency, 1971).

The first has been discussed above, while the latter was the product of a federally funded study of the California Department of Corrections conducted by the National Council on Crime and Delinquency in 1970. Among others, the report contained recommendations that the Adult Authority be abolished and that California prison terms be greatly reduced. Though never implemented, one result of these criticisms and others was a move by the Adult Authority to an early time fix in late 1971. This action resulted in over 70 percent of those appearing before the authority in that period receiving release dates, thus drawing heavy criticism from conservative groups.

In response to this criticism, Governor Reagan persuaded the authority to be more cautious. Release rates dropped and prison populations began to rise. This in turn led to increased and more vociferous criticism of the Adult Authority and indeterminate sentencing by both the Department of Corrections and liberal prisoners' rights groups.

Achieving Reform in California

The reform of sentencing in California resulted from a temporary coalition of groups and persons supporting determinate sentencing either as a means to insure increased community protection or to improve the situation of offenders incarcerated in the California system. The liberal, individual rights proponents dominated the reform process in its initial development. Conservative advocates of community protection became involved later, in part as a reaction to the "liberal" sentencing provisions of Senate Bill 42 (S.B. 42), later to be known as the Uniform Determinate Sentencing Act of 1976.

In 1974 the California Senate formed a Select Committee on Penal Institutions as part of an overall effort to rewrite the total California Penal

Code. A consultant to that committee discovered that most criminal justice personnel, lobbyists, and interest groups were dissatisfied with indeterminate sentencing. He and another consultant began to work toward modification of the California sentencing structure (Cassou and Taugher, 1978: 12). They drafted a working paper outlining a new sentencing law that was still indeterminate but with a reduction in the very wide ranges between minimum and maximum sentences for most offenses.

Hearings on this proposal were held in December 1974, with nearly every witness voicing opposition to the proposal. With the exception of a contingent of sentencing judges, almost every speaker called for a more radical restructuring of sentencing in California, a restructuring that would greatly reduce or abolish sentencing and parole release discretion (San Francisco Sunday Examiner and Chronicle, 1974; and see Parnas and Salerno, 1978).

In 1975 the consultants reworked this proposal with an emphasis on determinate sentencing. During this period, Governor Brown appointed Raymond Procunier Chairman of the Adult Authority and the authority adopted a parole release guidelines matrix. The governor supported Procunier's efforts at "determinacy from within," and although S.B. 42 passed the California Senate in May 1975, it never left the Assembly's Criminal Justice Committee.

The Assembly Committee was already considering a new sentencing bill proposed by its chairman, and S.B. 42 was merely another option. Further, there was no indication that Governor Brown would sign a determinate sentencing bill, given his public support of Procunier's efforts. Finally, the California District Attorney's Association, the ACLU, and the California Judiciary voiced opposition to the law. The bill was held over for review in the 1976 session.

Procunier resigned from the Adult Authority in late 1975 after failing to win confirmation by the California Senate. In January 1976 the California Supreme Court decided the case of In re Stanley. In that decision, the court ruled that mechanical application of parole guidelines without reference to inmate reform was a violation of the California Constitution. The drafters of S.B. 42 used this decision to convince Governor Brown's office that the parole guidelines were illegal. The governor then lent his support to S.B. 42.

In a series of meetings during the spring of 1976, representatives of law enforcement groups, prisoners' rights groups, and other interested parties hammered out a compromise on sentencing reform. This amended version of S.B. 42 was the bill that was finally passed into law. In the process of compromise and building political support for passage of S.B. 42, several critical issues were ignored or downplayed.

The drafters of S.B. 42 based penalties on average terms served by California inmates prior to the adoption of the new law. The issue addressed in the California reform process was limited to the question of who would set criminal penalties. The severity of criminal sentences was not at issue. Also, the questions of plea bargaining, misdemeanor procedures, and the power of sentencing judges to grant probation were avoided. These issues threatened to fragment the fragile coalition of liberal and conservative support that was critical to the passage of a determinate sanction law (Parnas and Salerno, 1978: 40-41).

The result of these compromises was a sentencing structure that reduced discretionary decisionmaking that the liberal groups felt supported discriminatory sentencing and denial of equal protection. It also allowed maximum penalties that were much shorter than those previously imposed under California law. Conservatives, on the other hand, had achieved a sentencing structure that called for definite sentences that could not be reduced by a parole board and should thus prove of more deterrent value. Also, dangerous offenders could be subjected to extended terms if elements of the offense justified enhancements of sentence (Casson and Taugher, 1978: 41-67).

The Aftermath of California Sentencing Reform

Almost immediately after it had been signed into law, conservative factions began to lobby for changes in the Uniform Determinate Sentencing Act of 1976. They sought stiffer penalties, a longer period of parole supervision, and safeguards on the retroactive application of the new law. Through Assembly Bill 476, sentences were lengthened, some judicial discretion was returned, and much of the early emphasis of the law on reducing penalty severity and enhancing equity was overturned.

Since then, every session of the legislature has seen new bills submitted to increase penalties for specified crimes or to add enhancements. There are also some pressures to return to some form of discretionary parole release, at least for specified offense/offender types (Barkdull, 1980: 21-23). The questions of prosecutorial power, judicial discretion in granting probation, and the scaling of penalties remain unresolved.

THE SENTENCING REFORM PROCESS IN OREGON

At nearly the same time as California was undergoing a sentencing reform movement, its neighbor to the north was also struggling with the issues of sentencing disparity and severity. In 1977 the Oregon state legislature passed a bill requiring proportionality in criminal sanctions and the structuring of parole release discretion through the promulgation of criteria including "ranges of imprisonment" to be used by the parole board in setting parole release dates.[17]

Historical Background of the Movement

Oregon was a latecomer of the turn-of-the-century movement to adopt indeterminate sentencing and parole. In 1905 the governor was given the authority to grant paroles to deserving prisoners, but this was basically no more than legislative acknowledgement of parole since the governor had the power to grant pardons and commutations (Lindsey, 1925: 64). In 1911 the first parole board in Oregon was created, to be comprised of the governor's secretary and two members appointed by the governor. This board was charged with investigating parole applicants and making recommendations for parole action to the governor.

The first state parole officer was authorized by the Oregon legislature in 1915. 1939 brought the creation of a three-member, part-time board whose function was to grant parole and administer parole and probation field services. This body was called the Board of Probation and Parole. In 1959 membership on the board was expanded to five part-time positions, and in 1969 the board was reconstituted.

This new board was comprised of three full-time members and had the sole task of granting and revoking parole. The management and administration of both probation and parole supervision was vested in the Corrections Division, as it was believed this division was better suited to these tasks, and that the reorganization would enhance correctional treatment in the state. In 1973 the board was renamed the State Board of Parole to more accurately describe its function.

In 1975, because of an ever-increasing workload and a desire to increase the use of parole as a method of release from prison, the size of the board was expanded to five full-time members (Taylor, 1979: 53). In 1974 an effort by the board to regain administrative control over parole supervision was defeated in the legislature. A report by the Legislative Fiscal Office (1974) argued that such a shift in control could alter the then current system's bias toward optimism and the expanded use of parole.

The Oregon State Board of Parole was under pressure to reduce growing prison populations but was expected to do so in a manner that would not result in the release of dangerous criminals. The Corrections Division felt that the board of parole was insensitive to the problems of prison overcrowding, while the law enforcement community, and presumably the general public, felt that the board was insensitive to the amount of risk to the community posed by these prisoners being released on parole. In an effort to increase the use of parole release, the size of the board was expanded from three to five full-time members in 1975.

Late 1974 and early 1975 saw two "spectacular" crimes by offenders on release status. Both were murders and both received a great deal of media coverage. One was participating in a work release program and the other had been released on a temporary social pass. The events focused attention on the release of prison inmates. The legislature, meeting for the 1975 session, felt compelled to take action in response to these crimes.

The increasing number of prisoners being housed in Oregon's correctional facilities was overburdening the Corrections Division. There was a suspicion, publicly voiced by some critics, that parole was being employed as a method of controlling the prison population without adequate regard for the protection of the public. A study of parole decisionmaking in Oregon noted the mounting political pressures to reform parole, one cause of which was the rising prison population (Moule and Hanft, 1976).

Public criticism of the Oregon sentencing structure as it existed in 1975 and 1976 prior to reform was primarily voiced by conservatives seeking to enhance public protection. The two outrageous murders noted above, the suspicion that parole release was being used to balance institutional population, and the lack of judicial control over length of incarceration were the principal reasons for this criticism. The conservative arguments were based on an incapacitative and deterrence rationale (Beatty, 1976).

As in California, the reform process in Oregon resulted from a consensus of groups and individuals advocating either an increased emphasis on societal protection or on the protection of individual rights in Oregon's sentencing policy. Again, similar to California, the Oregon reform was a product of competition and compromise. In Oregon, however, the reform process was somewhat less controversial, for a variety of reasons (Taylor, 1979: 53-55).

Achieving Reform in Oregon

In late 1975 Governor Straub appointed a task force on corrections in Oregon and, as previously noted, there was legislative interest in sentencing and release decisionmaking. Several mandatory minimum term bills were introduced, but none was passed. At the close of the 1975 session, despite intense legislative interest, not one mandatory minimum term law had been enacted, and the problem of prison overcrowding was worsening. The Interim Committee on the Judiciary had decided to investigate correctional law and attempt to draft legislation that would address the problems of Oregon's correctional system.

Public concern over rising crime, reaction to "spectacular" crimes by offenders on release status, in conjunction with a crisis of overcrowding in Oregon correctional institutions, placed pressure on elected officials, especially the governor and legislators, to "do something" about sentencing and corrections in Oregon. The initial steps taken by both the governor and the legislature were similar. The governor appointed a task force and the legislature designated a topic of its Interim Committee on the Judiciary to be the study of problems in corrections. Eventually, these two groups began to work together.

At the beginning, however, neither group had an official position or course of action. Both groups were aware of mandatory minimum sentence proposals, and both were also aware that concrete action against murders by released offenders was a requirement of any changes in Oregon law. But at that point there was no consensus about what the justice system in Oregon should look like after reform.

Both groups sought and received testimony from interested parties in public meetings and through mailed solicitations. There were no organized special interest lobbying efforts for parole reform as had been the case in California. Sentencing judges opposed the parole board's power to overturn judicial sanctions by granting release, and the prosecutors desired a reduction in the releases of inmates convicted of offenses against the person.[18] The parole board was viewed as too liberal in its release policies by conservatives and not liberal enough by the corrections division.

The kind of organized support for parole reform from the political left that characterized the California reform effort was absent in Oregon. Special interest groups representing prisoners in Oregon were either non-existent or ineffectual. Where liberal support did come into play was behind the scenes. Major actors in the reform process were motivated by the justice arguments associated with the liberal factions in parole reform.

An almost universal denial of any influence by scholarly writings about sentencing and parole was reported by those involved in sentencing reform in California. In Oregon, the reverse was true. Particularly those most influential in the actual reform proposal, H.B. 2013, had been impressed by *The Future of Imprisonment* (Morris, 1974), *Fair and Certain Punishment,* and *Doing Justice.* As a result of shared interests, it was almost inevitable that those most active in the movement to reform sentencing in Oregon would come to work together even though they began their efforts independently.

The board of parole developed and implemented parole decisionmaking guidelines in late 1975, and these guidelines were continually refined during 1976 and 1977. Before either the governor's task force or the interim committee had proposed any reforms, the board of parole had structured its discretion on its own initiative. The requests by both bodies for input from the board ensured they would learn about the guideline system. On its own initiative, however, the board set out to inform judges, prosecutors, correctional officials, inmates, and the general public about the new matrix system. What occurred over the next year was the establishment of linkages between these three bodies that resulted in a uniform "front" proposing parole reform legislation to the Oregon House of Representatives and the eventual passage of H.B. 2013.

By the end of 1976, the Governor's task force, the Interim Committee on the Judiciary, and the Oregon State Board of Parole all favored structuring parole release discretion through guidelines as a requirement of law. The Legislative Assembly of 1977 saw limited debate, the resolution of some differences, a tightening of the legislation, and final legislative approval. These things made the reform "official," but it had already been accomplished by January 1977.[19]

By August 1976, the parole board, through its chairman, the Interim Committee, through its chief legal counsel, and the Governor's task force were all working on the same idea: legislative requirement of structured release discretion. In September 1976, the Interim Committee met again, this time voting to endorse the parole reform measure and to submit it to the 1977 Legislative Assembly for consideration by the entire legislature.

The reasons behind these three groups coming to support the reform legislation are varied. The chairman of the governor's task force had always been interested in sentencing disparity, and the task force as a whole was interested in a system of sanctions that released minor offenders relatively early. The parole matrix did just that. It also allowed the task force to support a punishment-oriented justice system that would not lead to longer prison terms and that would avoid the mandatory sentence bills that had been the mainstay of legislative proposals up to that time.[20]

The parole board supported the legislation for an altogether different reason. Word of the Stanley decision in California had reached Oregon. There was some concern that the Oregon Supreme Court would invalidate the guidelines system, and legislative confirmation of the matrix was viewed as a way to avoid that.

When the Legislative Assembly in Oregon first met in January 1977, H.B. 2013, though not yet introduced, was an odds on favorite for passage. It had the seal of approval of the Interim Legislative Committee on the Judiciary, which had included the chairpersons of both the House and Senate Judiciary Committees of 1977. By its acceptance, the governor's task force had given H.B. 2013 support from the governor, and his chief legal counsel, who had chaired the task force, took an active part in the bill's movement through the legislature. Finally, the bill was also supported by the agency most affected, the parole board.

No strong opposition to H.B. 2013 ever emerged during the 1977 session. The legislative process produced amendments and compromises, but the basic intent of the bill's drafters remained. The committee process was important, however, not for the testimony received, but because of who testified. The process was a testing of the bill's general acceptability to the powerful political forces in Oregon.

Several compromise amendments to H.B. 2013 responded to the few criticisms voiced in hearings. One allowed judicial minimum terms up to half the legislative maximum that could be overridden only by an affirmative vote of four out of five board members. Another created an Advisory Commission on Prison Terms and Parole Rules ensuring judicial input into prison term policy. As with California, the difficult issues of identifying and assigning appropriate penalties for specific crimes, as well as the impact of plea negotiation and sentences to probation, were not addressed by the legislature.

The Aftermath of Oregon Sentencing Reform

Sentencing judges are required to state on the record their reasons for imposing sentences, to hold a hearing on the issue of factors in aggravation or mitigation of the sentence, and to disclose most of the information on which the sentencing decision is based.[21] If a sentence of incarceration in a state penal institution is imposed, the inmate is to be seen by the board of parole and informed of his or her parole release date within six months of admission to the institution.

The information on which the parole release date (prison term) decision is based is disclosed to the inmate. Board rules provide the inmate with notice, disclosure, the right to elocution, and a written statement of the decision and reasons therefore. An administrative review process was established, and final actions of the board are appealable to the courts. Only the right to representation has not been conferred on the inmate at prison term hearings.

The reform in Oregon, however, was very limited in that it principally affected the board of parole and did not specifically address judicial sentencing disparity. The impact of this reform on other aspects of the justice process, such as prosecution, judicial sentencing, and institutional programming, was minimized in order to enhance the likelihood of passage. Finally, it must be recalled that sentencing reform was an issue created out of a widespread concern in Oregon over prison overcrowding and crime control in general. H.B. 2013 was suggested implicitly, if not explicitly, as at least a partial solution to both those problems.

SOME OBSERVATIONS ON SENTENCING REFORM

It is still too early to determine whether or not the changes in the sentencing structures of California and Oregon will enhance fairness and reduce disparity. It may be that both types of sentencing structures will achieve these ends, or that neither will. It remains to be seen how these structured changes will affect the imposition of criminal sanctions in those two states. What can be seen, however, is that both reform movements appear to share some common characteristics.

Most important is that reform proponents limit the extent of the changes they seek, and that the reform process is structured so that change will generally be incremental in nature. The requirement of broad-based support for legislative action leads reformers to limit the scope of their proposals and to compromise with those who hold divergent opinions. The justice policymaking processes are structured so that radical or sweeping reform is unlikely.

In the brief sketches of sentencing reform in the two states presented above, it is apparent that not only reform advocates themselves limit the scope of policy change, but that the reform process almost requires such action. Particularly in terms of legislative change, it is typical that parties interested in reform, whether as advocates or opponents of specific proposals, arrive at a compromise solution through "bargaining" (see Edelman, 1964: Chs. 2, 4). Thus, the requirement of cooperation between opposing sides of a controversial policy issue results in a limitation of the scope of reform through the process of compromise.

The effect of compromise on the outcome of reform efforts is clearly visible in the cases of California and Oregon. In California, the compromise on S.B. 42 was the product of a series of meetings between liberal and conservative interest groups in the spring of 1976. In Oregon, compromise occurred on several points, most notably the authority of the parole board to override a judicial minimum and the separation of the heinous murder issue from the parole release guidelines issue.

The desire of reform advocates to see their efforts result in some form of policy change provides a strong motivation to acquiesce to compromise proposals. The relatively late entry of opposition groups to a reform debate often limits the ability to develop alternative solutions. This is due in part to the fact that the forces supporting the reform advocates are typically already mobilized. Therefore, they are willing to settle for compromises. These compromises often serve to allow time for a more concerted effort at redirecting a reform policy at a later date. As Cassou and Taugher (1978: 17) noted in California, regarding the ultimate passage of S.B. 42:

> The Governor became interested and agreed to support the legislation if law enforcement groups found the bill acceptable. These groups, led by the Attorney General and the District Attorney of Alameda County, had become concerned in recent years with the increasing willingness of the California Supreme Court to rewrite sentencing law and with the reforms of the Adult Authority. Moreover, these groups felt that the legislature would be more responsive to future proposals to increase terms than the Adult Authority bureaucracy had been.

The recent history of penal legislation in California suggests that this strategy was well founded. In Oregon, the legislature has been resistant to efforts to increase criminal penalties, passing only bills requiring a mandatory prison term for persons convicted of committing a felony while armed with a firearm.[22] This may be due to the fact that prison term-setting in Oregon is a parole board function, while in California it is a legislative one (von Hirsch and Hanrahan, 1979: 88-96).

Yet another important distinction between the Oregon and California reforms refers to the breadth of the changes enacted. Oregon's legislation dealt principally with the parole board and was thus more easily adopted (Taylor, 1979: 54-55). California's legislation, which was consciously written to avoid plea bargaining, the utility of parole supervision, and the issue of what constitutes an appropriate penalty all involved a more complex change and led to the initial formulation of A.B. 476.

What can be seen from this examination of sentencing reform in California and Oregon is that change, especially legislative change, requires broad-based political support. For this reason, reform advocates limit the scope of their reform proposals. Further, they are often required to secure the support of opposing parties, most often through compromise or avoidance of especially sensitive issues. Thus, it would appear that refinements to reforms adopted after the initial change may be more important to an understanding of the effects of reform than the proposal as originally presented.

The principal interest groups in sentencing reform appear to be liberals advocating an individual rights rationale and conservatives proposing societal protection models. Cloudy wording of proposals in terms of "determinacy," "certainty," or "justice" allow these traditionally antagonistic interests to coalesce around the issue of sentencing reform. This coalition leads to compromise and continued efforts to shape revised sentencing structures beyond the date of their adoption.

CONCLUSIONS

From the review of the process of sentencing reform in two states, it appears that the specific provisions of sentencing reform proposals attract the attention of a limited audience, although the issue of sentencing reform may be perceived to have widespread support. Further, several types of interest groups usually enter the reform process at different stages and attempt to alter proposals in ways that are most congruent with their respective definitions of reform goals.

To the degree that those who create sentencing reform as an issue have a concrete reform proposal and elicit support for it, they will be successful in seeing their proposal adopted. In an effort to maintain control and focus attention, reform proponents limit the scope of proposals by specifically avoiding broader issues such as plea bargaining and seek to minimize the possible negative impacts of reform on large agencies such as parole field services or penal institutions.

Finally, proponents of reforms are most successful when they co-opt opponents through compromise on specific provisions of a reform proposal rather than through attempts to contain issues by direct conflict or confrontation with opponents. Compromise exists on two levels. First, the different and relatively small groups that attend to justice system reform proposals must generally present a uniform position in order that action be taken. To do this, critical aspects of the issue are left ill-defined or unexplored to minimize conflict. Thus opposing expectations of reform are supported. Second, reform advocates, aware of the need for consensus, must often limit their proposals, thereby leaving open, or creating, mechanisms to control or circumvent the impact of reform.

Reform proposals enacted by policymakers are characterized by broad-based support. This support is generated through compromise and limiting the breadth of reform so that groups focus on sentencing decisions rather than involving significant alterations of prison term lengths, correctional programs, or trial procedures.

The most striking findings were the small number of persons involved in actually writing legislation and the importance of persistence to the control of legislative action. Partly because so few individuals actually write legislation, and because the legislative process is one of bargaining and compromise, it appears that if a person or group is determined enough, they can control the reform process.

In regard to the goals of sentencing reform, the central question that remains unanswered is one of how best to balance conflicting concerns. The question is not specific to the form or severity of appropriate criminal sentences, as the Twentieth Century Fund Task Force asked it ("How long is too long? How short is too short?"). Rather, Norval Morris (1978: 3) came closer to the essential question when he wrote:

> The purposes to be achieved by sentencing are not agreed upon nor are the procedures. A mixture of motives has led us astray: an exaggerated belief by some in the deterrent efficacy of punishment; an excessive belief by others in the reformative capacity of the criminal law.

What is most important and impressive about contemporary sentencing reform is that it is possible that we may finally begin to resolve this conflict. The variety of reforms adopted provide us with an opportunity to study the sentencing process that may never again be presented. The significant impact of current sentencing reforms lies in the results of an analysis of their impact on both public protection and individual rights.

A more important question relates to a pragmatic assessment of sentencing reform, and indeed, all aspects of criminal justice reform. That is, what can we reasonably expect from reform in the justice system and how can we improve the likelihood that our expectations will be met? It is quite likely that we all expect too much of reform efforts and thereby sow the seeds of our own disappointment. In the future, we should be forewarned when we notice that different people expect different outcomes of the same change.

NOTES

1. Maine Revised Statutes Annotated, Title 17-A, Sections 1251-1254.
2. In this chapter the authors identify "liberals" and "conservatives" in justice policy principally in that conservatives are more optimistic that existing justice

machinery can control crime, while liberals opt for a social reform approach to crime control.

3. This report was later published as *Prison Without Walls: Report on New York Parole* (New York: Praeger, 1975.

4. The Citizen's Inquiry, chaired by Ramsey Clark, saw the abolition of parole as a long-range goal, one which would follow increasing equity and fairness in the total American society. They identified a need for social services to be provided to the poor and minorities and for equality in educational, economic, and social opportunities to be achieved before any real progress in reducing crime could be expected.

5. Idaho Code Annotated, Section 20-223 (1971).

6. The matrix "ranges" are based on past decisions of the U.S. Parole Commission. These decisions are used as precedents for current decisionmaking, and the provision of written guidelines, with a requirement of written reasons for decisions incompatible with the suggested guideline ranges, supports a type of "state decisis" doctrine in that "normal" cases are generally decided within the applicable range.

7. These guidelines are revised periodically and are found in the Federal Register.

8. Most of these proposals would allow some discretionary power over sentence lengths. Generally this power is granted to the sentencing judge, and the Twentieth Century Fund is almost alone in retaining some paroling authority. Of course, control over any "good time" becomes crucial in these systems, and as will be shown, this control has generally been left with a modified version of a parole authority.

9. The "ideal" or "pure" type is a methodological concept popularized by the sociologist Max Weber. The ideal type is a device used to bring issues into focus and to allow for precision in the formulation of concepts and definitions. An excellent exposition of the use of ideal types is presented in Timasheff (1967: 177-181).

10. This conception of a criminal sentence as punishment and not for punishment is not new. Newman (1978: 331) has noted that: "In theory, however, prisons were not designed to be places *for* punishment but rather places of punishment." Regarding community supervision, Martinson (1976: 26) has been quoted as saying: "I suggest that probation and parole, rather than being a mitigation of punishment, be the punishment."

11. Two scholarly works are repeatedly identified as supporting the societal protection aspects of sentencing policy above those of individual rights. Nonetheless, both of these proposals include a great deal of attention to procedural fairness and controls on the exercise of sentencing power (see Van den Haag, 1975; and Wilson, 1975).

12. An account of David Fogel's reaction to a draft bill before the Alaska legislature in 1976 demonstrates this point. Upon hearing that Alaska was considering the "Fogel Plan," Fogel himself reviewed the provisions of the bill and hurriedly flew to Alaska to testify against it (see Corrections Magazine, 1977: 18).

13. California Statutes, ch. 149.

14. California Statutes, ch. 257. Much of the historical material included in this section is adapted from Hawkins (1971: 40-79).

15. "Report of the Investigating Committee on Penal Affairs," cited in Hawkins (1971: 77).

16. California Statues, ch. 483 (1931) recognized the utility of parole and indeterminate sentencing as a means to sanction institutional misconduct. Also see Wilcox (1929).

17. Oregon Revised Statutes, Section 144.780

18. The judges aired their complaints in a series of newspaper articles in the Portland, Oregon *Journal* beginning on June 7 and ending June 9, 1977.

19. The Oregon Board of Parole filed Administrative Rules with the Oregon Secretary of State on January 26, 1977. These rules contained the prison term matrix and were incorporated as Chapter 254, Oregon Administrative Rules.

20. In the 1977 Legislative Assembly, a total of twelve bills requiring mandatory terms for some or all felony offenders were introduced: S.B. 471 (all felons must serve maximum term), S.B. 900 (one-year minimum for criminally negligent homicide), H.B. 2011 (mandatory 15-year term for aggravated murder), H.B. 2286, H.B. 2294 (mandatory minimum terms for those convicted of committing or attempting felonies while armed), H.B. 2333 (all felons sentenced to prison would serve one-half of the maximum term), H.B. 2576 (required additional prison term consecutive to term imposed for offense to be imposed on all convicted of felonies while armed), H.B. 2589 (required 5-year minimum imposed on offenders convicted of certain offenses where victim was over 65 years of age), H.B. 2876 (allowed sentencing judge to impose a minimum term that would be binding on the parole board), H.B. 3037 (allowed judge to impose minimum term up to one-half of the maximum; could be overridden by unanimous vote of the Board of Parole), H.B. 3041 (minimum terms for felonies committed with a firearm). The final version of H.B. 2013 included a version of H.B. 3037, but the minimum could be overridden by a vote of four board members. Other than H.B. 2013, only H.B. 2011, the aggravated murder bill, was passed.

21. Oregon Revised Statutes, Section 137.079.

22. Oregon Revised Statutes, Section 165.065 (1979).

CASE

In re STANLEY (1976) 54 Cal. App. 3rd 1030

REFERENCES

ALLEN, F. (1964) The Borderland of Criminal Justice. Chicago: University of Chicago Press.

American Friends Service Committee (1971) Struggle for Justice. New York: Hill & Wang.

American Law Institute (1962) Model Penal Code: Proposed Official Draft. Philadelphia: American Law Institute.

BARKDULL, W. L. (1980) "The determinate sentence and the violent offender: what happens when the time runs out?" Federal Probation 44 (June).

BEATTY, J. C., Jr. (1976) "Concurring report and partial dissent," pp. 117-122 in Report of the Governor's Task Force on Corrections. Salem, Oregon, October.

CASSOU, A. and B. TAUGHER (1978) "Determinate sentencing in California: the new numbers game." Pacific Law Journal 9 (January).

Citizen's Inquiry on Parole and Criminal Justice (1974) Report on New York Parole. New York: Citizen's Inquiry.

CLEAR, T. R., J. D. HEWITT, R. M. REGOLI (1978) "Discretion and the determinate sentence." Crime and Delinquency 24 (October).

Corrections Magazine (1977) "Fixed sentencing becomes law in 3 states: other legislatures wary." Vol. 3.

DAVIS, K. C. (1969) Discretionary Justice: A Preliminary Inquiry. Baton Rouge: Louisiana State University Press.

DAWSON, R. O. (1969) Sentencing: The Decision as to Type, Length and Conditions of Sentence. Boston: Little, Brown.

EDELMAN, M. (1964) The Symbolic Uses of Politics. Urbana: University of Illinois Press.

FOGEL, D. (1976) We Are the Living Proof. Cincinnati: W. H. Anderson.

FRANKEL, M. E. (1973) Criminal Sentences: Law Without Order. New York: Hill & Wang.

GOTTFREDSON, D. M., C. A. COSGROVE, L. T. WILKINS, J. WALLERSTEIN, and C. RAUH (1978) Classification for Parole Decision Policy. Washington, DC: Government Printing Office.

GOTTFREDSON, D. M., L. T. WILKINS, P. B. HOFFMAN, and S. M. SINGER (1974) The Utilization of Experience in Parole Decision-Making: Summary Report and Supplementary Reports 1-13. Washington, DC: Government Printing Office.

GREENBERG, D. F. and D. HUMPHRIES (1980) "The cooptation of fixed sentencing reform." Crime and Delinquency 26 (April).

HAWKINS, K. O. (1971) Parole selection: the American experience." Ph.D. dissertation, University of Cambridge, England.

HOFFMAN, P. B. (1975) Federal Parole Guidelines: Three Years of Experience. Washington, DC: Research Unit, U.S. Board of Parole, Report 10.

KITTRIE, N. (1967) "The divestment of the criminal law and the coming of the therapeutic state." Suffolk University Law Review 1 (Spring): 43-76.

KRESS, J. M., L. T. WILKINS, and D. M. GOTTFREDSON (1976) "Is the end of judicial sentencing in sight?" Judicature 60.

LINDSEY, E. (1925) "Historical sketch of the indeterminate sentence and parole system." Journal of Criminal Law and Criminology 16 (May).

MARTINSON, R. (1976) "Critics of corrections speak out." Corrections Magazine 3.

McGEE, R. A. (1974) "A new look at sentencing—Part II." Federal Probation 38 (September): 3-11.

MORRIS, N. (1978) "Conceptual overview and commentary on the movement toward determinacy," in Determinate Sentencing: Reform or Regression. Washington, DC: Government Printing Office.

MOTLEY, C. B. (1973) " 'Law and order' and the criminal justice system." Journal of Criminal Law and Criminology 64 (September): 267-288.

MOULE, D. M. and J. K. HANFT, Jr. (1976) "Parole decision-making in Oregon." Oregon Law Review 55: 303-305.

National Advisory Commission on Criminal Justice Standards and Goals (1973) The Courts. Washington, DC: Government Printing Office.

National Council on Crime and Delinquency (1971) California Correctional System Study—The System. Sacramento: California Board of Corrections.

——— (1963) Model Sentencing Act. New York: National Council on Crime and Delinquency.

NEWMAN, D. J. (1978) Introduction to Criminal Justice (2nd ed.) Philadelphia: J. B. Lippincott.

O'LEARY, V. and D. DUFFEE (1972) "Correctional policy: a classification of goals designed for change." Crime and Delinquency 18 (October).

Oregon Legislative Fiscal Office (1974) "Study of the state board of parole." Salem.

PACKER, H. L. (1968) The Limits of the Criminal Sanction. Stanford, CA: Stanford University Press.

PARNAS, R. I. and M. B. SALERNO (1978) "The influence behind, substance and impact of the new determinate sentencing law in California." University of California Davis Law Review 11: 29-41.

Pilot Institute of Sentencing (1966) Federal Rules Decision 26.

RECKLESS, W. C. and H. E. ALLEN (1979) "Developing a national crime policy: the impact of politics on crime in America," in Criminology: New Concerns. Beverly Hills, CA: Sage.

REMINGTON, F. J. and D. J. NEWMAN (1962) "The Highland Park Institute on sentencing disparity." Federal Probation 26: 3-9.

San Francisco Sunday Examiner and Chronicle (1974) "Looks like the number's up for indefinite prison terms." Section A, December 8.

SMITH, J. F. (1973) "Prison reform through the legislature," in The Politics of Punishment. New York: Harper & Row.

STANLEY, D. (1976) Prisoners Among Us: The Problems of Parole. Washington, DC: The Brookings Institution.

TAYLOR, E. L. (1979) "In search of equity: the Oregon parole matrix." Federal Probation 43 (March).

TIMASHEFF, N. S. (1967) Sociological Theory. New York: Random House.

TRAVIS, L. F. III and V. O'LEARY (1979) Changes in Sentencing and Parole Decision Making: 1976-1978. Hackensack, NJ: National Council on Crime and Delinquency.

Twentieth Century Fund Task Force on Criminal Sentencing (1976) Fair and Certain Punishment. New York: McGraw-Hill.

VAN DEN HAAG, E. (1975) Punishing Criminals. New York: Basic Books.

VON HIRSCH, A. (1976) Doing Justice: The Choice of Punishments. New York: Hill & Wang.

——— and K. J. HANRAHAN (1979) The Question of Parole. Cambridge, MA: Ballinger.

WILCOX, C. (1929) "Parole: principles and practice." Journal of Criminal Law and Criminology 20: 345-354.

WILSON, J. Q. (1975) Thinking About Crime. New York: Basic Books.

——— (1968) Varieties of Police Behavior. Cambridge, MA: Harvard University Press.

Chapter 4

PAROLE GUIDELINES

IRA BLALOCK

Parole practices have been criticized on three grounds. First, it has been said that parole doesn't work; too many inmates enter the front door and leave through the back unreformed and bent on new criminal activity. Second, critics have said that indeterminate sentences leave everyone in the dark regarding the inmate's "debt." No one knows how long a person committed to the department of corrections will be in prison before the board of parole decides to release him or her. The justice of this practice is called into question, especially when offenders with essentially the same history and personality profiles receive widely disparate sentences from the courts and disparate prison terms from the parole board. Finally, parole decisionmaking policy is not explicit. In other words, the boards and commissions responsible for release operate in secret according to tacit policies unknown and unknowable to the public and the offender.[1] This contributes to cynicism, makes program planning impossible, and embitters offenders. Such embittered offenders, the argument goes, commit more, not fewer, crimes after release from prison (see American Friends, 1971; and von Hirsch and Hanrahan, 1979).

The Oregon Board of Parole, by adopting explicit guidelines pursuant to the passage of House Bill 2013 in 1977, has addressed two of these criticisms. The guidelines provide explicit structure to the discretion of the board without being procrustean, and offenders, as well as the public, know in advance the customary range of time to be served based on the seriousness of the instant offense and the prisoner's prior criminal history

and risk potential. Offense severity, already assigned three felony levels by
the Oregon legislature, is further broken down by the board's administrative rules.[2] Discretion is still possible within the durational range; variations are permitted because of aggravation or mitigation. However, the
aggravating or mitigating factors customarily considered by the board in
the exercise of its discretion are made explicit. The factors considered in
assessing the criminal history or risk of parole failure are likewise made
explicit. Rigidity is avoided by allowing the board to exercise its discretion, but only with explicit, reviewable, and written reasons (see Taylor,
1979).

This chapter addresses the problems created when only one criminal
justice agency, e.g., the Oregon Parole Board, implements guidelines. A
basic purpose of the guidelines is to introduce structure into a discretionary decisionmaking system—to produce more equity in the term-
setting decision. Obviously, the system can be undermined, at least partially, if only one agency articulates and adheres to structured policy
guidelines. As so often happens, the relationships among different actors in
the system resemble a quarrel or a fight. What happens if only one agency
uses guidelines is perhaps analogous to a boxing match in which only one
of the fighters has to follow the rules.

Some critics of the current effort to structure discretion are concerned
about piecemeal reform (see Foote, 1977: 133). Authority to allocate
punishments in Oregon is currently shared by numerous agencies: the
parole board, the Advisory Commission on Prison Terms and Parole
Standards, the sentencing judge, the prosecutor, and even the warden of
the prison, who can grant terminal leave and request increased sanctions or
reductions in prison terms for inmates. But so far it is only the parole
board's discretion that has been structured. Albert Alschuler (1977: 59),
one authority concerned about piecemeal reform, has written that
"although prosecutors' offices have in practice probably had a greater
influence on sentencing than any of the other agencies (not excluding state
legislators), the call for sentencing reform has largely ignored this extensive
prosecutorial power." Alschuler goes on to argue that the objectives of
reformers are likely to be frustrated as long as the reforms "leave the
prosecutor's power to formulate charges and to bargain for guilty pleas
unchecked" (1977: 59).

This chapter will explore the difficulty of piecemeal reform as it has
been experienced in Oregon. It is, I believe, an exaggeration to argue that
piecemeal reform will necessarily make things worse. However, the Oregon
reform is not complete, and there are problems because the power of the

parole board, which is in a position to reduce disparity and rectify abuses and inequities that occur at the front end of the system, is limited by explicit rules. There is no question that the Oregon reform could be enhanced with respect to equity in sentencing by structuring the discretion of judges and, most particularly, prosecutors.

PAROLE PRACTICE AND GUIDELINES

The parole board first has contact with an inmate at a prison term hearing held three to four months after the offender is received by the Corrections Division. At this hearing, several variables are considered in establishing a parole release date: the severity of the offense, the criminal history, and matters in aggravation or extenuation and mitigation. If the release date is within five years, the board will also decide whether to see the inmate again. If the board waives an "exit interview," the offender will be released without seeing the board again unless he or she is involved in misconduct or granted an administrative review (internal appeal). If the exit interview is waived, the board will decide how long the parole supervision period will be and establish any special conditions.

Offenders serving longer than five years will not be given the terms or conditions of their parole; they will be reviewed by the board after five years and then every three years as appropriate. At these subsequent reviews, the offender is eligible for a 20 percent reduction of the period under review (one year for five years and seven months for three years). If the offender's conduct has been good and if he or she has taken steps to rehabilitate (or habilitate) him- or herself, a reduction will be granted. Because of limited program opportunities, rehabilitation efforts are generously interpreted. In other words, faithful performance of a prison industry job, coupled with fairly clear conduct, is usually enough to earn a 20 percent reduction.

Offense severity and criminal history/risk are the two basic considerations in setting the initial parole release date. These two considerations are arranged in a matrix that is not unlike the mileage matrix appearing in the road maps that service stations used to give away. In a mileage matrix, you read down one side and find the name of a city you are leaving or approaching. Then you use the horizontal to find another city. The number of miles between the two cities is found where the columns intersect. Oregon's parole matrix works the same way (Table 4.1).[3] Down the left-hand side, crimes are arranged from low (Category 1) to high (Category 7) severity. The horizontal gives four levels of criminal history

TABLE 4.1 Criminal History/Risk Assessment Score

	11-9 Excellent	8-6 Good	5-3 Fair	2-0 Poor
Offense Severity Rating: (All ranges in Categories 1-6 shown in months)				
	Base Range			
Category 1	6	6	6-10	12-18
Category 2	6	6-10	10-14	16-24
Category 3	6-10	10-14	14-20	22-38
Category 4	10-16	16-22	22-30	32-44
Category 5	16-24	24-36	40-52	56-72
Category 6	30-40	44-56	60-80	90-130
Category 7 (in years)				
Subcategory 2	8-10	10-13	13-16	16-20
Subcategory 1	10-14	14-19	19-24	24-Life

or parole risk. They range from excellent (score between 9 and 11) to poor (score between 0 and 2). The score is determined by using the history/risk scoring device (Table 4.2).[4] Locate the criminal history/risk assessment score and then the crime category; at that intersection is a number that represents the range of time in months to be served.

If there are multiple, concurrently imposed sentences, the offense severity is established by using the most serious crime. The fact that concurrent sentences exist is generally considered an aggravating circumstance. Multiple sentences imposed consecutively are dealt with more severely. The sentence for the most serious crime becomes the principle or first crime in the series. The range for the principle crime is calculated as for any other crime. However, the subordinate range (or ranges, if there is more than one sentence) is taken from the base range, which is the shortest range for that crime category, as indicated in Table 4.1.[5] In other words, an offender is penalized by his or her prior record only once.

The legislature established other exceptions to the matrix. One of the most significant is the sentencing judge's authority under statute to impose minimum terms. The board can overrule minimum terms by a vote of four out of five members. However, it is often difficult to arrive at a term that four members will support. The 1981 legislature gave the board the same power to unsum ranges as it enjoys with respect to overriding minimum terms. Rules have been developed to aid the board in dealing with the decision to unsum ranges for consecutive sentences.

TABLE 4.2   Criminal History/Risk Assessment

Client's Name _____

Offense _____

A. No prior felony or misdemeanor convictions as an adult or juvenile: 3

One prior conviction: 2

Two or three prior convictions: 1

Four or more prior convictions: 0

B. No prior incarcerations (i.e., executed sentences of 90 days or more) as an adult or juvenile: 2

One or two prior incarcerations: 1

Three or more prior incarcerations: 0

C. Verified period of 3 years conviction free in the community prior to present incarceration: 1

Otherwise: 0

D. Age at commencement of behavior leading to this incarceration:

26 or older and at least one point received in Items A, B, or C: 2

26 or older and no points received in A, B, or C: 1

21 to under 26 and at least one point receivde in A, B, or C: 1

21 to under 26 and no points received in A, B, or C: 0

Under 21:   0

E. Present commitment does not include parole, probation, failure to appear, release agreement, escape, or custody violation: 2

Present commitment involves probation, release agreement, or failure to appear violation: 1

Present commitment involves parole, escape, or custody violation: 0

F. Has no admitted or documented heroin or opiate derivative abuse problem: 1

Otherwise: 0

Total History/Risk Assessment Score: _____

Departures from the guideline range are permitted when aggravating or mitigating circumstances are found. Variations are essential to equity in term-setting because of the diverse criminal behavior that can be encountered under any formal crime category or title. Deciding upon variations is part of the problem; making findings with respect to aggravation or mitigation is a very practical and immediate concern. Usually the front end of the criminal justice system exacerbates the situation. The police, prosecutors, and judges possess enormous discretion. The police, in the first instance, have to decide whether to charge on an offender or to send him or her home. The prosecutor, in turn, has tremendous discretion in charging and plea bargaining. The judge, in turn, has the option to place an offender on probation, commit him or her to jail, sentence him or her to prison for up to 5, 10, or 20 years (for class C, B, or A felonies), or to declare him or her dangerous, which carries a maximum of 30 years in prison. In Oregon, the prosecutor can request and the judge may impose multiple sentences in a consecutive or concurrent fashion. Moreover, the judge can impose a minimum sentence of one-half of the maximum term he imposes.[6] If the judge does this on consecutive sentences, the minimum can become enormously long.

The board's rules generally work efficiently to reduce disparate decisions. However, the lack of standards, rules, or guidelines at the front end of the system makes the board's work more difficult. The board's previously unchecked discretion has now been limited. Unfortunately, those limits sometimes work to prevent the board from reaching an appropriate decision, i.e., setting a just and equitable term. Variations from the range have been limited, and it is sometimes impossible to hold an offender for an appropriate length of time or to release him or her as early as desirable. The board can, of course, do nothing for equity if the offender's charge is reduced and probation is granted. Those who should not be in prison can be released when they first appear. However, that decision can only be made after the offender actually appears, and equity can be further frustrated by inappropriate minimum terms, consecutive sentences, or by minimum terms imposed consecutively.

In brief compass, the absence of judicial standards and unbridled prosecutorial discretion often frustrates the board's search for equity.

PROSECUTIONAL DISCRETION

Prosecutors in America are noted for possessing enormous discretion,[7] and the way they exercise their discretion significantly affects the parole board's term-setting practice. Prosecutorial discretion is of even greater significance now that the parole board's practices are constrained by standards and rules. Two areas of prosecutorial discretion—charging and plea bargaining—are of special interest to the parole board.

The prosecutor is umhampered by rules when filing charges against a defendant. He or she can overcharge an offender and then threaten to ask for mandatory sentences, threaten to recommend consecutive sentences, or threaten further investigation if a plea bargain is not entered into. Prosecutors unbounded by rules are in a very strong bargaining position, particularly when it relates to an offender who thinks he or she is guilty. The burden of producing evidence and the presumption of innocence do not function the same way in the prosecutor's office as they do in the courtroom.

It is a common experience for a parole board member to hear an offender complain bitterly about the sentence received on the guilty plea he or she made in court. When asked why the offender pled guilty, the response that "I had no choice" is frequently heard. Admittedly, the offender has different aims or objectives when he or she pleads guilty or no contest before the court than during the prayer made later before a parole board. In the first instance, the offender is avoiding a threat from the prosecutor by pleading guilty. In the second instance, he or she seeks a release from prison at the earliest possible time. One may question the sincerity or motives of a prisoner who argues that he or she was ill-served by a prosecutor and public defender striking a bargain on the offender's behalf. The judge will, of course, explain that the defendant has a right to a trial. It all looks "nice and legal" in the courtroom. Later, in the prison, it may not feel that way to the prisoner. It is difficult not to conclude that justice, rehabilitation, and public safety are ill served by unstructured discretion in the prosecutor's office and trial court. Such a system is all too often a "Bleak House" to the defendant, even if it appears to be an uncoerced plea accepted after warnings and explanations about waived rights.

Variations in plea bargaining practices also present enormous problems for the board in meting out equitable and uniform prison terms. A murder may be pleaded to manslaughter, a rape to attempted rape, and other serious crimes can simply be dropped. Occasionally, an offender will insist upon his or her constitutional rights and go to trial; by doing so, the offender risks an enormous increase in the penalty tariff. The pressure is enormous to take the plea; an experienced prosecutor may, for example, agree to a reduced sentence. Suppose a Burglary I has been committed.

The prosecutor can agree to forego the maximum of 20 years and recommend 10 years in exchange for a plea—an "excellent bargain," an inexperienced defense counsel might say to his client.

Later, while the prisoner is reflecting in his or her cell, a different picture may emerge, a picture that does not reflect the careful warnings, the informed notice, and careful questions from the judge before any rights were waived or pleas accepted. We are all familiar with pictures that present illusions. Some pictures can be perceived as one thing until a different pattern is discovered; a can-can girl can become a hag with a bonnet. After you have seen both images within the same picture, you can, by force of will, perceive the other. The exercise of rights in the court may sometimes be like that. For most offenders, the picture is that the plea ensures them some benefit. For others, particularly when the charge or bargain has been manipulated by a prosecutor, the disposition and sentence, even with careful warnings and the full panoply of due process, are more analogous to the hag in a bonnet than a can-can girl.

The operator of one of Oregon's drug treatment programs has convinced some prosecutors to recommend (and judges to use) the treatment program as an alternative to incarceration, and to provide the operator with a hammer to ensure the "enrollee" is motivated. The hammer is a suspended sentence. Some judges provide very big hammers. For example, recently a former enrollee appeared before the parole board for a prison term hearing. The sentence was two 20-year consecutive sentences with 10-year minimums suspended, pending successful completion of the program. In my opinion, the offender, who had committed two armed robberies, deserved to go to prison in the first place. However, two 10-year minimums imposed consecutively constitute a disproportionally harsh penalty for a probation failure. Many prosecutors do not recommend minimum sentences in that fashion. A few do, and the hammer sought by the program operator may ultimately lead to widely disparate dispositions. Leaving aside the morality of coerced treatment, the result can be shocking. The board's rules, of course, operate to make it more difficult than under the previous discretionary system to grant appropriate relief. In such cases, guidelines, in fact, create disparity.

Another source of disparity comes about when relatively unusual convictions are encountered, for example, incestuous rape between a father and daughter. Some prosecutions move forward and charge rape in the first degree. Other times, particularly if the crime is the first for a defendant, the charge will be bargained to Sex Abuse I. The difference in the maximum sentence is 15 years. Sex abuse is a class C felony carrying a 5-year maximum. Rape I is a class A felony carrying a 20-year maximum.

The difference between the two decisions is solely up to the prosecutor who charges or plea bargains the case.

Yet another source of disparity is found in the way aggravation is viewed; some prosecutors and judges see the typical case of incestuous rape as aggravated, because the criminal behavior is likely to have been engaged in over a protracted period of time. Some decisionmakers see the special relationship between a father and daughter as a violation of trust, and hence a greater degree of culpability is ascribed to the father than to a stranger who commits rape.

In other courtrooms, such behavior is seen as a misplaced pleasure bond and the protracted nature of the crime is not perceived as aggravating, because that is the usual nature of incestuous relations. The point is not what is the right view and disposition or even if there is a "right" answer; the issue is, lacking prosecutorial and sentencing standards, widely disparate treatment results. Further, following such disparate charging and sentencing, the guidelines then perpetuate that disparity. The parole board's guidelines, meant to limit and structure the board's powers, can enforce a disparate disposition. It is impossible for the board to raise the penalty for sex abuse to equal the sanction for rape in the first degree. The opposite is also true: The board cannot reduce the Rape I sanction to equalize the disposition. Not surprisingly, there is a division among the five members of the board on this issue, and this division further limits the power of the board to ameliorate the disparity between the dispositions in such cases. Additionally, one must consider the number of judges and prosecutors when disparity is the issue. There are 36 counties in Oregon, each with a district attorney. There are many more deputies. Each prosecutor has different policies (mostly tacit) about charging and plea bargaining. Some prosecutors will, for example, readily charge a gun and then take it away as a part of a plea; others are more reluctant to lose a gun in negotiations.

Now that the parole board's discretion is limited, these variations in charging and bargaining practices are very important. More than ever before, prosecutors can dictate or influence the prison term. As one example, the ranges for what is actually a rape in the first degree would be as follows:

		Disposition
—	Charge: Rape I (no prior crimes)	30 to 40 months
—	Plead to Rape II (no prior crimes)	10 to 16 months
—	Plead to Sex Abuse I (no prior crimes)	6 to 10 months

The matrix range is much lower for the sex abuse or Rape II crime title. It is very difficult for the board to aggravate the lower charges or mitigate the Rape I. Thus, disparity has, in some cases, been locked into the system by the rules.

LACK OF STANDARDS FOR THE JUDICIARY

Even though the parole board's term-setting discretion was structured pursuant to the 1977 legislation, the trial court judges have as much discretion as ever when imposing sentence. A representative of the trial judges was cautioned during the 1977 session that the legislature would come back to the question of judicial discretion at the next session. Further, the judges were warned to do something about adding structure on their own initiative or face the prospect of the legislature imposing structure on the courts. However, the warning wasn't followed up by the legislature and the judges did nothing. Now, finally, a task force is at work on the problem of judicial discretion.

And problem it is. There are about 100 trial court judges (circuit court) in Oregon; this does not include pro tem appointments. Because of a lack of standards, the sentencing practices and policies vary enormously. There are four areas in which the lack of an articulated and guiding philosophy and attendant standards for the judiciary particularly affects the parole board:

(1) lack of explicit sentencing philosophy,
(2) lack of standards to determine sentence length,
(3) lack of standards in imposing mandatory minimums, and
(4) lack of standards in imposing consecutive sentences.

The lack of standards is a problem at the most basic and philosophical level, because the judges do not have an articulated sentencing philosophy. House Bill 2013 set forth a just deserts (a modified just deserts) model for the parole board.[8] Rehabilitation, deterrence, and public protection can be taken into consideration, but not to an extent inconsistent with the basic principle of just deserts. However, the judiciary has no articulated principles of sentencing. Judges may take any rational goal into consideration when imposing sentence. One judge may emphasize rehabilitation, another just deserts, and another public protection. With this lack of articulated philosophy, it is inevitable that judicial sentencing practices vary enormously.

One problem area noticed by the parole board is the lack of guidelines for the decision to grant or deny probation—the "in/out" decision. There is a great deal of variation around the state, variation from rural to urban judges and from judge to judge within a certain locale. Not infrequently, the board reviews prisoners who should never have been sent to prison in the first place—and because of the guidelines, the board often has trouble dealing with such cases. Certainly the board can and does release some or even most of these prisoners at their first appearance. However, if jail time is considered, such inappropriately incarcerated defendants may serve as many as nine months and sometimes more before they first appear and can be released on parole.

The utilization of prison varies from county to county. During 1980, for example, the overall percentage of class C felonies received at the institution as a percentage of the total commitments was 47 percent. For some rural counties, the percentage was 100 percent. While absolute numbers from these counties were small, a wide differential is still revealed by the ratio. Other counties with substantially more volume were sending class C offenders at percentages of 55 percent to 68 percent. In fact, 12 of the 36 counties had 55 percent or more of their total commitments as class C felonies, nearly 10 percent above the arithmetic average. Five sent more than 60 percent of their commitments as class C felonies. These figures reveal a disparate use of prison.[9] The threshold, particularly in smaller counties and cities, for sending an offender to prison is, in some cases, too low compared to other jurisdictions.

Even more shocking is the disparate use made of prison for felonious driving offenses. If the use of probation is compared with incarceration, clearly disparate use of imprisonment is revealed. The overall percentage of driving convictions sent to corrections division institutions as opposed to probation was 11.5 percent for the years 1978, 1979, and 1980. Multnomah County, the largest and most urban Oregon county, sent 18.2 percent of their felonious driving offenders to prison. Washington County, on the other hand, sent just 3 percent of felonious driving offenders to prison. Lane County sent 17.4 percent, Coos County sent 22.5 percent, Union County sent 33.3 percent, and Tillamook County sent 1.8 percent to prison.[10] Clearly, the "in/out" decision follows very different patterns throughout the state.

There are also variations in the length of sentence. A review of seven "driving while suspended" sentences revealed: 1 at 2 years, 1 at 2.5 years, 3 at 3 years, 1 at 5 years, and 1 at 5.5 years. The highest sentence (5.5 years) is nearly three times the lowest penalty (2 years) recorded; this

TABLE 4.3

Number		Sentence Length
1	at	3 years
1		4 years
6		5 years
1		6 years
3		7 years
1		8 years
1		10 years
1		14 years

represents a significant variation in dispositions for driving while suspended.[11]

If more serious crimes are considered, the variation is even greater. For example, Table 4.3 reviews 15 Burglary I sentences.[12] The difference between the lowest and the highest is almost 500 percent. It is not unknown for a person convicted of a routine burglary to receive 20 years. If one were to examine the sentencing with respect to history/risk score (H/R score) and crime category, the picture is little, if any, improved. For example, the first 25 Robbery I sentences encountered appear in Table 4.4.[13]

Clearly, the board is encountering widely disparate sentencing, and much of the disparity is attributable to the county from which the prisoner was committed or to a particular judge within a county. Considerations such as urban or rural county and conservative or liberal judge explain much of the disparity. Some judges become known in court for their sentencing patterns, and the parole board soon learns each judge's idiosyncracies.

The judge's authority to impose minimum terms is the third area of concern to the parole board.[14] Under H.B. 2013, the sentencing judge is authorized to impose a minimum of one-half the maximum he imposes. For example, in a class A felony that carries a maximum of 20 years, the judge can impose a minimum of 10 years. This legal provision creates significant problems for the board because there are no standards governing the prosecutor's recommendation of the minimum term or the judge's imposition of the minimum.

In fact, recent efforts of the parole board to impose guidelines for presentence report recommendations with respect to minimum terms were

TABLE 4.4   Robbery I

	H/R Score (11-9) Excellent	H/R Score (8-6) Good	H/R Score (5-3) Fair	H/R Score (2-0) Poor	Sentencing in Years
1			x		5 years
2	x				6 years
3			x		7 years
4				x	8 years
5				x	8 years
6		x			10 years
7		x			10 years
8			x		10 years
9			x		10 years
10			x		10 years
11			x		10 years
12				x	10 years
13				x	10 years
14			x		11 years
15				x	11 years
16		x			15 years
17				x	17 years
18			x		18 years
19			x		20 years
20				x	20 years
21				x	20 years
22				x	20 years
23				x	20 years
24				x	20 years
25	x				40 years*

* Two Robbery I sentences were imposed consecutively

beaten back by the judges. The one fail-safe provision that was included in the 1977 Parole Reform Act (the power of the parole board to overrule a minimum term with four out of five votes) is difficult to exercise. Four out of five votes are difficult to secure. For whatever reasons, the board is sometimes reluctant to challenge a judicial sentence. Further, because there is no statutory principle with respect to minimums, extraneous considerations, or even changing moods or personality considerations within the board, can influence the board's decisions to sustain or override minimum terms. To date, the board has not developed rules or policies to structure the decision to override minimum sentences.[15] Without doubt, the most draconian terms are sure to arouse the board's sense of fairness. However, even with widely disparate minimum terms the board can only impose a reduced term that four members will support. This means that even if the board agrees to override a minimum term, the harshest judgment will prevail. The difference between what the majority wants and what one board member can arbitrarily insist upon can be quite substantial. This is particularly true if the crime is one that a board member holdout finds particularly or idiosyncratically reprehensible.

The issue of concurrent or consecutive sentences is of vital concern since the Parole Reform Act of 1977 was passed. The legislature mandated that if the sentences were imposed consecutively, then the ranges in the matrix shown earlier must be summed. If sentences are imposed concurrently, the range is selected by reference to the most serious crime. It is, therefore, a matter of great significance whether sentences are concurrent or consecutive.

Initially, no guidance with respect to consecutive sentences was provided by the legislature for any of the actors in the system, except that the parole board must sum the ranges. However, the 1981 legislative assembly addressed this problem.

The problem of disparity in prison terms because of the judicial decision to impose consecutive sentences was first discovered by the parole board soon after the 1977 law went into effect. Offenders with no discernible difference that the board could determine, either clinically or with reference to crime categories and criminal history, were being given quite disparate treatment. For example, it is not unusual for a youthful burglar serving his first term to cooperate with the police in "clearing" other burglaries by confessing to multiple offenses. Most often, such offenders are prosecuted on one or two burglaries and given concurrent sentences. The actual prison term for youthful offenders convicted of property crimes seldom exceeds 24 months and is often 10 to 14 months. However, one such offender who confessed and cleared a series of burglaries was, in fact, convicted of five such burglaries. He was, moreover, given five consecutive sentences and five minimum terms of one year each (minimums are summed in the same fashion as ranges). Therefore, the total of the minimum sentences was 60 months. The point is not only that 60 months is too long, which I believe is patently obvious where a first-time youthful offender convicted of property crimes is concerned, but that the disposition is so widely disparate with similarly situated offenders who received concurrent sentences. The resulting disparity is shocking to the conscience of anyone concerned about equity.

While there are no parole board standards to guide the decision with respect to minimum terms, the board has produced some guidance for consecutive sentences. In deciding whether it is proper to maintain summed ranges for consecutive sentences, the board has developed a set of questions:[16]

(1) Is the criminal history extensive (history/risk score 2 or less)?
(2) Are crimes separate episodes?
(3) Are crimes separate and distinct, i.e., rape and sodomy?
(4) Is minimum sentence below principal range?
(5) Is mitigation absent or minimal?
(6) Is aggravation substantial and weightier than mitigation that might be present?
(7) Does history/risk score understate the criminal history?
(8) Are the crimes characteristic of the offender or part of an uncharacteristic crime spree?

The board also requires that the requisite aggravation necessary to justify summed ranges increases with each sentence in the series. Further, the board is more likely to accept summed ranges when the crimes are person-to-person crimes. Property crimes, unless the potential harm or loss is exceptionally high, are more likely to be "unstacked."

To the board member, the experience of setting terms is an intensely collegial one. Members appear together in panels to review the work of other panel members on periodic reviews and appeals. They are constantly "checked" by a collegial body of only five members. This is in contrast to nearly 100 judges and 36 district attorneys and their deputies who see one another only at conferences where their criticisms are more likely to be directed at the parole board than toward each other. In short, the differences in the way the decisionmakers work is enormous. The large number of judges and prosecutors makes dealing with disparity more problematic. To the judge, sentencing is an individual matter dealing with comparatively rare individual sentencing decisions. Unfortunately, this disparity is aggravated in some respects by the parole board guidelines. Guidelines are, generally speaking, conducive to less disparity. However, if the board has to sum ranges or produce a greater quorum to override a judicial minimum, then it is apparent that for those cases, at least, greater disparity can be built into the ultimate prison term decision by the existence of the guidelines. When, for example, the board is confronted by a judge who is intolerant of guidelines or upset about the board's decision-making, the board, to recall our early analogy, is like a prize fighter entering the ring bounded by the Marquis DeQueensbury rules while the other combatant, the judge, is free to pursue the "fight" in any manner that he chooses.

"READING THROUGH" THE OFFICIAL RECORD

Discretion exercised at the prosecutorial or trial court level poses a serious problem for parole boards using structured discretion. The term-setting agent, whether the parole board or the sentencing judge or perhaps both, has to read through the bargain if equity and fairness in termsetting are going to prevail. Two offenders who have both been found guilty of unarmed robbery in fact may have committed quite different acts. One offender may have used a sawed-off shotgun and locked the proprietor in a walk-in freezer as compared to another offender who was "boosting" goods from a convenience store and broke loose from a security agent.

There are many other examples. Joyriding in an automobile that is not damaged is a category 1 offense. If the offender is in the worst history/risk category, the penalty is 12 to 18 months. One of the state's prosecutors discovered an anomoly in the guideline matrix. If a car is valued at over $5,000 and is taken by a joyrider, the penalty, if the prosecutor charges theft in the first degree, is 22-32 months (category 3 offense) for the worst history/risk category. Nothing has changed but the way the crime is charged by the prosecutor. In order to make an equitable decision, the board must look past the crime title and plea bargain to the "real" offense behavior.

Obviously, quite different behaviors may be represented by a crime title from a criminal code. If the purpose of guidelines is to introduce consistency in dealing with similarly situated offenders, then the actual offense behavior becomes more important than the crime title. This raises a concern over what data elements will be considered when classifying an offender.

The practices in guideline states differ as to the setting and categorizing of offense severity. In Minnesota and Oregon the crime category depends in large measure on the crime of conviction. Some crime titles that cover a wide range of behaviors (such as burglary and theft) are subcategorized by such elements as dollar loss, use of weapon, or confronting a victim. The U.S. Parole Commission ignores the crime title and classifies the offense with reference to the "real offense" behavior. This practice allows the parole commission to "read through" the bargain and categorize crimes based on what the commission believes really happened. Due process concerns are raised by this practice. Oregon uses aggravation and mitigation to deal with "real offense" behavior. This is a more limiting practice and means that the offender who plea bargains will probably receive a lesser penalty than called for by the actual offense behavior.

DISCUSSION AND CONCLUSIONS

The guidelines adopted by the board have reduced disparity, produced an early time-fix, and made the decision criteria more explicit. Guidelines do not reduce recidivism; they were not meant to reduce failure or eliminate new crimes by parolees. They provide for more equitable treatment and sanctions that are more proportionate to the crime severity and criminal history of the offender. To the extent that desert criteria allow, the Oregon guidelines allow for holding offenders who are more likely to reoffend longer before they are released on parole.

One way to help improve the image of the guidelines and the parole board, *and* to increase the likelihood of equity and uniformity in prison terms is to provide standards, guidelines, or rules at the front end of the system, i.e., at the arrest, prosecution, and sentencing levels.

Some steps to improve the exercise of discretionary decisions have already been taken. The most recent legislative session has expanded the board's powers to deal with sentencing decisions to impose multiple sentences in a consecutive fashion. The board can now unsum ranges with four concurring votes. This reform, however, expanded the parole board's powers; it did not attempt to structure the source of the problem—judicial discretion.

While much of the discretion to establish prison terms has appropriately been confined by the parole board's rules, other problems need attention. For example, the legislature has imposed minimum sentences for crimes committed with a gun. The legislation requires the district attorney to inform the court if the defendant used or threatened to use an operable or inoperable firearm during the commission of a felony. If the judge suspects a firearm was used, he is supposed to make an inquiry. If a firearm was used, a minimum sentence of 5 years for the first conviction, 10 years for the second, and 30 years for the third shall be imposed.[17] Disregarding the question of legislative intent, prosecutors often "swallow" the gun in the indictment or the judges overlook it in the sentence. Many times the offender "cops a plea" to avoid the enhanced penalty for the gun. Perhaps the minimums don't really enjoy the support of the prosecutors and the judges; the prosecutor, however, has found a marvelous tool to pressure defendants during plea bargaining. Let us suppose, however, that a sentencing judge knows about the statute requiring minimums if a firearm is used (some of them don't seem to) and is scrupulous about following the law. If the defendant used a gun, that scrupulous judge is to be avoided like the plague by the defense bar. A law-abiding judge in this case can hurt a client. Two or three Oregon judges are, in fact, scrupulous about following this statute. Sometimes the prosecutor also wants to follow the statute because he or she wants a longer term than would otherwise be imposed. Minimums, imposed because of a firearm, are not subject to being overridden by a parole board. It is a case of the legislature passing a guideline law and then overruling themselves on a particular category of crime. Again, equity is the loser.

In order to increase the chances that equitable and uniform periods of incarceration will be served, standards should be adopted at all decision points in the sanctioning system. We could start by requiring prosecutors to explain on the record why charges have been dropped. A prosecutor should be required to explain the original arrest, indictment, and subsequent charges pleaded to and explain the reasons or bargains that resulted in dropped charges. The magistrate should be empowered to order prosecution to proceed in cases where that appears appropriate. In fact, dismissed charges should be handled the same way. The magistrate could then provide a second-level review or check to ensure that political or otherwise influential defendants are not given special treatment.[18]

The power to be lenient is the power to discriminate. Currently, American prosecutors have unfettered discretion to be lenient. Prominent citizens, e.g., corporate executives, leading lawyers, or politically powerful defendants who have been charged with crimes, provide temptations for prosecutors to be lenient and dismiss charges. If the rule of law is to be expanded, then this area of discretion must be subjected to review and the discretion structured.[19]

Structuring discretion can be handled most efficiently through administrative rule-making. This could be provided within the attorney general's office or through a specialized task force or commission. Wherever it is provided, the rules that structure the prosecutor's discretion should be "owned" by the prosecutors. This could be accomplished by having prosecutors involved in the rule-making. Such rules can channel discretion and provide meaningful criteria for a review of the prosecutor's discretion.

The judge should be given the option to apply the prison term or parole guidelines at sentencing or allow the parole board to set them. This would allow the judge to apply the rules and set an initial release date or impose the maximum penalty and allow the parole board to apply the guidelines and set the initial release date. If the judge followed the guidelines and set the initial release date, the board should be limited to a specific variation, perhaps 20 percent of the term, unless four members voted to overrule the initial release date. However, I would allow the board to send the case back to the judge if the guidelines were not followed and allow the judge to amend or reject the board's position. The board should explain the reasons for any differing assessment with respect to application of the guidelines in the explanation sending the case back for reconsideration. Then appellate review could focus on cases where a divergence appeared. This would narrow the issue and provide for more meaningful review without increasing the workload of the court. In fact, because the issues on review have been sharpened, the workload should be reduced. These suggestions are moderate in scope, yet they would provide more structure without eliminating individual judgments. Moreover, they maintain the parole board as a safety net and otherwise allow for checks and balances.

Many persons believe that with the adequate guidelines, the judges could do the term-setting without recourse to a subsequent review by a parole board. I believe that this course is unwise. Parole boards provide an important review. They are collegial bodies more likely to be consistent than 100 judges scattered throughout a state. Currently, all 100 or so of these judges are white, predominantly Christian, males. There are no minorities, women, or persons of color making sentencing decisions. Parole boards provide for more representative participation than we have so far experienced within the ranks of the judiciary. They are also able to respond to post-incarceration changes. These are a few of the reasons I believe parole should be retained. If, on the other hand, the judges apply the guidelines and set initial dates accurately and subsequent modifications are not needed, then the decisionmakers can reexamine the role of the parole board in the light of the data. Experience in a more widely structured system is essential before a workable and effective agency, such as the parole board, can be eliminated.

The primary goal should be to make the entire system more equitable. I believe that this can best be accomplished by enhancing the rule of law within the judicial and prosecutorial ranks.

NOTES

1. For an objective analysis of the Oregon Parole Board practices prior to the adoption of guidelines, see Moule and Hanft (1976).

2. The current rules of the board may be reviewed in Oregon Administrative Rules (OAR), ch. 255.

3. OAR 255-35-025, Exhibit C.

4. OAR 255-35-015.

5. OAR 255-35-022.

6. ORS 144.110.

7. For a discussion of structuring discretion and in particular prosecutorial discretion, see Davis (1969: ch. 8).

8. ORS 144.780.

9. Oregon Corrections Division Periodic Report, "Class C Commitments to OSP, OSCI, OWCC (as reported)," ADP Support Services, March 10, 1980.

10. Oregon Law Enforcement Council published statistics.

11. Oregon Corrections Division printout of population showing population and including crime category and sentence length. The first seven sentences encountered are reported.

12. Ibid.

13. Ibid.

14. ORS 144.110.

15. OAR 255-35-020 (2).

16. OAR 255-35-022 presents the considerations in a slightly different format.

17. ORS 161.610.

18. ORS 135.405 requires that "similarly situated defendants should be afforded equal plea agreement opportunities." In the absence of explicit rules governing plea agreement procedures, it is impossible to challenge or indeed verify that "similarly situated" defendants receive the same opportunity.

19. Davis (1969: 188-189) points out that even when the prosecutor's discretion is confined, structured, and checked by statute, the major outlines of prosecutorial power are governed by a set of assumptions. The principal assumption is that the power to prosecute must be discretionary. Currently, prosecutors' decisions in Oregon are not effectively reviewed. Invariably, the prosecutors will, Davis points out, assert that unstructured discretion is, "as everybody knows," necessary. "Why," Davis asks, "should the discretionary power be so unconfined that, of half a dozen potential defendants he can prove guilty, he can select any one for prosecution and let the other five go, making his decision, if he chooses, on the basis of considerations extraneous to justice?"

REFERENCES

ALSCHULER, A. (1977) "Sentencing reform and prosecutorial power: a critique of recent proposals for 'fixed' and 'presumptive' sentencing," in Determinate Sentencing: Reform or Regression? Proceedings of the Special Conference on Determinate Sentencing, Boalt Hall School of Law, University of California at Berkeley, June 2-3.

American Friends Service Committee (1971) Report of Crime and Punishment in America. New York: Hill & Wang.

DAVIS, K. C. (1969) Discretionary Justice: A Preliminary Inquiry. Baton Rouge: Louisiana State University Press.

FOOTE, C. (1977) "Deceptive determinate sentencing," in Determinate Sentencing: Reform or Regression? Proceedings of the Special Conference on Determinate Sentencing, Boalt Hall School of Law, University of California at Berkeley, June 2-3.

MOULE, D. M. and J. K. HANFT (1976) "Parole decision-making in Oregon." Oregon Law Review 55 (3): 303-347.

TAYLOR, E. L. (1979) "In search of equity: the Oregon parole matrix." Federal Probation (March): 52-59.

VON HIRSCH, A. and K. HANRAHAN (1979) The Question of Parole. Cambridge, MA: Ballinger.

Chapter 5

REMOVING THE EFFECTS OF DISCRIMINATION IN SENTENCING GUIDELINES

BRIDGET A. STECHER
RICHARD F. SPARKS

The literature on the sentencing of criminal offenders has been concerned with "disparity" for longer than most of us care to remember.[1] Prominent among the causes cited for the supposed disparity in the sentencing process has been the consideration, by judges, of ethically irrelevant or discriminatory factors as grounds for their sentencing decisions.[2] Judges have been criticized for imposing different sentences on offenders who are similar in respect to the characteristics normally thought to be relevant to sentences, such as the nature and circumstances of the offense and the offender's prior record. In some cases, at least, this unfairness is thought to have been based on factors such as race or social class.[3]

Sentencing guidelines, one of the newer methods proposed to control sentencing disparity,[4] purport to provide a model of sentencing that is free

AUTHORS' NOTE: The research contained in this chapter was conducted using data obtained under grant 78-NI-AX-0147 from the National Institute of Justice (formerly the National Institute of Law Enforcement and Criminal Justice), Law Enforcement Assistance Administration, U.S. Department of Justice, and administered by Rutgers University, School of Criminal Justice, Newark, New Jersey. The points of view or opinions expressed in this chapter are those of the authors and do not necessarily represent the official position or policies of the National Institute of Justice or of the U.S. Department of Justice.

from the bias that results when judges consider ethically irrelevant factors in reaching their sentencing decisions. Since ethically irrelevant factors such as race or sex are not explicitly *included* as items in the guidelines model, it is often assumed that the resultant sentences derived from the model have *eliminated* the disparity that might be caused by such factors. The purpose of this study is to examine this claim in some detail. In so doing, we would also like to point out some ways in which guideline developers can completely subvert their aim of eliminating disparity by overlooking some statistical issues in removing the effects of discriminatory factors from empirically based sentencing guidelines.

SENTENCING GUIDELINES: SOME GENERALITIES

Decisionmaking guidelines have a relatively short, but varied history in criminal justice settings. Originally proposed to provide a general statement of the policies of the U.S. Board of Parole (now the U.S. Parole Commission) governing the release of offenders from confinement (Gottfredson et al., 1975), the concept was soon extended to the sentencing process, where guidelines were intended to provide a decisionmaking aid to judges (Wilkins et al., 1976: 20).[5] Sentencing guidelines have been said to be "empirically derived" (as they most commonly have been to date) from analysis of case-level data on past paroling or sentencing decisions.[6] (It is worth noting, in passing, that this need not be the case.)[7] The earliest sentencing guidelines were developed for use by judges on a more or less voluntary basis, in that the guidelines recommendation was said to be not legally binding on the decisionmaker.[8] More recently, sentencing guidelines have been instituted on a mandatory basis by statute law.[9]

Inspection of the sentencing guidelines developed to date makes it clear that, empirically derived or not, they represent a very mixed breed. What all of them have in common, however, is a clear intention to affect the policies governing decisions made in the future through the promulgation of stated decisionmaking rules.[10] Although the rhetoric that decisionmaking guidelines are "descriptive, not prescriptive" (Wilkins et al., 1976; Kress et al., 1976) has been attached to the concept since its origin, the very concept of guidelines shows that rhetoric to be false. At their simplest level of construction, empirically derived guidelines purport to describe past practice by noting factors that are strong predictors of past sentencing decisions. To describe past practice (to the extent that that can be done with accuracy) in a set of rules intended for *consultation* in future cases is also clearly to *prescribe* future sentencing policy. This fact is underscored by the methods most commonly used to determine which factors will be incorporated in the decisionmaking rules. If past practices were to be completely described, then obviously *all* of the factors that influenced the decision in each case—whether morally iniquitous or not—would have to be included in the model. This has not been the case; rather, most of the models developed have used only a *limited* number of factors in the guidelines model[11]—such as general items of information pertaining to the offense committed and the offender's prior record—and the items chosen have most often been those that could account for significant portions in decision variation across an entire sample of cases.

The more enlightened of the researchers involved in guidelines development have realized that both the concept and the use of the tool are heavily laden with prescription about sentencing policies. At a more advanced level, therefore, guidelines research results have been consciously modified to reflect policy decisions, not so much about past practices, but rather about how various factors *should* be used to create a just sentencing policy in the future.[12]

CONTROLLING VARIATION IN DECISIONMAKING: REMOVING CERTAIN VARIABLES FROM A SENTENCING GUIDELINES MODEL

One very good reason that past practice is often not fully described in a sentencing guidelines model is because it may have contained some variation in sentences due to the effects of items considered to be inappropriate or unethical influences on sentences. What sorts of items are to be considered inappropriate or unethical? We begin by considering "race" (using that term as a shorthand including ethnicity) because it is the most often-cited example of a cause of unwarranted sentence disparity, and we will use it as an example in a particular case study of the problem. But race is not the only thing that needs to be considered here. What else might be involved?

At the most simplistic level, the answer is quite clear. First, one would assume that sentence length variations caused by items over which even the offender has no control, such as race, or sex, or even length of big toe, would be clearly improper. After all, the offender cannot do much about the color of his skin or the length of his big toe. But the question cannot be answered as simply as this. Other types of factors, which may have nothing at all to do with the offender, may prove to be important considerations in judges' determinations of sentence lengths, though they may be ultimately thought to be inappropriate or unethical. In a statewide sentencing guidelines model, for example, it would seem clearly unethical to build county-based sentence variations into the final model. Similarly, most persons would agree that differences in correctional resources from one area of a state to another—that previously may have resulted in different sentences for offenders from one part of the state as compared to the other—should not be reflected in a set of statewide sentencing guidelines. Or should they? Unfortunately, the answers to even these relatively simple questions about the inclusion of appropriate guidelines factors are not readily clear, nor do we presume that they should be. But having decided upon the simplest types of factors that should *not* influence sentences, regardless of what those factors might be, how then does one remove their effects from a sentencing guidelines model?

We have noted that factors such as race, sex, and so forth represent the simplest types of unacceptable items that researchers must consider in order to exclude their effects from guideline models. To digress for a moment, it must be noted that these things are often, or even usually, highly correlated with other items that are often treated as acceptable decisionmaking criteria. Take, for example, the variable "race." The question of how one removes the effects of race from a sentencing guideline model is a particularly complex one in light of the sorts of factors that are included in most guidelines developed to date. These factors usually include the seriousness of one's prior adult criminal record, juvenile record, and one's social stability—all of them things that racial minorities tend to rack up pretty nasty scores on. These factors are nonetheless included in guidelines because there is some sort of *justification* for their inclusion; thus, for example, offenders (regardless of race) who have long prior records *should* have that fact considered against them. The question that is not usually addressed is whether prior discrimination against minorities has led to different prior arrest and conviction patterns that continue to reflect racial discrimination by their inclusion in guidelines.

Finally, a number of items, such as incarceration prior to trial as a result of the inability to make bail, are very clearly factors that negatively affect racial minorities and the poor. When factors such as these appear to be strongly predictive of the sentence decisions of judges, what options does a researcher have if he wishes to eliminate their effects from a guidelines model used to determine incarceration and sentence lengths in the future?

Unfortunately, the identification of precisely which items or sorts of factors should be thought of as "inappropriate" or unethical is, in the last resort, a matter of a policy decision by researchers (as are a number of other technical decisions having policy ramifications)[13] and the judicial or legislative (or other) oversight body. There are some general criteria that may be employed, however, to aid in identifying the general sorts of factors that might be candidates for exclusion from a guidelines model. Of course, one would want to exclude factors that, on the surface, have no real bearing on the culpability of the offender—such as factors like those we noted above, e.g., race, social class, or sex. Beyond excluding those items which appear to be improper in the first instance, researchers may be further guided in their choice of appropriate factors by legislatively prescribed lists of factors that have been determined to be appropriate things to consider in judicial sentencing decisions. These factors may be thought of as legally *relevant* items. Unfortunately, a good deal of the time such lists of legally relevant factors are not available in explicit form. The researcher must then resort to determining which items may be thought of as appropriate in view of either the stated purposes of punishment (if there are any) or the intended purpose of the guidelines model.

However it may be determined which items of information should be used in the guidelines ultimately developed, the question remains of how to remove the effects of inappropriate factors from models describing judges' past decisions. A number of different approaches have been tried in an effort to resolve this problem, and we will argue that some have been more successful than others. One of the most common approaches to the elimination of discriminatory variables from a sentencing guidelines model has been just to ignore them. Without intending to sound facetious, we must say there is a certain intuitive appeal to the simplicity of this approach. It makes sense somehow to think that if the factor is not there, i.e., is not included in a regression model, then neither is its effect. Unfortunately, this does not prove to be correct in practice. The effect of simply leaving out a factor like race from guidelines models turns out only to average the effects of discrimination that were present in the past. For example, if black offenders were given sentences that were on the average four months longer than the sentences given to white offenders in the past, and if their numbers were about equal, then both groups combined would in the future receive terms that were longer on the average by about two months for whites but two months shorter for blacks, if the sentencing guidelines based strictly on past practice were adopted.[14]

A second approach has been to examine the relations that discriminatory variables have with other items in the data. (This tactic is often followed by the "then ignore them" strategy anyway.) The purpose of this exercise is, apparently, to determine if certain items in the data that might be acceptable for inclusion in a guidelines model exhibit strong associations with "improper" items. For instance, does "release on bail before trial" show discrimination based on the race of the offender? Although the most common end result of an exercise such as this in practice has been to ignore the findings, when an association of this kind is found (after all, how can one exclude *just* prior record from guidelines, even though it shows discriminatory associations?),[15] the results of such analyses have at times led to the exclusion of items from guidelines, regardless of their predictive power. In the state of Massachusetts, for example, whether the offender was free (either on bail or recognizance) before trial proved to be able to account for the largest amount of variation in models of both the decision to incarcerate and the length of sentence; yet the item was excluded from the final guidelines model because of its evident discrimination on the basis of race. Of course, it may be argued that such an item might have been excluded from a guidelines model anyway, because there is not a separate ethical justification for its inclusion; but in the case of Massachusetts, the initial reason for its removal from the guidelines was quite clear (Marx, 1980a, 1980b).

A third approach to the elimination of the effects of discriminatory variables from a sentencing guidelines model is to examine the relationship of the discriminatory variable directly on the sentence decision; but to our knowledge this approach, despite its inherent logic, has never been tried. There are a number of ways in which it can be carried out. First, one may estimate the amount of variation in sentencing decisions that can be explained by an "improper" variable by simply including that item in a regression equation predicting the decision along with all of the other items that are to be in the model. Second, it is possible to remove the variation in the decision that can be attributed to a discriminatory item and subsequently regress the remaining guidelines factors on the sentences imposed in the past. Finally, it is also possible to remove the effects of a discriminatory item from each of the appropriate variables that are to be included in a guidelines model using the second technique described above. Although such an approach would doubtless be a rather complex and cumbersome one, it would help to ensure that all of the effects of the improper item had been purged, so to speak, from the final guidelines sentences.

The remainder of this chapter will be devoted to examining, in a case study, the first two of these last approaches. Using data on sentences given out in the state of Massachusetts in 1977-78, and factors included in the Massachusetts sentencing guidelines model, we will examine what happens to the weights associated with the guidelines factors when the influence of *one* discriminatory item—race—is removed from the model. We will first examine the proportions of variation in the decision to incarcerate and in sentence lengths when race is directly included in regression equations predictive of those decisions. We next will attempt to remove the variation that can be attributed to race from the sentence decisions and then regress the guidelines items on the residuals from that equation.

REMOVING THE EFFECTS OF RACE FROM THE MASSACHUSETTS SENTENCING GUIDELINES

The Massachusetts sentencing guidelines, like other guidelines, explicitly exclude the variable "race" from the guidelines model. In addition to the explicit exclusion of the item itself, the Massachusetts sentencing guidelines developers carried out some detailed analyses of the influence of race on other items of information predictive of sentence dispositions (Marx, 1980a, 1980b). One result of these analyses was the exclusion of the item "whether the offender was free before trial" from the guidelines model as well. The question we address here is whether the simple exclusion of the variable "race," and of other items associated with race, from the guidelines model does effectively remove disparity based on race or race-related factors from future sentences based on the guidelines. To answer this question, we simulate the regression analyses that would produce the factor weights associated with the items in the Massachusetts guidelines.

The Massachusetts sentencing guidelines, by way of background information, were constructed after analyses of data about 1440 defendants convicted in the Massachusetts Superior Courts between 1 November 1977 and 31 October 1978. The final sentencing guidelines developed in that state included four factors—offender scores on (1) the seriousness of the current offense(s); (2) the seriousness of any prior offense(s); (3) the amount of injury to the victim for each of the current offenses; and (4) whether the offender had used a weapon in the current offense(s) (Massachusetts Superior Court, 1980). The weights assigned to each of these factors in the final version of the Massachusetts sentencing guidelines were derived directly from estimated regression coefficients produced by regression sentence length on selected predictors, though there appears to be some confusion in the project's reports about the sample of offenders used as the base for these analyses.[16] The weights assigned to factors in the Massachusetts sentencing guidelines represent the number of months to which an offender has been, and thus should be, sentenced to incarceration. The specific question we examine here is: Will the weights assigned to the Massachusetts guidelines factors change when the sentence variation attributable to race is removed from the sentences received by offenders in the past?

Before we present the results of our statistical analysis of the effects of race, we note some of the conclusions drawn by the Massachusetts Sentencing Guidelines Project's researchers about the issue. The Massachusetts judiciary and the sentencing guidelines project staff were particularly concerned with the issue of racial disparity in their prior sentencing practices. The judges of the Superior Court considered the possibility that there might be racial disparity in their sentences during the early stages of the guidelines research. Charges had previously been leveled against the Superior Court judges of racially based disparity. Judges responded to these charges by saying that *if* such racial disparity did exist, it should be researched and corrected. Correction of racial disparity—through sentencing guidelines that were *not* racially biased—would, they said, reflect a sentencing policy statement by the court, a statement that the consideration of race in the imposition of sentences is clearly inappropriate.

The Massachusetts Sentencing Guidelines Project was assigned the task of investigating possible racial biases in sentences imposed in the state as one part of their research. The project prepared two reports on this issue. The first report, *A Study of Racial Disparity in Massachusetts Superior Court Department,* found that:

> The results indicate that although the race of the defendant by itself does not directly influence the length of sentences, race indirectly influences sentence lengths because of the way the judges weigh and combine the [guidelines] factors. White defendants receive an advantage of significantly shorter sentences after trials relative to black defendants, and black defendants receive an advantage after pleas of slightly shorter sentences relative to white defendants [Marx, 1980a: 3].

The second report, *The Question of Racial Disparity in Massachusetts Superior Court Sentences,* was released one month after the first, once additional research suggested by the judges had been completed. The research findings stated in the second report do not differ much in content from that of the earlier summary:

> The results demonstrate that the race of a defendant by itself does not directly influence sentence length. However, the variables that do account for sentence length are weighted differently for black

and white defendants. As a result, black defendants receive an advantage of shorter sentences relative to white defendants in the great majority of cases that are disposed of by a plea of guilty. White defendants, on the other hand, have the advantage after trials of substantially shorter sentences compared to black defendants. When pleas and trials are considered together, there is no disparity in sentence length between black and white defendants [Marx, 1980b: 2].

We must call attention to two of the research conclusions of the Massachusetts Sentencing Guidelines Project about the influence of race that are stated above. First, as our statistical analysis will indicate, race "by itself" *does* affect sentence lengths in Massachusetts, and in a rather dramatic manner. Second, the report notes that when pleas and trials are considered together, there are no discernible differences in the sentences of blacks and whites. Clearly, this is the same as noting that if one does not take into account the presence of a suppressor variable, such as race, then one does not notice that that variable makes a difference in sentence lengths. However, this is also clearly not the same as removing the effects of the variable from the sentencing guidelines model. It is, rather, a case of examining the improper item's relations with other items and then ignoring the findings.

Since the Massachusetts guidelines do not incorporate the item of "trial versus plea disposition" in their model, it would be something of a waste of effort for us to focus our analysis on the discriminatory effects of that item on subsequent sentences here. Rather, we have decided to examine what exactly happens to the weights of two specific guidelines variables when the item of race is incorporated into regression equations predictive of sentence length. The results of these analyses are presented in Table 5.1.

As is shown in the first column of Table 5.1, the two Massachusetts guidelines factors of offenders' current and prior offense seriousness scores are able to account for about 12 percent of the variation in the judges' decisions of sentence length for 721 cases. The offender will receive approximately 1.3 months for each level of current offense seriousness and about a half a month for each level of prior offense seriousness. Of particular interest, for comparative purposes, is the fact that the base incarceration rate, as indicated by the intercept figure, is approximately 8 months in this equation. That is, each offender sentenced under this model would receive an average of 8 months of incarcerative time *before* additional time was added, based on the level of the current offense seriousness and the seriousness of the prior record.

TABLE 5.1 Regression Analyses of the Effects of Race on Sentence Lengths in Massachusetts (Incarcerated Offenders Only)

Items Included:	All Cases (N = 721) Guidelines Items Only in Model	All cases (N = 721) Guidelines Items Plus Race in Model	Blacks (N = 261) Guidelines Items Only in Model	Whites (N = 460) Guidelines Items Only in Model
Seriousness Score — Current Offenses	1.28	1.31	1.35	1.30
Seriousness Score — Prior Offenses	.41	.40	.28**	.46
Race (0 = White; 1 = Black)	— —	4.67*	— —	— —
Intercept	8.12	6.27	11.58	5.95
R Square	.123	.135	.095	.145
F Value	50.35	37.28	13.59	38.86
Significance	.0001	.0001	.0001	.0001

All factors show significant explanatory power in the regression equation at the .0001 level unless otherwise noted.
* Significant at the .001 level
** Significant at the .04 level

Moving to the second column of Table 5.1, one can note that when race is included as a predictive item in the regression equation, the equation is able to account for a larger proportion of the variation in sentence lengths. Without race as a predictive item, the seriousness of the current and prior offenses is able to account for about 12 percent of the variation; when race is considered as a factor, that figure rises to about 14 percent. But of more interest to us, in this instance, is the fact that the regression estimates for the weights for current and prior offense seriousness do not change in the second equation. Race is able to account for an additional 5 months in the sentence lengths of black offenders, and the intercept term is proportionately reduced from 8 months to 6 months.

To make the results of this analysis more readily apparent, we have repeated the analysis of sentence length separately for black and white offenders, using only current and prior offense seriousness. These results are presented in the two right-hand columns of Table 5.1. As can be seen from a comparison of the estimates in both columns, the seriousness of the current offense appears to carry about the same weight for black offenders as it does for white offenders, while the seriousness score for prior offenses shows some definite differences in weight between the two groups. The seriousness of the prior offenses adds about five months to the sentence lengths of white offenders, while it adds only about three months to the sentence lengths of black offenders. Moreover, the predictive value of the item in the regression equation for black offenders is not highly significant. This suggests that while the seriousness of the prior record is an important consideration for judges when sentencing white offenders, the prior record of black offenders does not much matter in the determination of sentence length.

So what *does* matter? The other major difference between the estimates for black and white offenders is clearly the intercept term of the base number of months to which members of the group on the average will be sentenced to incarceration. As is shown in Table 5.1, black offenders have a base incarceration length figure of about 12 months; the comparable time for white offenders is only 6 months—a difference of 6 months. This suggests that, on the average, black offenders receive sentences that are about 6 months longer in length than sentences given to white offenders, *regardless* of the seriousness of the current offense or the seriousness of the prior record!

We conclude from these analyses that race *does* affect sentence lengths in Massachusetts. The question remains, however, how to remove those effects from a model to guide sentencing in the future. To backtrack a bit,

TABLE 5.2   Removing the Effects of Race from the Lengths of
Sentences in Massachusetts, Incarcerated Cases (N = 721)

	Regression Estimates of Factors On:	
Items Included:	Actual Sentence Lengths	Residuals from Sentence Length Regression
Race	3.74*	--
Seriousness Score — Current Offense	--	1.30
Seriousness Score — Prior Offenses	--	.41
Intercept	16.11	-9.47
R Square	.008	.128
F Value	5.59	52.57
Significance	.0183	.0001

All factors show significant explanatory power in the regression equation at the
.0001 level unless otherwise noted.
*Significant at the .01 level.

we noted earlier that it is possible, using traditional multivariate techniques, first to determine the influence of the improper item, then to
remove that influence from the decisions under inspection, and finally to
determine the influence of relevant or appropriate factors. This procedure
was the next step in our analysis.

Table 5.2 presents the results of two regression analyses of sentence
lengths. The first analysis incorporates only the factor of race as the
predictive item in the regression equation. As is shown in the left-hand
column, when race alone is used to predict sentence length, all offenders
have a base incarceration sentence length of about 16 months, and black
offenders would receive an additional 4 months by virtue of their being
black. We next took the residuals from that equation, i.e., the variation in
sentence lengths remaining after the effects of race are excluded from the
decision, and regressed those residuals on the two relevant guidelines
factors. The results of this analysis are presented in the right-hand column
of Table 5.2.

Two things are worth nothing about the tables presented concerning
this analysis. First, in comparison with the factor weights derived from our

initial analysis (refer back to the first column of Table 5.1) of the influence of the guidelines factors on sentence lengths without taking account of race at all, the weights presented for these items here are not that different. When no account was taken of race, the regression estimate for the seriousness of the current offense was about 1.3 months, and that for the seriousness of the prior offenses was about half a month. Here, when the effects of race have been removed from the variation in the sentence length decision, those same weights are about 1.3 months and .5 months, respectively—not much different from our earlier results. However, the weight that *has* changed is that attached to the intercept term, or the (average) base number of months of sentence length. In our earlier analysis, we noted that offenders were sentenced on the average to about 8 months of incarceration, regardless of their scores on the current and prior offense seriousness items. Now, note that the base sentence length weight is *minus nine months*. In other words, after removing the effects of race from the sentence length decision variation, offenders receive an initial *credit* of nine months to the amount of time that would be called for by their current and prior offense seriousness scores!

CONCLUSION

In this chapter we have considered a problem that ought to have been considered by all of those who, in the past few years, have tried to design "empirically based" sentencing guidelines that will, to some extent, reflect past sentencing practice, but which has been considered (so far as we are aware) by none of them. Plainly, nobody wants guidelines that explicitly include iniquitous factors like race. But this does not mean that such factors should be excluded from the statistical models of past practice from which the guidelines will eventually be derived. On the contrary, if such models do not include *all* of the things which have been influential, in one way or another, in sentencing in the past, they will not permit the accurate estimation of those things (such as seriousness of offense and prior record) which *are* generally agreed to be appropriate considerations in sentencing. There are several ways in which a "race effect" may turn up in data on sentencing. For example, blacks may get heavier sentences across the board, even though the effect of, say, prior record is the same for both blacks and whites. This should show up in a comparison of intercept terms in regression equations estimated separately for blacks and whites. Alternatively and more insidiously, race may be correlated both with sentence severity and with some relevant factor such as prior record.

In this case, unless "race" is explicitly included in the model, the effect (b coefficient) of that relevant factor may be misestimated. Exclusion of race and other such factors from modelling equations may thus build into the subsequently created guidelines the very kinds of things that guidelines are supposed to avoid.

NOTES

1. The issue of disparity in the sentencing of criminal offenders has been debated for as long as sentence lengths have depended on judicial discretion. As the literature on the subject is thus voluminous, we do not wish to review it here, though it cannot be dismissed with a casual wave of the hand, either. The reader is referred to Sparks et al. (1982).

2. Although any number of variables may be thought of as legally or ethically irrelevant to judges' sentence decisions, race is the most often cited example (see Bullock, 1961; Gibson, 1978: 437; Green, 1964; Greenberg, 1977; Hagan, 1974; Hopkins, 1977).

3. It is important to note that the term "disparity" is sometimes used to refer to unjustified or excessive variation in sentencing that is *not* due to the influence of morally iniquitous factors such as race. However, we are not concerned with these other cases in this chapter.

4. For a detailed discussion of the origin and subsequent adaptation of decision-making guidelines in the sentencing process, see Sparks et al. (1982: ch. 3).

5. For an overview of the early rationale for the promulgation of sentencing guidelines, see Gottfredson et al. (1978) and, later, Gottfredson and Gottfredson (1980).

6. The earliest parole guidelines were based on the subjective assessments of cases made by parole board hearing examiners. Later efforts put much more emphasis on the collection of objective data about offenders, both in the parole and sentencing research contexts (see Gottfredson et al., 1977). See also Sparks et al. (1982) for a discussion of empirically based sentencing guidelines developed in New Jersey, Massachusetts, Minnesota, Pennsylvania, and Michigan, as well as Wilkins et al. (1976) for a discussion of the sentencing guidelines feasibility efforts in four court jurisdictions.

7. This is in fact what happened with the Oregon parole board's guidelines, which were first developed in 1975 and given statutory authority in 1977. No analyses of past decisionmaking practices were carried out before these guidelines were formulated. Instead, the board, under the chairmanship of Ira Blalock (see Chapter 4, this volume), simply *made up* the ranges of time that they thought appropriate to be served by different types of offenders.

8. One reason that guidelines, both for parole and sentencing, were an appealing method for the control of discretion was because they were usually used as nonbind-

ing decision rules. This aspect of the early guidelines models is much discussed in Gottfredson et al. (1975) and Wilkins et al. (1976).

9. Compare, for example, the sentencing guidelines developed for the state of Massachusetts, where the guidelines were first promulgated for voluntary consultation by judges, and later for voluntary compliance with the guidelines developed in the state of Minnesota, where compliance with the guidelines-recommended sentence is mandated by statute. For a further discussion of this issue, see Sparks et al. (1982: chs. 3, 9).

10. This point is discussed in great detail in the final report of the Evaluation of Statewide Sentencing Guidelines Project (Sparks et al., 1982: chs. 3, 11).

11. Indeed, the only set of sentencing guidelines developed to date that may have been moderately successful at merely describing past practice rather than prescribing future policy is that of the New Jersey Sentencing Guidelines (see McCarthy, 1978, 1979).

12. The Minnesota sentencing guidelines, for example, were under a conscious mandate to ensure that prison populations would be either held stable or decreased by the sentencing guidelines model. To accomplish this end, some alterations in past general practices had to be made as explicit policy decisions. The Massachusetts sentencing guidelines were also the result of substantial policy modifications to the original research findings (see Sparks et al., 1982: chs. 7, 9 for further discussion of this issue).

13. A number of decisions face guidelines researchers that can heavily affect the policies stated in a final guidelines model. For a discussion of some of the potential policy issues, see Sparks (1981).

14. Of course, the figures we give here are hypothetical; the actual amount of the difference in future sentence lengths for both groups would depend on the relative weight of each group in the overall sample.

15. In New Jersey, for example, the associations that race exhibited with the sentence decisions and with other items was investigated, but *after* the initial guidelines had already been developed and implemented. Similarly, though the research proved that there was variation in sentence length, for offenders sentenced to county institutions on the basis of race (and that decision is one predominantly made in *urban* New Jersey counties, where county correctional facilities to detain offenders for up to 18 months exist, and where the overwhelming majority of offenders are minorities), the results of the research were subsequently ignored (see McCarthy et al., 1979). Similar research was conducted subsequent to the development of the Michigan sentencing guidelines (see Zalman et al., 1979).

16. When we replicated the analyses that supposedly produced the Massachusetts sentencing guidelines, using the original Massachusetts data, we were able to produce factor weights comparable (though not exact) to the weights assigned to the factors in the final guidelines model when only incarcerated cases were used in producing the sentence length weights. However, we were able to approximate more closely the weights assigned in the Massachusetts guidelines when we used all cases (N = 1440) in the sentence length analyses and scored those cases that were not incarcerated as zero on the dependent variable, i.e., indicating that those cases had received sentences of zero months.

REFERENCES

BULLOCK, H. A. (1961) "Significance of the racial factor in the length of prison sentences." Journal of Criminal Law, Criminology, and Police Science 52(4): 411-417.

GIBSON, J. I. (1978) "Race as a determinant of criminal sentences: a methodological critique and a case study." Law and Society Review 12.

GOTTFREDSON, M. R. and D. M. GOTTFREDSON (1980) Decision Making in Criminal Justice: Toward the Rational Exercise of Discretion. Cambridge, MA: Ballinger.

GOTTFREDSON, D. M., L. T. WILKINS, and P. B. HOFFMAN (1978) Guidelines for Parole and Sentencing: A Policy Control Method. Lexington, MA: Lexington Books.

GOTTFREDSON, D. M., C. A. COSGROVE, L. T. WILKINS, J. WALLERSTEIN, and C. RAUH (1977) Classification for Parole Decision Policy. Washington, DC: Government Printing Office.

GOTTFREDSON, D. M., P. B. HOFFMAN, M. H. SIGLER, and L. T. WILKINS (1975) "Making paroling policy explicit." Crime and Delinquency 21: 34-44.

GREEN, E. (1964) "Inter- and intra-racial crime relative to sentencing." Journal of Criminal Law, Criminology, and Policy Science 55: 348-358.

GREENBERG, D. F. (1977) "Socioeconomic status and criminal sentences: is there an association?" American Sociological Review 42(1): 174-175.

HAGAN, J. (1974) "Extra-legal attributes and criminal sentencing: an assessment of a sociological viewpoint." Law and Society Review 8: 357-383.

HOPKINS, A. (1977) "Is there a class bias in sentencing?" American Sociological Review 42(1): 176-177.

KRESS, J. M., L. T. WILKINS, and D. M. GOTTFREDSON (1976) "Is the end of judicial sentencing in sight?" Judicature 60(5): 216-222.

MARX, T. J. (1980a) A Study of Racial Disparity in Massachusetts Superior Court Department. Boston: Massachusetts Superior Court Department, April 8.

――― (1980b) The Question of Racial Disparity in Massachusetts Superior Court Sentences. Boston: Superior Court Department, May 16.

Massachusetts Superior Court Sentencing Guidelines Project (1980) Massachusetts Sentencing Guidelines. Boston: Massachusetts Superior Court Department. (mimeograph)

McCARTHY, J. P., Jr. (1979) Supplemental Report of the Sentencing Guidelines Project to the Administrative Director of the Courts. Trenton, NJ: Administrative Office of the Courts, March 29.

――― (1978) Report of the Sentencing Guidelines Project to the Administrative Director of the Courts. Trenton, NJ: Administrative Office of the Courts, October 23.

――― N. SHEFLIN, and J. J. BARRACO (1979) Report of the Sentencing Guidelines Project to the Administrative Director of the Courts on the Relationship Between Race and Sentencing. Trenton, NJ: Administrative Office of the Courts, September 4.

SPARKS, R. F. (1981) The Construction of Sentencing Guidelines: A Methodological Critique. Presented to the Panel on Sentencing Research, Committee on Research on Law Enforcement and Administration, July 27-29.

SPARKS, R. F., B. A. STECHER, J. S. ALBANESE, and P. L. SHELLY (1982) Stumbling Toward Justice: Some Overlooked Research and Policy Questions About Statewide Sentencing Guidelines. Final Report of the Evaluation of Statewide Sentencing Guidelines Project. Newark, NJ: Rutgers University.

WILKINS, L. T., J. M. KRESS, D. M. GOTTFREDSON, J. C. CALPIN, and A. M. GELMAN (1976) Sentencing Guidelines: Structuring Judicial Discretion. Final Report of the Feasibility Study. Albany, NY: Criminal Justice Research Center.

ZALMAN, M., C. W. OSTROM, Jr., P. GUILLIAMS, and G. PEASLEE (1979) Sentencing in Michigan: Report of the Michigan Felony Sentencing Project. Lansing: Michigan Office of Criminal Justice.

Chapter 6

CALIFORNIA'S DISPARATE SENTENCE REVIEW PROCESS
Conceptual and Practical Issues

MARY LOU FENILI

HISTORY

When California enacted the indeterminate sentencing law (ISL) in 1917,[1] it followed the lead of 41 other states that had enacted some form of indeterminate sentencing or parole (Council of State Governments, 1976; Lindsey, 1925). Throughout most of the history of the ISL, the courts generally deferred to the parole board's discretion in the exercise of its powers. Accordingly, the California Adult Authority enjoyed virtually unquestioned freedom in setting terms for state prison inmates. Prior to Morrissey v. Brewer (1972), courts recognized only the inmate's right to apply for and be properly considered for parole (In re Wilkerson, 1969; In re Schoengarth, 1967; In re Minnis, 1972).

Morrissey's guarantee of due process in the parole revocation process began a period of greater judicial scrutiny of discretionary decisions made in the prison setting, culminating in judicial rewriting of the ISL to require due process protection in a variety of previously sacrosanct matters: granting parole (In re Sturm, 1974); rescinding an unexecuted grant of parole (Gee v. Brown, 1975; In re Prewitt, 1972); revoking parole or extending a term for a new felony conviction (In re Croix, 1974; In re Winn, 1975); requiring disclosure of reports and records (In re Olson, 1974); holding revocation hearings for parolees facing new criminal charges (In re Coughlin, 1976; In re Dunham, 1976); or receiving out-of-state commitments (Moody v. Daggett, 1976; In re Shapiro, 1975).

Paralleling the exposure of parole decisionmaking powers to the harsh light of due process was the recognition of the punitive effect of the terms set by the Adult Authority and the delay in deciding when a prisoner was rehabilitated. With In re Lynch (1972) and In re Foss (1974), the California Supreme Court began to craft a theory of proportionality in term-setting. The ensuing deluge of appeals and writs upon the courts created chaos in the parole decisionmaking process. With In re Rodriguez (1975), which required promptness in term-setting and a term commensurate with the prisoner's culpability, life on the "installment plan" under the ISL was rendered more certain, and unfettered administrative discretion was finally shackled. In re Stanley (1976), criticizing the procedures adopted by the Adult Authority in response to Rodriguez, gave new life to previously moribund efforts to enact a determinate sentencing law and tolled the death knell of the ISL (see Cassou and Taugher, 1978; Messinger and Johnson, 1978).

Judicial intrusion into parole decisionmaking caused the Adult Authority to justify its decisions with reasons and to record its decisions. This rendered the decisions more accessible and therefore more susceptible to judicial scrutiny. The resultant accountability inspired greater emphasis on considering facts and making rational decisions. Although arbitrary decisions still occurred, they were fewer and less likely to survive the due process filter through which the courts strained them. However, this increased judicial oversight of the term-setting process led many observers of and participants in the criminal justice system to fear that the courts would soon begin to determine what was an "appropriate" term. Since these decisions would be unpredictable and insulated from public accountability, many believed a more certain sentencing scheme would serve to minimize further judicial activism in this area.

In enacting the Uniform Determinate Sentencing Act of 1976 (DSL), the California legislature abandoned its nearly 60-year experiment with rehabilitation and changed the purpose of imprisonment for crime to punishment. It also designed a system to avoid the pitfalls of the ISL while retaining the judicially erected safeguards of the post-Morrissey/Lynch-Foss period:

> The legislature finds and declares that the purpose of imprisonment for crime is punishment. This purpose is best served by terms proportionate to the seriousness of the offense with provision for

uniformity in the sentences of offenders committing the same offense under similar circumstances. The Legislature further finds and declares that the elimination of disparity and the provision of uniformity of sentences can best be achieved by determinate sentences fixed by statute in proportion to the seriousness of the offense as determined by the Legislature to be imposed by the court with specified discretion.[2]

Adhering to the requirements of Lynch-Foss and their progeny, the legislature reserved to itself the establishment of terms through the political process, subject to public debate in a public forum and responsive to public opinion, rather than in the rarefied air of bureaucratic towers. Actual term-setting was removed from the administrative arena to the trial courts and carefully defined and described judicial discretion replaced administrative discretion.[3] Due process guarantees previously delineated by the courts for the exercise of administrative discretion were applied to the exercise of judicial discretion.[4]

The legislature also included a unique feature: a systematic administrative review of all sentences to state prison.[5] This review would be more comprehensive, faster, and allow broader comparisons among cases than normal case-by-case review in the appellate courts, where the defendant's decision to appeal selects and limits the cases to be reviewed. This administrative review would alleviate court congestion that would result from appellate review of all state prison sentences and would free appellate courts to focus on questions of legal error, abuse of discretion, and cruel or unusual punishment. The irony of the review was its assignment to the Community Release Board (now Board of Prison Terms), successor to the Adult Authority, the administrative agency whose excesses in implementing the Indeterminate Sentencing Law led to the development and enactment of the Determinate Sentencing Law.

BACKGROUND

Section 1170(f) provides:[6]

(1) Within one year after the commencement of the term of imprisonment, the Board of Prison Terms shall review the sentence to determine whether the sentence is disparate in comparison with the sentences imposed in similar cases. If the Board of Prison Terms determines that the sentence is disparate, the board shall notify the judge, the district attorney, the defense attorney, the defendant, and

the Judicial Council. The notification shall include a statement of the reasons for finding the sentence disparate.

Within 120 days of receipt of this information, the sentencing court shall schedule a hearing and may recall the sentence and commitment previously ordered and resentence the defendant in the same manner as if the defendant had not been sentenced previously, provided the new sentence is no greater than the initial sentence. In resentencing under this subdivision the court shall apply the sentencing rules of the Judicial Council and shall consider the information provided by the Board of Prison Terms.

(2) The review under this section shall concern the decision to deny probation and the sentencing decisions enumerated in paragraphs (2), (3), (4), and (5) of subdivision (a) of Section 1170.3 and apply the sentencing rules of the Judicial Council and the information regarding the sentences in this state of other persons convicted of similar crimes so as to eliminate disparity of sentences and to promote uniformity of sentencing.

This section requires the Board of Prison Terms to perform three simple tasks: (1) to compile information regarding sentences superior court judges impose on defendants whose offenses are governed by the DSL; (2) to compare the cases of DSL defendants convicted of and sentenced to state prison for similar crimes under similar circumstances; (3) to report to the sentencing judge in all cases whose sentences the board finds to be disparate.

The California attorney general advised the board that its responsibility pursuant to Section 1170(f) was to review each DSL sentence to state prison to determine if a "substantial difference" exists between the subject sentence and the sentences imposed on other DSL defendants convicted of similar crimes under similar circumstances (Opinions, 1977: 143).

The inquiry in the disparate sentence review process poses two factual questions: (1) To which cases is a subject case comparable? and (2) How does the sentence in the subject case relate to the sentences of other comparable cases? To answer these questions, the board makes "real" rather than "theoretical" comparisons, using as its yardstick the actual sentences imposed by superior court judges around the state. The board does not utilize an abstract or artificial standard based on some notion of an "appropriate" sentence.

An example may help clarify the nature of the disparate sentence review process. Figure 6.1 shows several cars on a highway: a single car, followed by a group of cars, followed by another single car. The group of

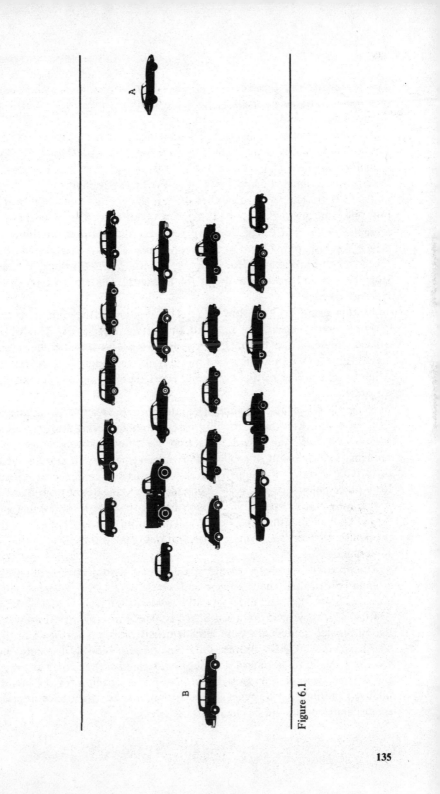

Figure 6.1

135

cars represents the flow of traffic for a given set of road and weather conditions. Imagine yourself to be a traffic officer monitoring traffic on this particular stretch of freeway.

For our purposes, it is 10 o'clock at night. It has been raining for several hours and the road surface is quite wet; heavy patches of fog limit visibility. The flow of traffic at this time is 45 mph. Car A is traveling at the legal speed limit of 55 mph; Car B is traveling at 30 mph.

Car A is traveling at a speed that the law allows. However, that speed is not safe for present road and weather conditions. The safe speed is 45 mph, the flow of traffic. You will stop Car A and ticket the driver for driving too fast for road and weather conditions. Car B is also traveling at a speed that the law allows. However, this driver is overly cautious. You will stop this car and ticket the driver for failing to maintain an appropriate highway speed.

In this example, the flow of traffic represents the sentences that superior court judges have imposed on certain DSL cases. The traffic officer represents the board. Car A represents a case found to be disparately high; Car B represents a case found to be disparately low. A "ticket" is the board's notice to the sentencing court that the sentence imposed is disparate.

To apply this example to the disparate sentence review process, assume that the board is reviewing robbery cases. After collecting information on all robbery cases, the board finds that the "flow of traffic" for cases involving a single count of robbery with enhancements is 60 months. After performing a series of comparisons among prisoners sentenced to prison for a single count of robbery with enhancements, the board finds that Car A is traveling at a "speed" of 84 months and that Car B is traveling at a "speed" of 24 months. The board will therefore issue a "ticket" to the two courts that sentenced these cases, informing them that these sentences are disparate.

The apparent simplicity of the board's tasks, its objective, and its line of inquiry disguises the complex and subtle issues that have beset the board's efforts to design, develop, and implement the review process. More significantly, they have confused board staff who must review cases once the automated sentence review has identified them for further scrutiny; board panels who must decide if the sentence is, indeed, disparate and therefore ought to be referred to the sentencing court; district attorneys and defense counsel who must attempt to refute or reinforce the board's findings; and judges who must decide if the sentences they have imposed are disparate and should be changed.

ASSUMPTIONS

Courts have traditionally reviewed sentences in criminal cases for three elements: legal error, abuse of discretion, and cruel or unusual punishment. The review for legal error focuses on the court's failure to apply appropriate statutory and decisional law in imposing a sentence. In this situation, the sentence is void because it is beyond the court's authority (People v. Superior Court [Duran], 1978).

Review for abuse of discretion seeks those situations where, after calm and careful reflection on the issues, one can fairly state that no judge would have reasonably made the same decision under the same circumstances (In re Marriage of Lopez, 1974). Review for cruel or unusual punishment concerns itself with the proportionality of the sentence (In re Lynch, 1972; In re Foss, 1974), and with whether it is commensurate with the defendant's culpability and the nature of the criminal conduct (In re Rodriguez, 1975). The administrative review of sentences for disparity pursuant to Section 1170(f) is different from all of these.

The disparate sentence review assumes the legality of the sentence imposed and the court's compliance with all appropriate requirements. Any legal errors found in the course of the process are corrected through usual legal means. The review recognizes the reasonableness of the sentence imposed. Considering the circumstances of the case, the charges found to be true or admitted by the defendant, the sentence components available to the court for sentencing, and the sentencing rules for the superior courts,[7] any judge could have reasonably imposed the same sentence.

The disparate sentence review acknowledges that convicted felons have performed acts that society abhors and condemns, that such persons are often dangerous and have little regard for the well-being of others, and that they may deserve the sentence imposed upon them. The board is, in reality, seeking to discover distinctions, if any, among comparable convicted felons sentenced to prison under the DSL. These people are, by definition, not upstanding members of their communities. However, the board endeavors to find those who are sentenced either more harshly or more leniently than others who are similarly situated and notifies the sentencing court of this fact.

CONCEPTUAL ISSUES

Error versus Difference

A frequent misconception regarding the disparate sentence review is that "the judge didn't sentence the prisoner wrong." This is a correct observation but quite beside the point, since the review assumes that the prisoner's sentence is legally proper. The court has, however, sentenced the prisoner differently. This is a crucial distinction. Many things can be different without being wrong. A man and a woman differ as to sex, but that doesn't mean that one is wrong. Differences are a matter of degree and kind, but things that are different are not necessarily wrong.

The board sorts cases by principal convicted offense. All penal provisions of all California codes have been arranged into 33 groups for comparison pusposes, so that there are sufficient cases in each group for meaningful comparison. For example, there are sufficient numbers of persons sentenced to prison for robbery and for second degree burglary so that each of these is in a group of its own. There are, however, relatively few cases sentenced to prison for grand theft, hence it is grouped with other theft offenses that are similar in nature. Within these larger groupings are subgroups of offenders having comparable factors as to juvenile and adult criminal histories, the nature and extent of the criminal behavior involved in their offenses, the use of weapons, and the causing of injury. The board compares cases on these and other points to determine where differences exist, if at all, among cases.

The board does not look at a particular factor in isolation and decide on the basis of that one factor that a case is different enough to warrant being labeled "disparate." Rather, the board examines the full combination of factors in reaching a decision of disparity.

In our traffic example, it is not simply that one car is going faster than the others that leads to the conclusion that its driver should be given a ticket. Rather, it is the interplay of all relevant road and weather conditions that leads to that conclusion.

Same versus Similar versus Unique

Section 1170(f) requires the board to compare those convicted of "similar crimes under similar circumstances." It does not require the board to compare cases which are the "same." "Similar" indicates that two items (cases) have factors or characteristics in common, while "same" indicates that two items (cases) are identical.

It would be virtually impossible to find two cases that are the same. Even "identical" twins are not identical in all ways. Crime partners will occasionally not appear in the same subgroup for comparison purposes because of differences in their participation in the criminal activity, in the number and type of offenses for which they are convicted, and in their adult and juvenile criminal histories, to name only a representative sample of factors.

Factors relating to the defendant are a relevant and appropriate consideration for sentencing purposes.[8] The board collects over 150 pieces of information on each case, including extensive information regarding the prisoner's adult and juvenile criminal histories, social and demographic history, and family background. The board also collects information on the nature and extent of the prisoner's participation in the criminal activity resulting in the DSL commitment to state prison, including the use of a weapon, the infliction of injury, and the amount of loss.

The board uses a variety of these factors to define a subgroup of cases for comparison purposes. For example, if the board is reviewing cases involving a single count of robbery, it may define a subgroup to have the following factors in common: criminal activity occurring in one event; one victim; no injury to the victim; two or fewer prior adult convictions; no prior prison terms; defendant armed with a firearm at the time of the offense; on probation at the time of the offense.

Generally, the board uses five or more factors to define a subgroup for comparison. This allows the board to use factors relating to the criminal behavior, prior criminal history, and the victims. It also enables the board to interpret the statute so as to effect the review process. If the board were to require too many factors to define a comparison subgroup, it could define a subgroup containing only the case being reviewed. This would render the review a nullity and would be an abuse of the board's discretion.

Occasionally a case contains a factor that appears to make the case unique. "Unique" indicates that an item (case) is the only one of its kind. It is, of course, theoretically possible to find a factor in every case that causes it to differ from every other case. However, this is merely another way of attempting to define a comparison group with "same" rather than "similar" cases.

If there is an unusual factor present in a case, the board examines the other cases in the comparison subgroup to ascertain if there is a similar factor in the other cases. The board also determines whether the unusual factor is involved in the disparity of the sentence in the case being reviewed. For example, assume the case being reviewed involves three counts of a theft offense and $1.5 million in loss. The court imposed the upper term, ran the second and third counts consecutive to the principal term, and imposed a two-year enhancement for the great loss. The source of disparity in the sentence is the number of consecutive terms imposed. The amount of loss appears to be an unusual factor rendering the case "unique." However, it is eliminated as a unique factor for two reasons: It is accounted for by the additional two years for the great loss enhancement and it is not the source of the disparity in the sentence.

Another example may underscore the point. Assume the case under review involves a conviction for a single count of assault with a deadly weapon on a peace officer. The fact that the case involved injury to a police officer is not a unique factor, because every case in the comparison group involved that factor.

Fine versus Gross

When Section 1170(f) was initially enacted, everyone assumed that extremely long sentences would be the ones referred to the courts for modification. However, it has been the board's experience that cases with extremely long sentences contain very unusual circumstances that are accounted for in the sentence. These are invariably cases with large numbers of convicted counts resulting from a lengthy period of criminal behavior; with serious injury to several victims; or with a long criminal history reflected by numerous prior prison terms.

Referring to our traffic example, assume that a car is in front of all the cars in Figure 6.1 and that this car is traveling at 85 mph. An obvious conclusion would be that this speed is excessive for the road and weather conditions and that this car should be ticketed. However, closer examination indicates that this car is a police vehicle responding to an emergency, a fact that clearly distinguishes this vehicle from the others. Disparity, therefore, need not be gross in absolute terms. This is only logical, since the board's determination is to be based on comparisons among cases. Therefore, disparity is always expressed in relative terms.

The DSL allows for relatively small differences among sentences. The provision for computing consecutive terms employs one-third of the middle term for the offense sentenced consecutively. As a result, the difference between sentences can be merely four months or eight months.[9] Limits on terms also contribute to the fine distinctions among sentences, as total terms for certain offenses are limited to twice the base term imposed for the principal offense,[10] while the amount of time imposed for nonviolent consecutive terms is limited to five years.[11]

Because the DSL is so mathematically complicated, it allows courts to impose sentences with relatively fine distinctions among them in temporal terms. Because these distinctions are not obvious, they can easily become buried in the great mass of sentences imposed in DSL cases. It seems appropriate, therefore, for the board to find disparities involving fine rather than great distinctions. Furthermore, were the board to find disparities in cases with long sentences, its recommendation for modification would likely be for a small reduction in the sentence.[12] Long sentences generally involve additional punishment for enhancements, which are mandatory in the absence of mitigating circumstances. This leaves both the board and the courts with little room for recommending or making changes.

Appropriate versus Disparate

Another misconception of the disparate sentence review is that a sentence cannot be disparate if the prisoner deserves the sentence imposed. As indicated earlier, the board assumes that the prisoner deserves to be punished because he or she has committed antisocial acts. Furthermore, the board assumes that the prisoner may deserve the punishment received. Therefore, the sentence is appropriate when considered in isolation. However, since the DSL's predominant policy is to promote uniformity of sentencing, a sentence cannot be viewed in isolation when its possible disparity is at issue. Rather, it must be viewed in relative terms, in relation to other similar cases. In other words, the issue is not whether the sentence is appropriate in an absolute sense, but whether it is appropriate when compared with the sentences other judges imposed in comparable cases.

The board's finding of disparity indicates that other judges sentenced comparable cases differently. That is, the speed at which Car A is traveling exceeds the flow of traffic. The prisoner in the subject case received more punishment from Judge X than other comparable offenders received from other judges. The logical question at this point is whether the sentences imposed in the other cases are appropriate: Judge X maintains the appropriateness of Prisoner A's sentence and the inappropriateness of the sentences imposed by the other judges. Whether Judge X is right or wrong is irrelevant to the board's finding of disparity. It is not the board's function to make a value judgment about the sentences imposed in the comparable cases. The board merely reports what the majority of judges have done in sentencing comparable cases and informs Judge X where

Prisoner A's sentence stands in relation to that of comparable cases. The board simply reports the flow of traffic without comment as to whether the flow of traffic is too fast or too slow. The board then indicates whether the subject case is traveling too fast (the sentence is too long) or too slow (the sentence is too short) in relation to the flow of traffic.

No Compulsion versus DSL Imperative

The statute does not compel the court to follow the board's recommendation for recall and resentencing because of disparity. Section 1170(f)(1) requires the court to schedule a hearing within 120 days of receiving the board's notice. The court must apply the sentencing rules for the superior courts and consider the board's information in determining whether to recall and resentence. If the court decides to recall and resentence, the new sentence cannot be longer than the initial sentence.

Juxtaposed to the statute's minimal guidance in this area is the DSL's imperative against disparity and in favor of uniformity. As originally enacted in Senate Bill 42, the provision for disparate sentence review stood by itself in Section 1170.1b. When the legislature amended the DSL in Assembly Bill 476, it moved the provision for disparate sentence review into Section 1170. This section contains the legislature's policy statement regarding punishment as the purpose of imprisonment, a purpose best served by uniform terms.[13]

Many other provisions in the statutory scheme echo and underscore this emphasis on uniformity: limits on the total term and the amount of time to be served for certain consecutive terms;[14] uniform reduction of a DSL term for good behavior and program participation;[15] specified loss of good time credits;[16] the Judicial Council's mandate to promote uniformity in sentencing by adopting sentencing rules;[17] the superior court's mandate to apply the sentencing rules;[18] the Judicial Council's mandate to conduct annual sentencing institutes to help judges impose appropriate sentences;[19] the Judicial Council's mandate to publish a quarterly report on statewide sentencing practices and to consider this information in adopting sentencing rules;[20] and the Judicial Council's mandate to review statutory sentences and proposed legislation affecting felony sentences.[21] Taken together, these provisions appear to imply that the board's recommendation ought to be followed.

In two cases in which the board's motions[22] for recall and resentencing were denied (People v. Herrera, 1982; People v. Craig, 1982), the California state public defender has argued that the board's findings create a rebuttable presumption in favor of recall and resentencing. If the board's information is not rebutted, then the presumption becomes conclusive.

The Herrera case provides a partial answer to this issue. The First District Court of Appeal held there that the board's motion[23] does not create a rebuttable presumption in favor of recall and resentencing. The court reasoned that the legislature could have provided guidance in Section 1170(f) as to what procedure should be followed in the hearing on the board's motion and could have required the sentencing judge to make findings in ruling on the motion. Since the legislature did not do so, the court found that it did not intend the motion to create a presumption. The court further held that the board's determination that a sentence is disparate is entitled to great weight. The court reasoned that the construction of a statute by the officials charged with its administration, although not controlling, is entitled to great weight. Since the board is essentially construing the meaning of the term "disparate," the board's determination is entitled to serious consideration.

In determining the merits of a board motion, the sentencing judge must undertake a two-part analysis: (1) The judge must determine whether the sentence imposed is, indeed, disparate, giving the board's finding of disparity great weight; (2) If the judge finds that the sentence imposed is disparate, the judge must give this fact great weight in the decision whether or not to recall the sentence. A sentencing judge will have met the obligation under (1) if the record shows that the judge seriously considered the information provided by the board and attempted to discern whether, when compared to sentences imposed by other judges, the sentence imposed in the subject case was disparate. The judge is not required to make findings as to the reasons for disagreeing with the board's determination that a sentence is disparate, although the opinion suggests that the judge will want the record to show the reasons for disagreement, so as to provide evidence that the judge undertook the necessary inquiry to meet the standard.

If, after meeting the burden required by (1), the judge finds that the sentence imposed is not disparate, the judge is not required to conduct further inquiry and may deny the motion. If the judge finds that the sentence imposed is disparate, then he or she must undertake the second part of the analysis.

To meet the great weight standard in (2), the judge should treat observed sentencing patterns as guidelines to help promote uniformity of sentencing rather than as immutable rules that place judicial discretion in a straitjacket. The sentencing judge may find the sentence to be disparate, but need not recall and resentence.

Although the board will no longer file motions in disparate cases, the sentencing judge must schedule a hearing on the board's recommendation.

Accordingly, the procedures Herrera established for consideration of the board's findings will continue to apply.

PRACTICAL ISSUES

Even though the board identifies and attempts to clarify the conceptual issues, judges and lawyers often do not understand these issues. This leads to several practical problems during hearings in disparate cases.

"I Did It Wrong."

A sentencing judge rarely considers a case a second time unless an appellate court has found an error and remanded the case for further action. As a result, when the judge receives notice of a disparate sentence, the judge's natural reaction is: "They think I did it wrong." This feeling does not endear the board to the judge.

Judges have difficulty accepting that there is no legal error in the sentence and no abuse of discretion in imposing the sentence, but that the sentence should be changed nonetheless. This difficulty leads judges to conclude that the other judges are out of line and, therefore, the subject sentence is not disparate. The only solution to this problem is the education of judges about the process and patience in explaining its complex and subtle issues.

New Information

The board's notice provides the court with new information regarding sentencing that was not available to the court at the time of sentencing. The review process is so constituted that the board is providing this information one year after sentencing, when the court's recollection may be cloudy and the district attorney and the defense attorney at sentencing no longer available.

It would be preferable to have information regarding disparate and nondisparate sentences available in advance of sentencing, so that the court could consider it along with other relevant information. Section 1170(g) affords courts the opportunity to request information from the board prior to sentencing. Probation officers could request this information for their presentence reports. Although this information is a year old and may not be valid at the time the subject case is sentenced, it will provide the courts with information not presently available. Of course, requesting this information does not ensure that the subject case will not be found disparate when the review is conducted one year later.

Ideally, the board would like to complete its review of each case within four to six months after sentencing. However, the crush of commitments to state prison hampers the board's ability to make faster progress. This problem is unlikely to abate as the courts respond to public outcry against crime by committing more defendants to state prison.

To provide some advance information to courts, the board has published two Sentencing Practices Reports to illustrate selected sentencing characteristics. The board uses the major offense groups, which represent 80 percent of all persons received in prison during the time period studied. The reports are almost exclusively concerned with charging, pleading, and sentencing decisions.

Disparately Short Terms

The statute only allows the court to reduce a term. Therefore, disparately short terms go uncorrected. If uniformity is to be achieved, then disparity ought to be a two-edged sword. This issue arises every year but has never been seriously addressed by the legislature. The major stumbling blocks remain a variety of constitutional issues that must be resolved before a sentence could be increased.

A more important obstacle may be opposition by district attorneys; disparately short sentences generally result from plea bargains specifying the sentence, and increasing the term would appear to require allowing the prisoner to withdraw the plea. One year after sentencing, the district attorney may no longer be able to make a case, assuming that one could have been made a year earlier.

The board notifies courts of all cases whose sentences it finds disparately short. The board does this to educate the courts and the other participants in the criminal justice system.

A New Role for the Board

The board's predecessor, the Adult Authority, is the culprit whose excesses under the ISL led to the adoption of the DSL. Now the board, successor to that arbitrary and capricious agency, suggests reducing a term. Courts are frequently confused and bemused over this state of affairs. In hearings, the district attorney has often remarked: "I thought you were on my side." Board counsel would carefully explain that the board appears as a friend of the court and is a neutral party in the proceedings. However, the district attorney opposed reducing the term and carried the burden of refuting the board's evidence.

Frequently, when a prisoner arrived in the courtroom, the judge would remark to board counsel: "Your client is here." Counsel would carefully deny this, reminding the court that the board is the client, that the board was the moving party but was not an adversary in the proceedings. Defense attorneys always considered the board their ally and were absolutely astounded and dismayed when board counsel agreed with the court that a prisoner's behavior was reprehensible. Counsel always assured the court that the board had considered that behavior and the behavior of the other prisoners in the comparison group in determining whether the sentence in the subject case was disparate.

As of January 8, 1982, the board had sent letters to courts regarding 18 disparately short cases involving four counties (Los Angeles, Alameda, Orange, and San Francisco). The board has filed motions in 31 disparately long cases involving fourteen counties (Los Angeles, San Bernardino, Santa Clara, Tulare, San Francisco, Orange, San Diego, Santa Barbara, Kern, Santa Cruz, Butte, Sacramento, Lake, and Ventura). The board's motion was granted in 14 cases (45 percent), resulting in a total reduction in prison terms of 296 months, or 24 years and 8 months. The average reduction was 9.55 months.

Judge versus Computer

When the DSL was enacted, many judges feared that it was so mechanical and complicated that sentencing would be better handled by computer. Once judges realized how very complicated the DSL was, many wished a computer would do the sentencing. With the board using an automated sentence review process for its preliminary screening in the disparate sentence review, many judges believe a computer in Sacramento is second-guessing their sentencing decisions. They fear that the decision regarding disparity is being made by a machine rather than by people.

The board uses the automated sentence review only to identify cases for further scrutiny by individuals employed in the disparate sentence review process. Cases are initially reviewed by analysts trained to read and interpret information of various kinds, including board decisions made in other types of cases. Hearing representatives are also involved; their responsibilities, training, and experience include setting terms under the ISL, setting terms for life prisoners, and revoking parole. At this first level of review, the decision that a case, identified by the computer as possibly disparate, ought to be reviewed further is the result of the exercise of discretion by these individuals.

The final determination that a case is disparate and should be referred to the sentencing court results from the exercise of discretion by a panel of two board members and one hearing representative. Although the computer is utilized in the review process, it is only the first filter through which the cases are sifted. At all subsequent stages, individuals sift the cases for disparity.

Plea Bargains

Section 1170(f) requires the board to use a statewide standard for comparing cases of similar crimes under similar circumstances. The legislature believes that punishment should be uniform, regardless of the location in which criminal behavior occurs. It may well be that one important "circumstance" is that an offense occurs in a "cow county"[24] rather than in a large urban county like Los Angeles, Santa Clara, or Alameda. However, the legislature has not altered its emphasis on statewide uniformity, despite having amended the DSL every year.

The problem that location causes is a matter of volume of cases. In large urban counties, the sheer volume of cases necessitates plea bargaining in nearly all cases. In smaller counties, cases are more likely to go to trial. Judges feel very uncomfortable being told that the sentence they imposed is disparate when that sentence may have been part of a plea bargain or negotiated disposition.

The statute requires the board to review all DSL sentences to state prison, not merely those resulting from trials. Although the judge is rarely involved in the negotiation of a plea bargain, whether for the determination of a conviction or a sentence, the judge's approval of the bargain is essential for it to become effective (People v. Orin, 1975). Board data indicate that 74 percent of criminal cases are resolved by some form of negotiated disposition. If the board were to interpret the statute so that it did not review cases resolved by plea bargain or negotiated disposition, the board would severely limit the benefit the legislature conferred upon DSL prisoners.

CONCLUSION

The Board of Prison Terms has designed, developed, implemented, and refined the only systematic statewide review of all state prison sentences under a determinate sentencing law. In the process, it has amassed a superior data base of criminal justice and sentencing information and gained the respect, however grudging at times, of the California judiciary. The board's thoughtful anticipation of and response to significant conceptual and practical issues is directly responsible for its success.

NOTES

1. California Statutes 1917, ch. 527, s. 1, at 665 (formerly California Penal Code, Section 1168).
2. Penal Code, Section 1170(a)(1).
3. Penal Code, Sections 1170 and 1170.1. All references are to the California Penal Code unless otherwise specified.
4. Sections 1170(b), 1170(c), and 1170.1(g).
5. Section 1170(f).
6. The provisions quoted here were effective January 1, 1982. Statutes 1981, ch. 1111, s. 1. As originally enacted, this section required the board to file a motion in any case whose sentence the board determined to be disparately long. Statutes 1976, ch. 1139, s. 273; Statutes 1977, ch. 165, s. 15.
7. California Rules of Court 401-453.
8. California Rules of Court 421(b) and 423(b); People v. Cheatham (1979).
9. Section 1170.1(a).
10. Section 1170.1(f).
11. Section 1170.1(a).
12. The longest sentence reduction recommended by the board as of January 8, 1982 was 60 months on a term of 248 months.
13. Section 1170(a)(1).
14. Sections 1170.1(a), (d), (f).
15. Section 2930.
16. Section 2931.
17. Section 1170.3.
18. Section 1170(a)(2).
19. Section 1170.5.
20. Section 1170.4.
21. Section 1170.6.
22. The original version of Section 1170(f) required the board to file motions in cases whose sentences were disparately long.
23. Herrera was the first disparate case.
24. This is a county with three or fewer superior court judges. The appellation is of their own choosing and they are very proud of it.

CASES

In re COUGHLIN (1976) 16 Cal. 3d 52
In re CROIX (1974) 12 Cal. 3d 146

In re DUNHAM (1976) 16 Cal. 3d 63
In re FOSS (1974) 10 Cal. 3d 910
GEE v. BROWN (1975) 14 Cal. 3d 571
In re LYNCH (1972) 8 Cal. 3d 410
In re MARRIAGE OF LOPEZ (1974) 38 Cal. App. 3d 93
In re MINNIS (1972) 7 Cal. 3d 639
MOODY v. DAGGETT (1976) 429 U.S. 78
MORRISSEY v. BREWER (1972) 408 U.S. 471
In re OLSON (1974) 37 Cal. App. 3d 783
PEOPLE v. CHEATHAM (1979) 23 Cal. 3d 829
PEOPLE v. CRAIG (1982) 2 Crim. 39879
PEOPLE v. HERRERA (1982) 1 Crim. 20170
PEOPLE v. HERRERA (1982) 127 Cal. App. 3d 590
PEOPLE v. ORIN (1975) 13 Cal. 3d 937
PEOPLE v. SUPERIOR COURT [Duran] (1978) 84 Cal. App. 3d 480
In re PREWITT (1972) 8 Cal. 3d 470
In re RODRIGUEZ (1975) 14 Cal. 3d 639
In re SCHOENGARTH (1967) 66 Cal. 2d 295
In re SHAPIRO (1975) 14 Cal. 3d 711
In re STANLEY (1976) 54 Cal. App. 3d 1030
In re STURM (1974) 11 Cal. 3d 258
In re WILKERSON (1969) 271 Cal. App. 2d 708
In re WINN (1975) 13 Cal. 3d 694

REFERENCES

CASSOU, A. and B. TAUGHER (1978) "Determinate sentencing in California: the new numbers game." Pacific Law Journal 9 (January): 61, 71-78.

Council of State Governments (1976) Definite Sentencing: An Examination of Proposals in Four States (March).

LINDSEY, E. (1925) "Historical sketch of the indeterminate sentence and parole system." Journal of Criminal Law and Criminology 16 (May).

MESSINGER, S. L. and P. E. JOHNSON (1978) "California's determinate sentencing statute: history and issues," in Determinate Sentencing: Reform or Regression? Proceedings of the Special Conference on Determinate Sentencing, June 2-3. Washington, DC: Government Printing Office.

Opinions of the Attorney General (California) (1977) Volume 60.

Chapter 7

AUTOMATED SCREENING
The California Experience

WILLIAM PANNELL

Under the provisions of California's Uniform Determinate Sentencing Act of 1976, the Board of Prison Terms is required to review the sentences of persons committed to prison with determinate sentences to determine if those sentences are substantially different from the sentences imposed on other offenders convicted of similar crimes under similar circumstances.[1] By statute, this process includes a review of the trial court's decision to deny probation. The Determinate Sentencing Act does not, however, require the board to review persons received in prison with "life" sentences (e.g., murderers), who represent 5-10 percent of the yearly intake at adult state-level correctional facilities. (For a complete review of California's sentence disparity review law, see the previous chapter.)

The wording of the legislative mandate to review sentences offered little hint of how the sentences should actually be reviewed. Meetings were held shortly after passage of the law to discuss the conceptual and practical aspects of disparate sentence review. Attending these meetings were representatives from the Board of Prison Terms (then called the Community Release Board), the Department of Corrections, and the Rand Corporation. Other consultants were also sounded by the board.

It was assumed in 1977, when the disparity review process got underway, that a great number of factors might be associated with sentencing practices in general, and sentencing disparity in particular. An extensive list of potentially useful data items was developed. Most of the variables originally suggested exist in the board's data base today. A practical conceptualization of the review mandate was also developed. Board of Prison Terms staff determined that the review would be limited to the exercise of judicial discretion, not to the exercise of discretion by other actors in the criminal justice system. For example, prosecutorial discretion in charging and plea bargaining, which might lead to sentencing disparity, would not be included in the review. Analysts and legal staff felt, although not unanimously, that the legislative mandate was to review the sentences of persons "*convicted* of similar crimes."

It was clear from the beginning that some sort of computerized statistical approach was appropriate, although exactly *what* approach was not at all apparent. Among the suggestions were: regression analysis to predict sentences, log linear modeling, numerical taxonomy to group offenders, factor analysis to group variables, discriminant analysis, and various combinations of the above. After some experimentation with different standard statistical approaches (e.g., regression analysis), the board developed an approach which it felt best suited the statutory mandate. The resulting model, a sentencing simulation model called Automated Sentence Review, will be discussed shortly.

To develop a statistical model and to review the sentences of over 10,000 determinately sentenced prisoners entering state correctional institutions each year, the board concluded that in-house technical staff and computer capability was a necessity.

STAFF

The board initially hired a small staff comprised of three analysts, two data processing people, and a secretary. Staff to collect and code data were also hired. Over the past four years, staffing has remained essentially at this original level.

COMPUTER FACILITIES

The board uses a IV-Phase mini-computer connected to the Teale Data Center, a state-owned, multipurpose facility. The current configuration is as follows:

Mainframe and memory:

484 K bytes main memory

67.5 mega-bytes disc space

Peripheral devices:

18 video display units

300 LPM printer

3 55 CPS printers

Communications:

RJE line to Teale Data Center

3270 line to the Data Center

The in-house computer facilities are used for data entry, word processing, and program development. Most programs used by the board are written in SAS (Statistical Analysis System). These programs, along with the necessary JCL (IBM Job Control Language) are stored locally on disc. This is a very effective, efficient way of processing and analyzing the board's data.

DATA BASE

The board collects at least 172 variables on every case coded. The information collected includes all legal information contained in the committing court's Abstract of Judgment. Extensive information is also collected from the probation officer's report, the sentencing transcript, the California Department of Corrections "face sheet," the Bureau of Criminal Statistics "rap sheet," and charging documents (information, indictment, complaint, and so forth). The board also uses on occasion the Department of Corrections incident reports and parole violation reports.

The data collected are key-entered into a video display terminal with a formated screen. The data are edited extensively when entered. Two types of edits are performed. Validity edits verify that the type and length of fields entered are consistent with the variables being entered. Consistency edits logically compare values of different variables when appropriate. The data are then reentered for verification. The result of this process is a very "clean" set of records. This extensive editing is necessary for more than the usual reasons, since specific case information can result in alteration of a person's sentence. In all, 1400-2000 cases are entered each month.

Once the data are entered, they are transmitted in batch each month to Teale Data Center, where they are formated for SAS (Statistical Analysis System) data files. SAS is a proprietary software package for data management and statistical analysis. It is user-oriented and extremely easy to learn and use. All analyses of the data, with the exception of the simulation model (Automated Sentence Review), are done with SAS. Although many languages can be successfully used in simulation modelling, PLI was chosen by the board because of previous staff experience with that language.

Since individual records can be of variable lengths, a relational data base consisting of five SAS files was designed. One file contains fixed length demographic, prior criminal history and offense information, while the other four contain detailed information on each offense charged, each offense of conviction, each personal victim, and each business victim. The first or "master" file also contains summary information from each of the four detailed files, such as the number of victims seriously injured or number of offenses charged.

SENTENCE REVIEW

Eventually, the board decided to develop several different methods of sentence review to be used in "series" with one another. The first type of automated review to be developed was a Monte Carlo simulation model (see, for example, Fishman, 1978). This model attempts to replicate the decisions that a judge makes when sentencing. Currently under development is a factor analysis model for grouping variables within offense categories. Other sentence review models are now in the planning stage.

The simulation model, called Automated Sentence Review, was implemented in PLI, a high-level IBM language. It is top-down modular in design, and the code is rich in comment and lacking in go-tos. It is a complex program that is understood and used by more than one staff member. Another program, written in SAS, checks offender sentencing information for arithmetic errors.

Automated Sentence Review (ASR) calculates a sentence for each prisoner, using Monte Carlo techniques. Sentences for each offender are calculated 10,000 times. If, according to the simulation, fewer than 10.5 percent of those 10,000 theoretical sentencings would have resulted in a sentence as high or higher than the actual sentence imposed in that case, the case is identified as potentially disparate and requiring further review. A similar process identifies cases that may be disparately low. Cases identified by the ASR for further scrutiny are submitted to a secondary screening by a hearing representative of the board and other board staff. (See the previous chapter for further details of the secondary screening process.)

INPUT FOR THE SIMULATION MODEL (ASR)

The Automated Sentence Review (ASR) model reads two types of data. First, it reads inmate-specific data, describing a prisoner to be reviewed. This information includes the detailed legal circumstances of the offense, as well as information such as injury inflicted to victims, criminal justice status of the offender at the time of his or her conviction, and the prior prison experiences of the offender. The second type of data used by the model consists of odds or probability distributions that relate to the several sentencing decisions. These probability distributions are derived from observed sentencing practices and address the several decision components of the Determinate Sentencing Law.

Sentencing under California's Determinate Sentencing Law is a precisely defined process. There are three possible "base" sentences for any particular felony offense, for example, burglary—2 years, 3 years, 4 years; robbery—3 years, 4 years, 5 years. This base sentence can be enhanced or increased by specified lengths of time under a variety of conditions. For example, enhancements include increasing the sentence for use of a firearm, infliction of great bodily injury, prior prison terms, or excessive financial loss. Time may also be added for offenses in addition to the primary offense, e.g., consecutive sentences. The law also provides complex limitations to sentencing under specified circumstances. Thus, a judge sentencing an offender is typically faced with many choices. His or her decisions compound to produce a sentence. Considerable variation is possible in the sentence finally selected.

The simulation model is programmed in PLI to replicate the logic and special limitations of the law. The model calculates sentences for every offender received in prison under the Determinate Sentencing Law, and then compares the calculated sentences to the actual sentence received by that person. Sentences are calculated on the basis of the particular conviction circumstances of the offender and the observed historical sentencing patterns or probabilities drawn from the data base.

OUTPUT

The output of ASR consists of an OS (Operating System) file, each record of which contains a distribution of 10,000 sentences for each offender. Additionally, the records contain statistics describing each distribution. These statistics include several measures of central tendency, such as the mean; several measures of dispersion, such as the standard deviation; the most likely sentences, and the least likely sentences. Most importantly, the records contain a comparison of the actual sentence that the offender received with the mean simulated sentence. Several statistics describing the distribution of sentences and the sentence position of the offender being reviewed are produced (see Figure 7.1). An SAS file is created from the OS file. The SAS file is then used to produce special reports describing potentially disparate cases.

Sentences identified as disparately "low" cannot legally be lengthened. The law provides only that disparately "high" sentences can be lowered. To date, several prisoners have had their sentences reduced as a result of the disparate sentence review process. A total of 24 man-years of reduction in sentence as of January 11, 1982 have resulted in a state savings of at least $312,000. It is anticipated that ultimately, when the system is perfected, at least 20 persons per month will be found to have disparate sentences.

DOCUMENTATION

The board's data base and sentence review function are documented in a manner similar to that expounded by DeMarco (1978). This method involves descriptive hierarchically ordered "Bubble Charts" (see Figures 7.2, 7.3, 7.4, and 7.5), along with detailed specification of the low-order processes, or bubbles (see Figures 7.6, 7.7, and 7.8).

CDC=C9999   VARIANT SCORE=   −1.3227
               STANDARDIZED SENTENCE SCORE=1.3915

CDC=C000   VARIANT SCORE=   1.5444
               STANDARDIZED SENTENCE SCORE=0.9992

CDC=C1111   SENTENCE   NUMBER

                  36   5
                  48   58
                  52   1
                  60   343
                  64   2
                  68   27
                  72   836
                  76   21
                  80   177
                  84   1559
                  88   72
                  92   707
                  96   1481
                 100   163
                 104   1444
                 108   673
                 112   148
                 116   1282
                 120   120
                 124   72
                 128   652
                 136   19
                 140   138

               ACTUAL SENTENCE = 124
               SIMULATED MEAN SENTENCE = 98
               SENTENCE MIDRANGE = 88
               MOST LIKELY SENTENCE(S) = 84 MONTHS
               LEAST LIKELY SENTENCE(S) = 52 MONTHS
               HIGHEST SENTENCE = 140
               LOWEST SENTENCE = 36
               STANDARD DEVIATION = 17.8717
               SENTENCE DIVERSITY = 2.4459
               STANDARDIZED SENTENCE SCORE = 1.4598
               VARIANT SCORE = 3.5705

FIGURE 7.1   SAMPLE OUTPUT

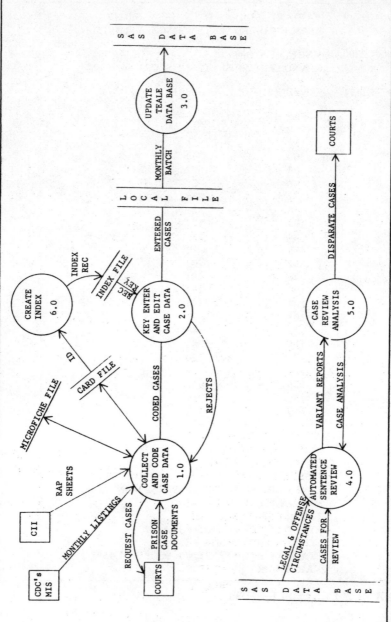

Figure 7.2

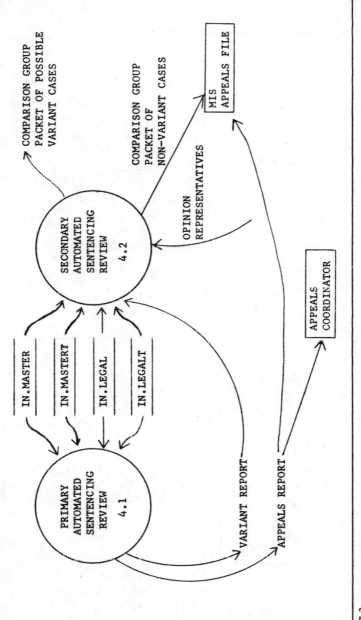

Figure 7.3

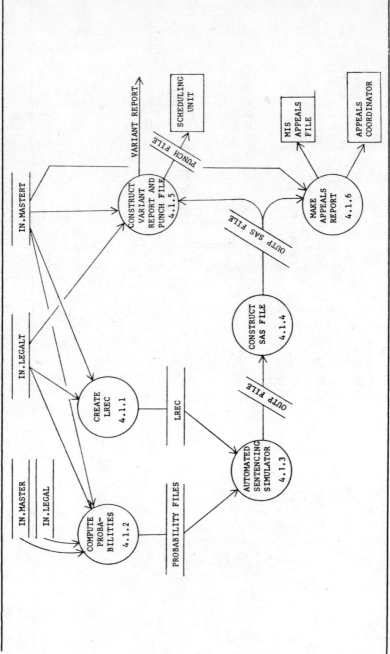

160

Figure 7.4

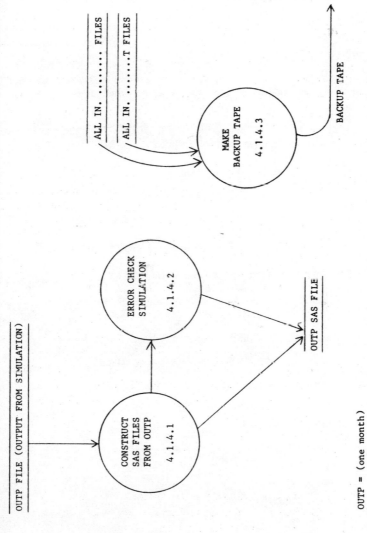

OUTP FILE (OUTPUT FROM SIMULATION)

CONSTRUCT
SAS FILES
FROM OUTP

4.1.4.1

ERROR CHECK
SIMULATION

4.1.4.2

OUTP SAS FILE

MAKE
BACKUP TAPE

4.1.4.3

ALL IN. .... FILES

ALL IN. ......T FILES

BACKUP TAPE

OUTP = (one month)

Figure 7.5

161

PROCESS NUMBER: 4.1.3

PROCESS NAME: AUTOMATED SENTENCING SIMULATOR

In this program written in PL/I the computer sentences everybody who came to prison during a certain month 10,000 times.

If, according to the computer, fewer than 10.5% of these 10,000 sentences would have resulted in a sentence equal to or higher than the actual sentence imposed, the case is printed out.

Similarly, if fewer than 10.5% of the theoretical sentences were equal to or lower than the actual sentence imposed, the case is printed out.

STEPS:

1. In FILE NAME change the names of the four probability input files.

> Example: //LI DD DSN=FILE NAME (MMMYY)
> //SI DD DSN=FILE NAME (MMMYY)
> //SCI DD DSN=FILE NAME (MMMYY)
> //SPI DD DSN=FILE NAME (MMMYY)

and change the name of the partitioned output file.

> Example: //OFILE DD DSN= FILE NAME (MMMYY),

2. Send: FILE NAME

For special JCL, FILE
change CDC # and DREC
send HASP, FILE

FIGURE 7.6

PROCESS NUMBER: 4.1.4.1

PROCESS NAME: SAVE OUTPUT FROM AUTOMATED SENTENCING SIM-
ULATOR IN SAS FILE

The automated sentencing review process is written in PL/I. This program translates
the output from ASR in SAS and creates a SAS dataset. It further adds the Z-score
computed by the simulator to this month's MASTERT file.

STEPS:

1. In FILE NAME change name of the partitioned dataset that the simulator has
created for the current month.

Example: //OUTP DD DSN= FILE NAME (MMMYY)

Change name of monthly SAS file to new month's name.

Example: MACRO MONTH IN.MMMYY %

2. Send: FILE NAME

FIGURE 7.7

PROCESS NUMBER: 4.1.4.2

PROCESS NAME: CHECK IF AUTOMATED SENTENCING SIMULATOR MADE
                ERRORS

If the 10,000 theoretical computer sentences do not include a sentence equal to the
actual sentence, at least once, something suspicious might be going on. These cases
(possible errors) should be analyzed and reviewed manually for disparity.

STEPS:

1. In FILE, ERRORS change new month's SASFILE name.

    Example: SET FILE .MMMYY;

Send: FILE, ERRORS

FIGURE 7.8

NOTE

1. Section 1170(f) of the California Penal Code.

REFERENCES

DeMARCO, T. (1978) Structured Analysis and System Specification. New York:
    Yourdon.
FISHMAN, G. S. (1978) Principles of Discrete Event Simulation. New York: John
    Wiley.

Chapter 8

JUDICIAL RESPONSE TO
SENTENCE REVIEW
A Test Case

FRANCES TERNUS

In 1976, the California legislature replaced the state's 60-year-old indeterminate sentencing system with the comprehensive Uniform Determinate Sentencing Act. In replacing the former system, where the Adult Authority made determinations of parole readiness based on punishment and rehabilitative factors, the legislature declared in Senate Bill 42 that the purpose of imprisonment under the new system is punishment and that

> this purpose is best served by terms proportionate to the seriousness of the offense with provision for uniformity in the sentences of offenders committing the same offense under similar circumstances. The Legislature further finds and declares that the elimination of disparity and the provision of uniformity of sentences can best be achieved by determinate sentences fixed by statute in proportion to the seriousness of the offense as determined by the Legislature to be imposed by the court with specified discretion.[1]

Both in the code sections providing statutory determinate sentencing rules and in the sections providing for retroactive application of determinate terms, the legislature stressed one of its major goals—the elimination of disparity and greater uniformity in sentencing.

As the author of S.B. 42 stated:

> Punishment should be fair and consistent. This fairness should exist regardless of the county in our state in which conviction was effected. . . . Incarceration terms should not be set at the caprice of the [parole board] or vary incident to the subjective views of any person or group. This is the essence of SB 42 [Nejedly, 1977: 25-26].

Uniformity, then, is a paramount objective of the new law. Judicially, in the exercise of their "specified discretion," sentencing courts were provided with both statutory and administrative guidelines to direct their sentencing determinations.[2] However, the guidelines were broad rather than very specific, and the rules lacked precision. Furthermore, the unavailability of statewide information concerning actual sentencing decisions as opposed to rules and guidelines constituted a major stumbling block to an achievement of uniformity, since courts in different areas of the state and judges in the different courts would still sentence according to local practice rather than in accordance with uniform statewide practice.

To remedy this problem and to insure the "fair and consistent [punishment] regardless of the county . . . in which conviction was effected," the legislature passed two additional provisions in S.B. 42. First, the legislature directed the Judicial Council to gather and disseminate sentencing statistics, conduct training, and engage in an ongoing review of sentencing practices.[3] Second, the legislature included as part of the determinate sentencing process itself a systematic administrative review of all sentences of persons determinately committed to state prison. Enacted as Penal Code Section 1170(f), this provision, which was in effect until December 31, 1981, provided:

> In all cases the Board of Prison Terms shall, not later than one year after the commencement of the term of imprisonment, review the sentence and shall by motion recommend that the court recall the sentence . . . if the board determines the sentence is disparate.[4]

The review mandated by this statute was to concern all "sentencing decisions" and was to include a compilation of "information regarding the sentences in this state of other persons convicted of similar crimes so as to eliminate disparity of sentences and to promote uniformity of sentencing."[5] Thus the board's review and motion to recall a sentence was one more mechanism to ensure that the sentence imposed by the court fell within the "specified discretion" outlined by the legislature and was not disproportionate to the statewide sentencing pattern that arose under the new law. All of these provisions together were part of a complex and elaborate scheme to eliminate disparity and promote uniformity and a fair and just system of punishment (see Guzman v. Morris, 1981).

Following the judicial act of imposing a given sentence within the statutory framework, the determination of the disparateness of a sentence was a complex matter that the legislature delegated to the Board of Prison Terms (Opinions, 1977: 143, 145). As successor to the Community Release Board and Adult Authority, the board has a long history of experience and expertise in the sentencing area (Azeria v. California Adult Authority, 1961; In re Grey, 1974). The legislature therefore gave the board broad discretion in this new task, subject only to certain general considerations, of determining which sentences were disparate.[6]

The board's regulations[7] mandate it to accumulate in-depth information concerning statewide sentencing practices and to compare sentences imposed in similar cases. Through its comprehensive study of sentences, the board is in a unique position to make the kind of comparison that trial and appellate courts, in their individual case analysis, could not accomplish. However, under the California scheme the trial court still remains the ultimate arbiter of sentencing matters. This chapter describes the response of the judiciary to the first motion for recall and resentencing because of disparity in sentencing brought by the Board of Prison Terms.

PEOPLE v. RAMON HERRERA: CASE HISTORY

The Trial Court

Ramon Herrera was convicted by jury of robbing two people and attempting to rob a third person at a Taco Bell restaurant in San Jose, California on December 13, 1977. He was also convicted of robbing two people at a Straw Hat Pizza parlor in San Jose the same evening. On June 21, 1978 the trial court sentenced Herrera to consecutive terms in state prison for each individual conviction for a total prison term of nine years, four months.

On June 29, 1978 Herrera was received in prison. Following its own procedures, the board reviewed Herrera's sentence to determine if it was disparate pursuant to the requirements of Penal Code Section 1170(f). The board defined disparate as a "substantial difference, as the result of the exercise of judicial discretion, between the subject sentence and the sentences imposed on other offenders committing similar offenses under similar circumstances."[8]

The board began the procedure to determine if a sentence is disparate by examining the factual and legal information relevant to the sentencing decision in a given case and comparing that information with similar information obtained from all other criminal commitment cases. After this comparison is completed, the board can then determine whether the sentence in the given case is substantially different from the sentences imposed in other cases that have been found to be similar to the given case.

If the sentence imposed in the given case is initially found to be disparate by the board staff compared to the other cases, the matter is set for further review by a panel of board members. If that panel review determines that the sentence imposed is disparate, the panel, by motion filed with the sentencing court, must ask that the sentence be recalled and the disparity eliminated.

In Herrera's case, the board's motion and supporting documents established that the normal sentencing pattern in cases involving multiple robberies was to impose consecutive sentences for separate incidents and concurrent sentences for multiple victims involved in each separate incident. Variances from this pattern were few: Only 13 percent (six, excluding Herrera's) of 54 cases deviated from the sentencing pattern. The board's attachments demonstrated that these six cases involved factors far more aggravating than the factors present in Herrera's case. All six involved actual physical injuries or mistreatment of one or more victims or a lengthy criminal history. Herrera's crimes involved no actual injury, and his criminal history was more similar to those of the defendants in cases that followed the pattern than to those in the six variant cases.

The board summarized that Herrera's sentence of consecutive terms for each of the victims in each of the two robberies not only fell outside the normal sentencing pattern but was also substantially different from the sentences imposed in similar cases. Furthermore, Herrera's case was factually dissimilar from the 13 percent of the cases in which sentencing outside the normal pattern was found. Herrera's sentence, the board found, should have been within the normal pattern. Such a nondisparate sentence would total six years, eight months rather than nine years, four months. This sentence included three years as the middle base term for the principal offense, two years for the weapon enhancement, and one year, eight months as a consecutive enhancement for one of the counts arising from the second incident.

At the hearing on the motion, the prosecutor argued that comparisons could not be made because some sentences, unlike Herrera's, resulted from plea bargaining, while others followed jury trials. His reasoning was that the cases that led to convictions based on pleas would result in more lenient sentences. The board attorney responded that they were prohibited by a Supreme Court decision from separating sentences based on plea bargains from those resulting from jury trial convictions.

The trial court, in denying the motion, stated that it imposed the sentence recommended by the Probation Department and that it did not believe that the disparity, if there were any, was substantial. The court stated that Herrera had had contact with juvenile authorities, had one commitment to the California Rehabilitation Center, two county jail terms, had escaped on one of the terms, and had used a gun in the charged robberies.

Appeal

In August 1980, Herrera's appeal, prepared by the California State Public Defender's Office, was filed. On appeal, Herrera argued that if sentences are to be uniform in that similar crimes are to be punished with similar sentences, and if disparity is to be corrected by the operations of the disparate review statute and the board review encompassed therein, it necessarily followed that a motion to recall the sentence created a presumption in favor of the defendant that his sentence was disparate in violation of the prescriptions of the determinate sentencing act.[9] The presumption therefore would be that such a defendant would be entitled to have that sentence recalled to be resentenced in accordance with the law. Without this presumption, Herrera further argued, this entire statutory and administrative scheme would be reduced to nothing more than a meaningless gesture. Once the board sends a case back to court with a finding of disparity, the only way disparity can be eliminated would be to create a presumption that the sentence is disparate and must therefore be recalled.

In this case, Herrera contended, the trial court failed to overcome the presumption that the sentence was disparate. The court merely repeated the factors originally used to impose the nine-year prison sentence. Every one of these factors had been examined by the board in his case and in the 54 other cases. The board had established that none of these factors created a dissimilarity between Herrera's case and the cases that were sentenced under the normal pattern, and that none of these factors was as serious in his case as they were in the cases of the six persons whose sentences were longer than the pattern would otherwise allow.

In summary, Herrera stated, the court therefore failed to show the existence of any factor that was either not considered by the board or, if considered, lent justification to the imposition of the disparate sentence.

The board conclusively established that, utilizing the factors cited by the court, as well as all other relevant factors, Herrera's sentence was disparate and not in conformance with the statutory requirements. In denying the motion, the court simply disagreed with the board, disagreed that the sentence was disparate, but did so without any supporting factual basis. The court could point to nothing to indicate that the board was in error or had ignored some crucial point. Other than expressing the gut feeling that Herrera's sentence was correct, the court could point to nothing in the record to show that the sentence was not disparate. The board's determination that Herrera's sentence was disparate and that he must be resentenced created a presumption that was not rebutted by the trial court or the prosecutor.

The attorney general, respondent in the appeal, initially responded that an order denying a disparate review motion is not appealable. He further submitted that the appellate courts should hold that the sentencing courts should not exercise their power to adjudicate a disparate sentence review motion for recall of sentence where a pending appeal from the judgment exists unless a continuance pending appellate finality would prejudice opportunity for resentencing to a nondisparate term.

In specific response to Herrera's contention that a motion for recall created a presumption of disparity, the attorney general argued that this contention finds no support in the plain language of the statute, in the intent underlying the entire legislative scheme of which it is a part, nor in the historical background of the scheme. The statute not only fails to create a presumption, but there is also no burden to be met by the trial court in denying the motion. Furthermore, the attorney general contended, such argument, if adopted, would have a wholly unpredictable, possibly adverse impact on the overall level of sentencing uniformity in this state; would introduce contradictory sentencing criteria; and could frustrate the practical implementation of various sentencing objectives. Finally, adoption of such rule was not warranted in this case given the experimental nature of the board's administrative and statistical process.

The board, filing an amicus curiae brief, argued that their finding of disparity should be given great weight and that it was an abuse of discretion for the court not to accord this finding its appropriate weight.

The Court of Appeal, in its opinion filed January 8, 1982, first held that the order denying the motion to recall was appealable (People v. Herrera, 1982). The court additionally declined the attorney general's request to establish a rule of criminal procedure requiring that a defendant's appeal be finalized before a motion to recall could be adjudicated because the issue was not raised in the trial court.

The court rejected Herrera's contention that the board's finding of disparity created a rebuttable presumption that the sentence was incorrect and should be recalled. The court found that there was no authority in the statute for the finding of a presumption and stated that the statute neither specified what procedure should be followed in hearing the motion nor required the trial judge to make findings in ruling on the motion.

The court pointed out that the legislature has, when it wished, created presumptions in sentencing procedures that are contained in other statutes. The court found that the absence of such language in section 1170(f) indicated that the legislature did not intend to create a presumption when the motion was brought before the trial court. The court, however, also rejected the attorney general's contention that the trial court had no burden to meet when denying the motion. The court found that if the trial court could deny the motion without giving any consideration whatsoever to the board's finding of disparity, the purpose of the entire Determinate Sentencing Law—the elimination of disparity—would fail to be effectuated.

Rather than holding that the statute created a rebuttable presumption, the court found that the trial court must give "great weight" to the board's determination that a sentence is disparate. The court also set out a two-part analysis that trial courts must follow in determining the merits of a motion to recall. First, it must determine if the sentence is indeed disparate. Second, the fact of disparity, if found, must be given great weight in the court's decision to recall the sentence.

While the court found no California case that defined the meaning of great weight, it stated that the trial court would have met its burden of giving great weight to the board's finding in the first part of the analysis if it had seriously considered the board's information. However, the court did not require the trial court to make findings as to why it disagreed with the board's findings.

To meet its burden in the second part of the analysis, the court required the trial judge to question the "observed sentencing patterns" of other judges relied upon by the board. The statewide sentencing patterns, the court felt, should be treated as guidelines in the quest for uniformity of sentencing. They should not be used to limit a judge's sentencing discretion.

In applying this analysis to the facts of Herrera's case, the court found that the trial court had accorded the board's findings great weight by seriously considering the information provided by the board and attempting to discover whether the sentence imposed was disparate. The court therefore affirmed the denial of the board's motion.

Herrera's Petition for Hearing to the California Supreme Court was filed by the California State Public Defender's Office on February 17, 1982. The petition asked the Supreme Court to hear the case because the Court of Appeal's opinion offers no real guidance to trial courts, limits the board's functions to mere information gatherers, forecloses appellate review by failing to require the trial court to make specific findings when it denies a motion, and essentially takes the teeth out of the one mechanism in the law that assures uniform sentences. The Supreme Court denied the petition on April 1, 1982.

THE FUTURE FOR DISPARATE SENTENCE REVIEW IN CALIFORNIA

A convicted felon in California had a very slim—if not negligible—chance of having his sentence considered disparate by the Board of Prison Terms and, if considered disparate, an even slimmer chance of having the trial court reduce his term under the law as it read before January 1, 1982. Now with changes in the statute and the Herrera decision, the future for disparate sentence review in California appears to be very dark indeed.[10]

From January 1978 to December 1981, 34,454 persons were committed to the California Department of Corrections. From August 1979, when the board brought their first motion for recall before the trial court to December 1981, the board filed 31 motions. Of these, 15 motions were granted and the defendants' terms were lowered.

Under the Herrera decision, it is postulated that even fewer terms will be lowered than before. The "great weight" standard established by the Court of Appeal is far too minimal and vague a standard for such a substantial interest as liberty. A defendant's right to a fair and consistent punishment cannot be properly protected by such a standard. Furthermore, the opinion of the board in this context is more than the opinion of "the construction of a statute by the officials charged with its administration," as noted by the Court of Appeal. When determining that someone has been sentenced to prison 50 percent longer than is fair for his crime, the board's opinion is more than an administrative interpretation and should be given far more consideration than the mere "great weight" standard.

Additionally, it is clear that the Court of Appeal's required two-step procedure is fatally flawed. The trial court is apparently not required to give the board's finding of disparity great weight until after it determines the sentence is disparate. This procedure, when coupled with the failure to require a trial court to state reasons when it disagrees with the board's determination, virtually gives the trial court carte blanche to ignore the board's findings, without any risk of reversal at a later time. The trial court will, for the most part, have very little statistical information of its own to refute the board's elaborately gathered information.

The vagueness of both the standard and the procedure is apparent from the opinion. The opinion fails to define great weight and vaguely analogizes it to serious consideration. Furthermore, the failure of the Court of Appeal to require specific findings when the trial court disagrees with the board's determination that a sentence is disparate makes reversal almost impossible. The Court of Appeal, however, stated that as a practical matter the judge will want the record to show why he or she disagreed with the board. This polite request is hardly sufficient to assure that appellate review can be effectuated.

The new amendments to section 1170(f) further reduce the likelihood that a defendant's prison term, once found disparate by the board, will be reduced. Under the old law, the board was required to file a motion for recall and resentence with the sentencing court. This motion included all the documents the board staff relied upon in finding the sentence disparate, including case histories of the defendant in question, case histories of those similarly convicted, and the statistical analysis used to determine disparity. For instance, in the Herrera case, the board's motion and supporting documents numbered 57 pages. Additionally, the board counsel was the moving party and the board statistician testified as to the procedure used in determining disparity.

Under the new statute, the board is no longer the moving party. The board simply notifies the sentencing court that a disparity has been found in a sentence imposed by that court and states the reasons for the finding. The defendant's trial attorney, often a beleaguered public defender, has the burden of making the motion. The board's statistics, which were formerly appended to their motions as a matter of course, will be available only if requested. The board counsel and statisticians will appear only if subpoenaed.

This latter point will make a substantial difference at a hearing on a motion to recall. One cannot overestimate the emotional impact on the trial court of the Board of Prison Terms, hardly viewed as a traditional ally of prisoners, coming before the court with a motion stating that a prison term should be lowered. The trial attorney, who has presumably already argued at sentencing that the term should be lowered, will again be before the court. He simply will not have the effect or the prestige of the board.

When the miniscule number of motions for recall brought by the board is considered with the Herrera decision and the new disparate review statute, one cannot help but feel that there is no real commitment in California to uniformity of sentencing. The legislature, while constantly referring to the avoidance of disparity in the sentencing statutes as one of its main goals, has failed to put procedural safeguards in the disparity review statute to effectuate this goal. The effect of the statute and the case law is practically to return term-setting to the old days of unfettered discretion of the Adult Authority. Unless another appellate court in the future rules differently than the Herrera court, the abuses of the Adult Authority will be perpetuated.

NOTES

1. California Penal Code, Section 1170(a)(1). All references are to the California Penal Code unless otherwise noted.
2. Penal Code, Section 1170(a)(2), 1170.1; California Rules of Court, 410-453; In re Gray (1978).
3. Penal Code, Sections 1170.3-1170.6.
4. On January 1, 1982, Section 1170(f) was amended to read as follows:

(1) Within one year after the commencement of the term of imprisonment, the Board of Prison Terms shall review the sentence to determine whether the sentence is disparate in comparison with the sentences imposed in similar cases. If the Board of Prison Terms determines that the sentence is disparate, the board shall notify the judge, the district attorney, the defense attorney, the defendant, and the Judicial Council. The notification shall include a statement of the reasons for finding the sentence disparate.

Within 120 days of receipt of this information, the sentencing court shall schedule a hearing and may recall the sentence and commitment previously ordered and resentence the defendant in the same manner as if the defendant had not been sentenced previously provided the new sentence is no greater than the initial sentence. In resentencing under this subdivision the court shall apply the sentencing rules of the Judicial Council and shall consider the information provided by the Board of Prison Terms.

The effect of this change will be discussed later in this chapter.
5. Penal Code, Section 1170(f).
6. Penal Code, Section 1170(f).
7. California Administrative Code, Title 15, Sections 2100-2107.
8. California Administrative Code, Title 15, Section 2100 et seq.
9. See People v. Ramon Herrera, California Court of Appeal, First Appellate District, Division Two, Crim. No. 20170, the record filed therein.
10. See note 4 for new amendments to Section 1170(f).

CASES

AZERIA v. CALIFORNIA ADULT AUTHORITY (1961) 193 CA 2d 1
In re Gray (1978) 85 CA 3d 255
In re Grey (1974) 11 Cal. 3d 554
GUZMAN v. MORRIS (1981) 9th Cir., 644 F.2d 1295
PEOPLE v. HERRERA (1982) 127 Cal. App. 3d 590

REFERENCES

NEDJEDLY, J. (1977) "Senate Bill 42." Peace Officer Law Report (January).
Opinions of the Attorney General (California) (1977) Volume 60.

Chapter 9

JUDICIAL REVIEW
A Case for Sentencing
Guidelines and Just Deserts

PETER A. OZANNE

One of the earliest proposals for legal reform of our penal systems was judicial review of sentences.[1] By evaluating sentences in light of the reasons given for them and by comparing sentences in similar cases, proponents of sentence review contend that appellate courts will regulate the exercise of the broad discretion given to trial judges and parole boards.[2] In the process, appellate courts are expected to develop coherent sentencing policies and principles, to reduce sentence disparity, and to contribute to the equitable distribution of punishment and the rational allocation of corrections resources.

Judicial review was an axiom of sentence law reform by the early 1970s. Judge Marvin Frankel (1973: 5) had published his influential essay, *Criminal Sentences: Law Without Order,* in which he urged the adoption of measures, including appellate review, to "regulate the almost wholly unchecked and sweeping powers we give judges in the fashioning of sentences." As Judge Frankel, a federal trial judge, saw it:

> The sentencing powers of the judges are, in short, so far unconfined that, except for frequently monstrous maximum limits, they are effectively subject to no law at all. Everyone with the least training in law would be prompt to denounce a statute that merely said the penalty for crimes "shall be any term the judge sees fit to impose."

A regime of such arbitrary fiat would be intolerable in a supposedly free society, to say nothing of being involved under our due process clause. But the fact is that we have accepted unthinkingly a criminal code creating in effect precisely that degree of unbridled power [1973: 8].

The legal establishment apparently agreed. With the assessment that "no other country in the free world permits this condition to exist," the American Bar Association (1968: 2) published a detailed set of standards for appellate review of sentences designed to regulate the discretion exercised by sentencing judges. In the ABA's view, judicial sentence review could make substantial contributions to reducing sentence disparity in two ways:

First, it can level off the peaks by reducing the excessive sentence.... Second, and most importantly with respect to the problem of disparity, sentence review can contribute to the development of sound sentencing principles and thus lead closer to the goal of approaching each defendant on the same basis [1968: 28-29].

The second contribution of judicial review was to be accomplished by requiring trial judges to set forth the reasons for their sentences on the record and by directing appellate courts to write opinions that contain reasons for sentence modifications. Not only would this process reduce disparity, "but on a much broader scale it can also contribute significantly to the development of sound sentencing policy (1968: 30).

Although there is substantial evidence that differences in sentences are caused as much by decisions outside the courtroom, such as the charging decisions of prosecutors, plea bargains between attorneys, and the presentence investigations of probation officers (see Alschuler, 1978: 550; Gaylin, 1974: 13), it is not surprising that lawyers and judges would propose judicial review as a primary means to reform criminal sentencing. Lawyers are trained to focus on the roles played by lawyers and judges in courtrooms rather than the informal, less visible, and perhaps more important processes that are a part of any complex social system. Furthermore, judicial review is the traditional legal mechanism to reconcile the myriad of individual decisions by trial judges and to limit the exercise of discretion by formal decisionmakers.

At the time it published its standards for appellate review, the American Bar Association (1968: 13) estimated that judicial sentence review was "realistically available" in fifteen states. In the next decade, only eight more states enacted sentence review statutes (Singer, 1979: 116, n. 10).

An explanation for the limited acceptance of judicial sentence review is not hard to find. Appellate judges do not welcome additions to a caseload they already consider overwhelming. They see the call for judicial sentence review as the invitation to a flood of new appeals, and they make this view known to their legislatures. In the words of one prominent federal appeals court judge:

> I hope there will be enough good judgment in Congress to realize that adoption of [appellate sentence review] would administer the "coup de grace" to the courts of appeals as we know them [Friendly, 1973: 36].

Proponents of sentence review point out that many appeals already result from excessive sentences, although the appeals are expressed in terms of other legal issues (see Coburn, 1971). Studies in jurisdictions with judicial sentence review suggest that this specter of a flood of new appeals may be exaggerated (e.g., O'Donnell et al., 1977: 60). Nevertheless, many appellate judges remain convinced that substantive sentence review will overwhelm them with new appeals, and many legislatures apparently agree. Given the available evidence, it is difficult for the proponents of sentence review to deny the possibility that an increase in judicial workload will be a cost associated with its adoption.

In the jurisdictions that have adopted a system of sentence review, the performance of the courts in regulating sentencing decisions and reducing disparity has not been encouraging. One of the most thorough studies of sentence review systems made the following assessment:

> Even where appellate review exists, it has not resulted in the development of a body of principles, which serves to articulate criteria for important corrections decisions. In decisions reducing sentences, no principle emerges that can be used as a guide for future action. . . . In brief, judicial review of correctional decisions is likely to have a limited impact upon the daily operation of the correctional process [Dawson, 1969: 388-389; and see Dix, 1969].

The primary reason for the failure of sentence review to meet the expectations of its proponents is not hard to find, either. The U.S. Supreme Court recently described the problem facing appellate courts:

> Legislatures have traditionally set high maximum penalties within which judges must choose specific sentences, but generally have provided little guidance for the exercise of this choice. Although the

purposes of sentencing have often been defined as including deterrence, retribution, incapacitation, rehabilitation and community condemnation to maintain respect for law, legislatures have been silent regarding which purposes are primary and how conflicts among purposes are to be resolved [Hoffman & Stover, 1978, cited in Bullington v. Missouri, 1981].

Legislatures have failed to develop a sentencing policy from the theories of punishment that make up this country's "jurisprudence of sentencing," and the appellate courts have been unwilling to do so on their own. As a result, the nature and diversity of the recognized theories of punishment have presented two obstacles to the reduction of disparity and the regulation of sentencing through judicial review. First, it is impossible to identify sentence disparity or determine its significance without knowing what theory of punishment is being pursued as a matter of sentencing policy. Second, without such policy guidance, sentencers, in the first instance, have no uniform standards under which uniform sentences can be imposed, and reviewing courts, on appeal, have no standard to identify and measure disparate sentences.

There is little disagreement that some variation in sentences for the same crime is inevitable in order to account for differences in the circumstances surrounding the commission of particular offenses. Treating everyone the same, as well as treating everyone differently, raises a claim of disparity. However, at some point necessary sentence variation becomes unjustified sentence disparity. That point is determined by judgments of value.

When variations in sentences are caused by factors such as an offender's race or social status, for example, values more important than the prevention or punishment of crime are at stake. This kind of sentencing variation has been universally condemned as unjustified disparity, in theory if not in practice (Bullock, 1961: 411; Washington Law Review, 1973: 857; Wolfgang and Riedel, 1973: 119).

A less invidious but perhaps more pervasive form of sentence disparity occurs when two persons who are similarly situated are sentenced differently for the same crime (Wilkins et al., 1978: 1). The existence of this form of disparity depends on a determination that two persons are in fact "similarly situated." That determination in turn depends on a value judgment—the judgment of what theory of punishment should form the basis of the sentencing policy in a penal system.

Every recognized theory of criminal punishment makes a unique set of factors relevant to the sentencing decision. It is this set of factors that determines who is "similarly situated" for the purpose of identifying sentence disparity. Under a retributivistic theory of "just deserts," for example, it is those circumstances of the crime that relate to its severity and any prior criminal record of the offender. On the other hand, under a theory of rehabilitation, it is the characteristics of the offender and the offense that reveal the offender's potential for rehabilitation.

The existence of these differences in relevant sentencing factors among the recognized theories of punishment means that different offenders will be considered similarly situated and that different sentence variations will be considered disparate, depending on what theory underlies the sentencing policy in a penal system. For example, two offenders with identical criminal records are both convicted of felony theft of property valued at $1000 and are sentenced to one year in prison. Under a just deserts system, the offenders are similarly situated and the sentence is not disparate. The fact that one offender has a third grade education and has been unemployed for three years, while the other has two Ph.D.s and is the president of a university, would be irrelevant. If these socioeconomic factors had caused a difference in their sentences, then the difference would amount to sentence disparity in a just deserts system. On the other hand, in a rehabilitative penal system, these offenders are not similarly situated because they differ with respect to factors relevant to potential for rehabilitation, at least when rehabilitation is defined as behaving like persons with an education and a job. Under a theory of rehabilitation, these two offenders should receive different sentences. Imposing the same sentence in these cases would constitute disparity in a rehabilitative penal system.

The peculiar substance of some of the recognized theories of punishment are also bound to frustrate the search for disparity when they are used to justify sentences. The theory of rehabilitation, though never an exclusive justification for the institution of criminal punishment, has, over the past fifty years, attained preeminence among the competing theories of punishment. When rehabilitation is the justification for a sentence, it becomes virtually impossible to distinguish sentence disparity from acceptable sentence variation by comparing one sentence with another. It is not that rehabilitation theory rejects the value of equal treatment for similarly situated offenders outright; according to the theory, differences between sentences for offenders in the same circumstances frustrate rehabilitative objectives because the offenders will compare notes and many will become discouraged, cynical, and resistant to treatment. However, in order to determine an offender's rehabilitative potential, the theory of rehabilita-

tion justifies the consideration of a limitless array of individual characteristics, psychological needs, and socioeconomic circumstances. As a result,
it is impossible to tell whether any two offenders who are convicted of the
same crime are similarly situated.

Moreover, because many of the factors relevant to a rehabilitative
sentence are, at least in theory, dependent on the direct observation and
assessment of individual offenders, there is a compelling rationale to defer
to, rather than question, these individualized sentencing decisions. When
the agency chosen to review these decisions is an appellate court, its
customary resistance to substituting its judgment for the judgment of any
initial decisionmaker with respect to questions of fact makes the rationale
even more compelling.

Two other recognized theories of punishment present obstacles to
reducing disparity, because they explicitly subordinate the value of equal
sentencing treatment to the goals of crime prevention. Under the utilitarian theories of general deterrence and incapacitation, sentences that would
otherwise be considered disparate are justified when they serve the objective of reducing crime in the future. It is not that sentence variation has
positive value; sentence variation is a necessary evil when it contributes to
the prevention of the greater evil of future crime.

The exemplary sentence is a common cause of sentence variation under
a theory of general deterrence. The following statement has probably been
made, in one form or another, in every criminal court in this country:

> Young man, I am sentencing you to prison for six months longer
> than I normally would in order to send a message to other young
> people who might be considering this kind of conduct that . . . the
> community is fed up and isn't going to take it any more . . . [or, a
> person of your stature in this community can't get away with this
> and they won't either.]

In other words, if particular criminal conduct is considered an acute
and intractable social problem, or if the offender's circumstances increase
the likelihood that the deterrent message will be heard, then the utilitarian's calculus justifies an otherwise disparate sentence if it deters the
greater evil of future crime (Hart, 1973: 172).

The utilitarian theory of incapacitation also relegates uniform sentencing treatment to secondary status in an effort to protect society from
dangerous offenders. Trial courts often invoke this theory when sentencing
sex offenders, bad check writers, and alcoholics who persist in driving with

suspended or revoked driver's licenses. Parole boards usually consider this theory their "raison d'être."

Incapacitative sentences produce suspect variations in sentences for different crimes which are unrelated to the blameworthiness of the criminal conduct. For example, on the basis of predicted recidivism, an alcoholic motorist may find himself sharing prison space with a rapist, and the repeat property offender may remain in prison longer than a cellmate who killed in passion. Just two years ago, the U.S. Supreme Court upheld a mandatory life sentence imposed under a recidivist statute for the commission of three felonies over a nine-year period: fraudulently presenting a credit card with the intent to obtain approximately $80, passing a forged instrument in the amount of $28.36, and obtaining $120.75 by false pretenses (Rummel v. Estelle, 1980).

Incapacitative sentences also produce sentence variations that would otherwise amount to disparity due to the state of the art of predicting human behavior. As many critics of incapacitative sentencing strategies have pointed out, the devices used to predict future danger and to select those to be restrained are fallible. Under any method for assessing danger, a number of offenders will be classified as dangerous who, if left alone, would not prove dangerous. Treating these nondangerous "false positives" in the same way as the truly dangerous is an injustice that even the incapacitative penologist would label as sentence disparity in the abstract. Once again, however, there is a utilitarian justification for accepting a margin of error in predicting danger. The excessive punishment of false positives is a lesser evil in comparison to the future harm to society averted by the incapacitation of the truly dangerous.

Faced with silence from the legislature or a laundry list of the recognized theories of criminal punishment as a statement of sentencing policy, it is not surprising that sentence disparity is a hallmark of our penal system. Without an internally consistent statement of policy to guide the system, each sentencer becomes an independent policymaker who is free to choose a theory or purpose of punishment that seems to suit the circumstances in a particular case. In short, there is sentence disparity in our penal system because there is disparity in our sentencing policies.

What should we expect appellate courts to do when called upon to review sentences for disparity by finding that a particular sentence is too harsh or too lenient? Returning to the earlier hypothetical of two offenders with identical criminal records who are convicted of the felony theft of $1000 worth of property, assume that one offender is sentenced to one year in prison and the other to six months of unsupervised probation. In the first case, the trial judge's reason for the sentence is that "the sentence is proportionate to the seriousness of this offense and is similar to sentences for offenses of equal seriousness." In the second case, the trial judge reasons that "the defendant's prospects for rehabilitation are good and she has learned her lesson without spending any time behind bars." When confronted with a claim of disparity in one case in light of the other, should an appellate court choose to apply the set of factors relevant to sentencing under a retributivistic system or a rehabilitative system? The typical response of an appellate court in these circumstances is to defer to the "sound discretion" of the trial judge and uphold either sentence on review.

This was not the response that the early proponents of sentence review promised. By holding out the prospects of the development of "sound sentencing principles" and a "sound sentencing policy," the American Bar Association apparently expected the appellate courts to regulate sentences and reduce disparity by approaching the thicket of our jurisprudence of sentencing, selecting from among the competing theories of punishment, formulating a coherent sentencing policy, and developing rules consistent with that policy. Perhaps out of fear of increased workloads, perhaps due to a healthy respect for the processes of representative government, few appellate courts have taken up the challenge (Campbell, 1978: 386).

When appellate courts are directed by statute to review sentences, these courts do not respond by thumbing their noses at their legislatures and refusing to entertain sentence appeals at all. Instead, they respond by diligently undertaking "procedural" reviews of sentences to determine if sentences are imposed in conformity with established legal procedures. In cases where a sentencer fails to follow legal procedures, such as considering a presentence investigation report or stating reasons for the sentence on the record, sentences will be reversed or modified (Campbell, 1978: 390, 395; Dawson, 1969: 388; State v. Dinkel, 1978).

However, when an appeal calls upon these courts to even out disparities by reducing an excessive sentence, this "substantive" review of sentences is undertaken with great hesitancy. The typical response of an appellate court is to fashion a deferential standard of review that upholds sentences unless they are "clearly mistaken," outside "the zone of reasonableness," or reflect an "abuse of discretion" (Campbell, 1978: 393; see also State v. Dinkel, 1978; State v. Waldrip, 1975). If the substance of a sentence does not exceed the broad limits of the indeterminate sentence, it will usually be affirmed under these standards of review. Given the lack of intensity of substantive review, it is not surprising that "intuitive and hence vague Gestalt perceptions ... inform the review process," "word-reasons [become] full explanations" (Zeisel and Diamond, 1977: 881, 938), and sentence disparity persists in most of this country's penal systems.

Proponents of sentence law reform have been quick to blame the courts for sentence disparity because of their aversion to reviewing the substance of sentences. However, legislatures ought to share the blame. The appellate courts' failure to undertake substantive sentence review reflects not just a reaction to the prospects of more work, but a collective wisdom about the respective roles of courts and legislatures in formulating public policy in our representative systems of government.

If it is necessary to choose a theory of punishment and to formulate a general sentencing policy before disparity can be identified and sentencing discretion can be regulated, then our elected representatives in the legislature should perform these tasks. In systems where legislatures enact the laws defining crime, establish the procedures to prosecute it, and make up the sentence ranges to punish it, it is reasonable to expect the same branch of government to formulate a criminal sentencing policy. A public policy of criminal punishment is too important and controversial to leave to the courts. If legislatures assume this responsibility, they can provide an important role for appellate courts to play in regulating sentencing practices and reducing disparity: not the role of sentencing jurisprudentialist and rulemaker that the early proponents of judicial review envisioned, but a significant role nonetheless.

Two changes have taken place in contemporary penology that increase the prospects of a meaningful role for appellate courts in the regulation of sentences and the reduction of disparity. First, a consensus has emerged among proponents of sentence law reform that the indeterminate sentencing system and its underlying theory of rehabilitation must be eliminated (see Allen, 1978: 147). As a result, one of the greatest obstacles to identifying sentence disparity and reviewing sentencing decisions would also be eliminated.

Although there is considerable evidence that indeterminate sentencing systems do not rehabilitate (see Lipton et al., 1975; Martinson, 1979: 243), at least with the resources that society is now willing to devote to the task, this is not the reason for rejecting the theory of rehabilitation. Most critics of the theory are willing to continue offering rehabilitative programs in our penal systems (e.g., Packer, 1968: 67). The reason for rejecting the theory of rehabilitation is that, as the primary justification for the institution of punishment and the indeterminate sentencing, it provides sentencing decisionmakers with too much discretion.

The conclusion that there is too much discretion is based on a variety of assessments about the sentences that the theory of rehabilitation produces: indeterminate sentences are, depending on one's perspective, inequitably disparate, dangerously lenient, or oppressively harsh. There is also common ground for rejecting the current level of discretion in rehabilitative penal systems. In a system with unstructured sentencing discretion and the inconsistent sentencing decisions it produces, it is impossible to allocate scarce corrections resources rationally or to control prison populations.

A second change taking place is the increasing recognition among those interested in sentence law reform that the rule of law must replace unstructured discretion in our penal system. Nearly fifteen years ago, Kenneth Culp Davis (1969: 133), this country's foremost administrative law expert, focused his attention on our penal systems and concluded:

> The power of judges to sentence criminal defendants is one of the best examples of unstructured discretionary power that can and should be structured. The degree of disparity from one judge to another is widely regarded as a disgrace to the legal system. All the elements of structuring are needed—open plans, policy statements and rules, findings and reasons, and open precedents. Application to sentencing of what I have learned about structuring of other discretionary power leads me to believe that structuring the sentencing power is feasible.[3]

Proposals to abolish parole and adopt determinate, "flat-time" sentences represent the most radical response to excessive sentencing discretion. However, a purely determinate sentencing system has several drawbacks.

By eliminating the possibility of considering mitigating or aggravating circumstances in individual cases, the determinate sentence is too inflexible for most people's taste. Davis (1969: 27-29) would consider such a system an example of "an extravagant version of the rule of law" that led to excessive discretionary power in the first place. The law's objective should not be to eliminate all discretion, or even to impose the maximum amount of regulation possible. The objective of any form of regulation is to find the optimum balance between structure and discretion (Davis, 1969: 4).

Other commentators have suggested that discretion in the penal system is like liquid in a hydraulic system: If you squeeze all discretion out of the sentencing process, it will reappear and augment discretion exercised at other points in the system. Two of the most obvious points are where the prosecutor exercises his or her discretion to charge and to plea bargain (see, e.g., Alschuler, 1978: 550).[4]

Furthermore, as California's recent experience seems to indicate (see Cassau and Taugher, 1978), by making the legislature the exclusive sentencing rulemaker with the only formal discretion in the sentencing process, a determinate, flat-time sentencing system creates the likelihood of a distorted and incoherent scale of sentences. If the sentence set by the legislature is the sentence imposed by the judge, as it is in a flat-time system, then all sentencing hearings are, in effect, conducted on the floor of the legislature. It is not unusual for a legislature to respond to the voters' latest perception of a crime wave or the most recent atrocity of a parolee by increasing sentences for particular crimes (see von Hirsch, 1981: 591, 631).

A sentencing guidelines system provides much of the determinacy of a flat-time system without the inflexibility and susceptibility to crime-wave politics of flat-time sentences. Endorsed by some of the earliest proponents of judicial sentence review (Frankel, 1973: 118-123; Zeisel and Diamond, 1977: 935), sentencing guidelines have evolved from the pioneering work of criminologist Leslie Wilkins and his colleagues (see Wilkins et al. 1978; and Gottfredson et al., 1975: 34).

Sentencing guidelines provide an outline for sentencing practices by communicating the sentencing norms for particular crimes to individual sentencers. In legal terms, guidelines represent rules that structure the exercise of discretion by those legally authorized to make sentencing decisions without eliminating all discretion. In other words, guidelines attempt to strike "a proper balance between rule and discretion" (Davis, 1969: 42). By assuring "that *similar* persons are dealt with in *similar* ways in *similar* situations" (Wilkins et al., 1978), sentencing guidelines can promote consistent sentencing practices and reduce disparity.

The feature of sentencing guidelines that most obviously contributes to the reduction of disparity is the normal or presumed sentence. This sentence represents the punishment that is expected in the majority of cases for a particular crime. The sentence appears as a narrow range, rather than a point, on the guidelines scale of punishment. Ordinarily derived empirically from the prevailing sentencing practices in the jurisdiction in question, presumed sentence ranges in the guidelines system could also be derived from a sentencing policy that a legislature chooses as a matter of value.

Out of fear that sentencers might reject mandatory guidelines or out of respect for the limitations of anticipating exceptional cases by written rule, most systems make the guidelines standards advisory rather than binding (Wilkins et al., 1978). For similar reasons, lists of aggravating and mitigating circumstances are not exclusive, and sentences outside the guidelines' ranges are permitted if recorded reasons accompany extraordinary sentences.[5]

A legislature could make these sentencing guidelines rules and enact them into law as statutes. However, the rules need to be detailed and complex. In light of this need and the political pressures that are associated with the administration of a penal system, it is not surprising that someone would suggest "one of the greatest inventions of modern government"—administrative rulemaking (Davis, 1969: 65). By establishing a sentencing guidelines commission to make the rules, a legislature can create an administrative agency with representatives from the criminal justice community and the public who have the interest and expertise to develop specialized sentencing rules and who are sufficiently distant from the body politic to design a rational and consistent system of punishment (see Zalman, 1977: 266).

A sentencing guidelines system brings a rule of law to the criminal sentencing process. Furthermore, it preserves a realistic amount of discretion to varying sentences in individual cases. If it is administered by a sentencing commission, the system also increases the likelihood that the sentencing rules will be based on reason rather than crime-wave politics. It is these features that explain why an increasing number of states are adopting guidelines systems.[6]

Judicial sentence review, as a means of assuring fair and accurate individual sentencing decisions and as a check on the discretion exercised by administrators in making rules, is a natural ingredient in a sentencing guidelines system. Furthermore, because of the nature of sentencing guidelines, the traditional obstacles to substantive sentence review can be substantially reduced, if not eliminated.

Sentencing guidelines relieve the appellate courts of the burden of creating specific rules in pursuit of a general sentencing policy. The legislature and its administrative agency, the sentencing commission, must perform this task. Guidelines provide "operating rules that translate mitigating and aggravating circumstances into points on a sentencing scale" (Zeisel and Diamond, 1977: 933). Instead of asking the sentencer to fashion the kind of sentence needed to blame, deter, incapacitate, or rehabilitate within the wide ranges typically provided by legislatures, a guidelines matrix table directs the sentencer's attention to the intersection of the axes to a narrow range on the scale of possible sentences. The framework of the guidelines, as we shall see, also provides a means of establishing disincentives to appeal and thereby reduces the threat of a flood of new appeals.

With provisions for judicial sentence review, sentencing guidelines can be something more than an empirically derived feedback mechanism that communicates statistical norms to sentencers and encourages them to follow the norm. Guidelines can become the rule of law for a sentencing system. Necessary sentencing discretion can be preserved, but sentence variation without reason and sentencing rules without a basis in public policy will give rise to legal sanctions under a system of judicial review. In the final analysis, it is up to the legislatures to realize this potential by enacting a statute that promotes the functions of sentence review.

Appellate courts can perform three important review functions in a sentencing guidelines system. First, they can review sentences imposed within the ranges prescribed by the guidelines to determine if the guidelines were applied erroneously. This kind of error occurs, for example, when the sentencer incorrectly decides that aggravating or mitigating circumstances exist that justify variation from a presumed sentence. The task of identifying errors in applying a rule of law to a set of facts is one that appellate courts frequently perform. When that task is performed in a guidelines system, sentences that treat offenders the same when they should be treated differently are corrected and disparity is reduced in spite of a guidelines sentence's "appearance of regularity" (People v. Cox, 1979).

Second, extraordinary sentences outside the guidelines' range can be reviewed by an appellate court to determine if the sentencer's reasons justify an exception to the rule and if the circumstances of the offense and the terms of the sentence are comparable to other extraordinary sentences outside the guidelines. This function is important in order to prevent the exceptions from swallowing the rule in penal systems where sentencers are not always eager to have their discretion limited by rules.[7]

Appellate courts will face the same set of problems in reviewing sentences outside the guidelines that they have traditionally faced in reviewing indeterminate sentences. For example, if the sentencer justifies a sentence that exceeds the upper limit of the guidelines range because "the prominence and respect that this offender enjoys among our youth provides the opportunity to send out a strong deterrent message," how should the court evaluate this sentence? Is it excessive and therefore disparate? Legislatures will have to establish a sentencing policy to serve as a standard if they expect courts to perform this function. Lawful exceptions to the guidelines provisions, like the existence of disparity, will depend on the theory of punishment that a system chooses to pursue.

Third, appellate courts can review the sentencing guidelines themselves to determine whether or not, as rules of an administrative agency, they comply with public policy. Under recognized principles of administrative law (Davis, 1969: 152; see also Davis, 1976), an appellate court can serve as a check on a sentencing guidelines commission by holding that agency accountable to the policy under which the legislature delegated its authority to make sentencing law. Once again, this review function will depend on a statement of sentencing policy. Because a sentencing guidelines commission can create systemwide sentence variation under its rules, "checking and balancing" may be the most important review function that an appellate court can perform in a sentencing guidelines system.

A legislature that decides to adopt a sentencing guidelines system as a means of reducing sentence disparity, and that is attracted to the regulatory potential of judicial sentence review, should adopt a special appeals statute with conscious regard for the potential functions of review. The Oregon legislature, having ratified an intricate set of parole release guidelines, failed to enact such a special review statute. Although the proponents of Oregon's parole guidelines system intended to provide for review, it took three years and some artful reinterpretation of existing review statutes by Oregon's appellate courts before parole release decisions finally became subject to judicial review (see Harris v. Board of Parole, 1980a, 1980b, 1979).

When a legislature does enact a special sentence review statute, it sometimes appears to be an afterthought. A statute should explicitly state the relationship between the possible review functions of the appellate courts and the sentencing guidelines. It should also avoid the vague and elastic language that has traditionally been an obstacle to serious sentence review in jurisdictions with sentence review statutes.

After enacting one of the most comprehensive systems among the recent wave of sentencing guidelines systems, the Minnesota legislature provided for sentence review with the following language:

An appeal to the Supreme Court may be taken by the defendant or the state from any sentence imposed or stayed by the district court.

On an appeal pursuant to this section, the Supreme Court may review the sentence imposed or stayed to determine whether the sentence is inconsistent with statutory requirements, unreasonable, inappropriate, excessive, unjustifiably disparate, or not warranted by the findings of fact issued by the district courts.[8]

Should the Minnesota Supreme Court interpret this provision to mean that it is to review sentences that fall inside the guidelines, outside the guidelines, or both? Alternatively, is the court free to disregard the guidelines and use an "abuse of discretion" standard under which almost any sentence within the ranges provided by the legislature will survive review? Minnesota's review statute tempts an appellate court to continue a practice of upholding all but the most shocking or irrational sentences.[9]

In order for an appellate court to understand clearly the extent of its reviewing responsibility in a sentencing guidelines system, a legislature should explicitly include in a statute the sentence review functions it expects the courts to perform. Washington recently established the area of guidelines sentencing review with the following language:

(1) A sentence within the standard range for the offense shall not be appealed.

(2) If a sentence is outside of the sentence range for the offense, the defendant or prosecutor may seek review of the sentence before the court of appeals.[10]

Pennsylvania's new review statute provides a broader area of judicial review:

Determination on appeal.—The appellate court shall vacate the sentence and remand the case to the sentencing court with instructions if it finds:

(1) the sentencing court purported to sentence within the sentencing guidelines but applied the guidelines erroneously;

(2) the sentencing court sentenced within the sentencing guidelines but the case involves circumstances where the application of the guidelines would be clearly unreasonable;

(3) the sentencing court sentenced outside the sentencing guidelines and the sentence is unreasonable.

In all other cases the appellate court shall affirm the sentence imposed by the sentencing court.[11]

The Uniform Law Commissioners' Model Sentencing and Corrections Act (1978) provides for all three functions of judicial review in a guidelines system:

> An appeal from a sentence may be on one or more of the following grounds:
>
> (1) The sentencing court misapplied the sentencing guidelines.
> (2) The sentencing court deviated from the sentencing guidelines and the sentence imposed (i) is unduly disproportionate to sentences imposed for similar offenses on similar defendants, or (ii) does not serve the purposes of this Article and the principles of sentencing better than the sentence provided in the guidelines. . . .
> (4) The applied sentencing guidelines are inconsistent with the purposes of this Article and the principles of sentencing.[12]

As a comparison of Washington's and Pennsylvania's new sentence review statutes demonstrates, the extent of sentence review will vary from state to state, depending upon the legislature's perceptions of the relative importance of efficiency and fairness. The Washington legislature has gained the efficiency of fewer potential appeals at the expense of some fairness by precluding review of alleged errors in applying the sentencing guidelines to individual offenders. Pennsylvania, on the other hand, accepted the potential cost of an increased volume of appeals in exchange for greater assurances of accuracy by including sentences inside the guidelines within the area of review.

However, every state legislature should consider Washington's use of the sentencing guidelines framework to reinforce the guidelines and, at the same time, to make sentence review more attractive. By varying the access to sentence review in relation to sentences inside and outside the guidelines, the Washington legislature has created an additional incentive for sentencers to follow the guidelines and has eliminated the major practical objection to appellate review of sentences. Extraordinary sentences outside the guideline carry the risk of reversal on appeal, while normal sentences within the guidelines, which raise the specter of a flood of new appeals, are excluded from the scope of judicial review.

There is another way to strengthen the guidelines and make sentence review more attractive without foreclosing all possibility of correcting errors in sentences inside the guidelines as Washington has done. Legal terms of art can be used by legislatures to indicate the intensity of review they wish appellate courts to undertake. While these terms communicate differences in degree rather than kind, they can create variations in the likelihood that appellate courts will overturn sentences between sentences inside and outside the guidelines. This variation in the intensity of review establishes incentives to comply with the guidelines and disincentives to take frivolous sentence appeals.

For example, an appellate court can be told to take a deferential approach to the review of sentences inside the guidelines by resorting to the kind of language that appellate courts now use in reviewing sentences. A review statute could provide: "The appellate court shall modify a sentence within the guidelines' ranges if it concludes that the sentence is arbitrary, capricious, an abuse of discretion or otherwise not in accordance with law."[13] On the other hand, a more intensive approach to the review of sentences outside the guidelines could be communicated in the following terms: "The appellate court shall modify a sentence outside the guideline ranges to conform to the guidelines if it concludes that the sentence is clearly erroneous or that the sentence is inconsistent with the legislature's statement of sentencing policy." "Clearly erroneous" is a test that appellate courts have developed in reviewing the finding of facts of trial judges sitting without juries (Davis, 1972: 528). It has become a term of art in administrative law to communicate an intensity of review greater than "abuse of discretion," though considerably less than the complete substitution of a decisionmaker's judgment that is associated with "de novo" review (Davis, 1972: 530). Applied to sentences outside the guideline ranges, it would mean that "although there is evidence to support [the sentence], the reviewing court on the entire evidence is left with the definite and firm conviction that a mistake has been committed" in finding extraordinary aggravating or mitigating circumstances to justify the sentence which are similar to the circumstances in other cases of extraordinary sentences (United States v. United States Gypsum, 1948, cited in Davis, 1972: 528).[14]

By varying the intensity of review in relation to sentences inside and outside the guidelines, rather than limiting the area of review, a legislature can encourage conformity to the guidelines because of sentencers' desire to avoid the greater likelihood of reversal on appeal. At the same time, it can remove the threat of a flood of new appeals by reducing the chances of successful appeals in the majority of cases. Under such a scheme, there may be more sentence appeals than under Washington's statute, but there will also be a potential remedy for flagrant errors in applying the guidelines.

A legislature can try to communicate the intensity of review it wants its appellate courts to undertake in terms as clear as language and legal doctrines permit. Whether or not appellate judges take the message seriously and act upon it will be influenced by, and may depend on, their attitudes about the relative importance of equity and sentencers' prerogatives in the penal system and the resources they are given to perform the functions of sentence review.

Because of a recent U.S. Supreme Court decision, legislatures have another possible feature of a sentence review statute to consider. In United States v. DiFrancesco (1980), the court held that a federal statute that established extraordinary sentences for "dangerous special offenders" and provided for government appeal of those sentences did not violate the Double Jeopardy Clause of the Fifth Amendment to the U.S. Constitution. This clears the way for state legislatures to enact review statutes that provide for appeal by the prosecutor in all criminal cases, unless their state constitutions prohibit such provisions.

The right to appeal sentences that the government considers too lenient furthers the logic of a sentencing system designed to reduce disparity; sentences at the low end of the sentencing scale, as well as the high end, can be regulated. However, the opportunity for government sentence appeals also increases the potential workload of the appellate courts.

An alternative to government sentence appeals that will permit increases in some overly lenient sentences and, at the same time, add another disincentive to frivolous sentences appeals by defendants is a provision in a sentence review statute that permits the appellate courts to decrease or increase sentences. Illinois' sentence review statute provides, in part:

> The court to which such appeal is properly taken is authorized to modify the sentence and enter any sentence that the trial judge could have entered, including increasing or decreasing the sentence or entering an alternative sentence to a prison term.[15]

The attractiveness of such a provision will depend upon a legislature's perception of the current rate of sentencing errors on the side of leniency. If lenient sentences are common in a penal system, many of them will be left undisturbed by a statute like Illinois' because they will not be appealed by defendants.

After considering these relatively mechanical means to promote the role of judicial review in a sentencing guidelines system, a legislature still must address the basic reason for the failure of judicial sentence review to structure discretion or reduce disparity. Judicial review, or any other regulatory mechanism, can do little to tame the sentencing system until the purpose of sentencing is identified and a coherent policy from which sentencing standards can be derived is established. This task should be the responsibility of the legislature.

As we have already seen, disparity can take three forms in a guidelines system: first, the guidelines can be incorrectly applied to offenders; second, offenders who should be sentenced within the guideline ranges may receive extraordinary sentences; third, the guidelines administrators may make rules that categorize offenders similarly who should be treated differently. Judicial review can reduce all three forms of disparity. However, to deal with the last two forms of disparity, in particular, appellate courts will need a clear statement of sentencing policy to serve as a standard for substantive review. To review extraordinary sentences, the courts will need a standard under which they can evaluate the reasons for these sentences and a standard that serves as a basis for comparing extraordinary sentences with other sentences outside the guidelines. To review the content of the guidelines' rules, the courts will need a standard to determine the level of sentence variation that the system should tolerate as a matter of policy.

For the legislature that recognizes the need for a statement of sentencing policy, its policy options are limited. Of the theories that make up our jurisprudence of sentencing, rehabilitation has been banished as unmanageable or unfair, and deterrence theory has failed to provide the practical means to translate the deterrent effect into a scale of actual sentences (Gardner, 1976: 781, 783). That narrows a legislature's choice between the theory of incapacitation and the contemporary version of retributivism known as "just deserts."[16]

If the purpose for adopting sentencing guidelines is to minimize sentence disparity, as well as the inequitable distribution of punishment and irrational allocation of resources that disparity produces, then a legislature should choose the theory of just deserts as the basis for its sentencing policy. There are two reasons for this assertion. First, the idiosyncratic nature of incapacitative sentencing decisions and the technical nature of empirically derived, incapacitative guidelines make it unlikely that appellate courts will be able or willing to distinguish between sentence disparity and sentence variation. Instead, it is likely that they will defer to incapacitative guidelines in the same way that they have deferred to rehabilitative sentences. Second, the retributivistic principle of proportionate punishment, with its intolerance for sentence variation and its limitations on the number of factors that can justify variations in sentences, provides reviewing courts with a comprehensible basis for comparing sentences outside the guidelines and for questioning the apparently technical decisions that underlie the guidelines' rules.

Under an incapacitative sentencing policy, even one that incorporates the value of equal sentencing treatment, appellate courts are as likely to defer to decisions to sentence as they traditionally have been to defer to the allegedly individualized sentences designed to rehabilitate. When a sentencing judge explains an extraordinary sentence as an attempt to protect society from an offender whom he or she has predicted to be dangerous and incorrigible, there is the same temptation on appeal to respect the judge's first-hand assessment of an individual's personality and his or her evaluation of the myriad factors that are arguably relevant to predicting danger. In upholding the constitutionality of a death penalty statute that required a jury to predict whether or not there was "a probability that the defendant would commit criminal acts of violence that would constitute a continuing threat to society," the U.S. Supreme Court recently displayed this kind of judicial deference to strategies of incapacitation:

> The petitioner argues that it is impossible to predict future behavior and that the question is so vague as to be meaningless. It is, of course, not easy to predict future behavior. The fact that such a determination is difficult, however, does not mean that it cannot be made. Indeed, prediction of future criminal conduct is an essential element in many of the decisions rendered throughout our criminal justice system. The decision whether to admit a defendant to bail, for instance, must often turn on a judge's prediction of the defendant's future conduct. And any sentencing authority must predict a convicted person's probable future conduct when it engages in the process of determining what punishment to impose. For those sentenced to prison, these same predictions must be made by parole authorities [Jurek v. Texas, 1976].

Under an incapacitative sentencing policy, the task of judicial review is further complicated by the technical nature of modern incapacitative guidelines methodology. There is a strong legal tradition of "unreviewability" when the decisions in question involve "specialized subjects which are beyond the range of legal training" (Davis, 1972: 523). As a result, appellate courts will probably accept the substance of the sentencing guidelines at face value, in spite of evidence that offenders who would otherwise be treated differently will be treated the same under the guidelines.

The U.S. Parole Commission's guidelines demonstrate the nature of the problem that courts face in reviewing administrative decisions in an incapacitative guidelines system. The federal parole guidelines not only classify offenses in terms of severity and categorize offenders based on prior criminal acts; they also categorize offenders according to their statistical likelihood of recidivism. The prediction of offender, rather than sentencer, behavior in the construction of a Salient Factor Score, through the isolation, refinement, and validation of predictive variables, requires a mastery of the art and science of statistics (see, e.g., Hoffman and Beck, 1974: 195). It is unlikely that most citizens, legislators, sentencers, or appellate court judges will understand the process. As a result, categoric risk prediction represents a decisionmaking process that will be immune from review.

By acknowledging the desire of sentencers to incapacitate, and by trying to refine the practice through categoric risk prediction, incapacitative guideline systems present a "joker in the deck" for reviewing courts. When questions are raised on appeal concerning the effect devices such as the Salient Factor Score have on the distribution of punishment, appellate courts will most likely respond with deference toward the technical decisions of guidelines instead of subjecting their decisions to serious review.

There are two reasons why categoric risk prediction calls for a governmental restraint, or check, that judicial review can provide. First, the limited predictive power of categoric risk prediction methods results in a sufficient number of offenders who are erroneously treated the same under incapacitative guidelines so as to raise claims of an inequitable distribution of punishment and an irrational allocation of corrections resources (Underwood, 1979: 1408; Monahan, 1978; Morris, 1974: 66; Simon, 1971: 14). Second, the construction of categoric risk prediction devices such as the Salient Factor Score requires judgments of value by unelected administrators that can influence the levels of sentence variation and disparity throughout a penal system (Coffee, 1976: 975).

The basic question is not whether particular decisions of guidelines researchers and administrators are correct; the question is whether or not the underlying value judgments that balance fairness against efficiency ought to be left to the discretion of sentencing guidelines administrators who have neither the popular mandate of elected legislators nor the detachment from their administrative enterprise of appellate judges. Under a representative system of government in which laws defining crime and the purposes and procedures of the criminal law are considered important enough to be enacted by the legislature, and in which compliance with the legislative intent behind these laws can be enforced by judicial review, the answer ought to be no.

In the face of claims of excessive punishment based on arguments that incapacitative guidelines treat offenders similarly who should be treated differently, reviewing courts must pierce the veil of expertise that surrounds the methodology of categoric risk prediction and address the fundamental questions of value upon which judgments of disparity and excessiveness depend. Appellate courts will have to answer questions such as how many false positives in a particular category of risk are too many and whether or not more accurate but more expensive statistical methods should be used to construct devices like the Salient Factor Score. However, like the sentencing decisions in the rehabilitative sentencing systems of the past, the decisions of the guidelines administrators that include these questions of value will probably be good enough for most appellate courts.

There are two reasons why appellate courts are as likely to defer to sentencing decisions that cause sentence variation in an incapacitative guidelines system as they have been in a rehabilitative sentencing system. First, the statistical methods associated with construction of categoric risk prediction devices create an aura of expertise equal to, if not greater than, the aura surrounding individual sentencing decisions purportedly derived from first-hand assessment and tailored to rehabilitate the offender. Most appellate courts will be tempted to regard the decisions and the value judgments in constructing categoric risk prediction devices as "technical" and to defer to the "sound discretion" of the experts in categoric risk prediction. Second, under a formal sentencing policy of incapacitation, the implicit acceptance of errors in prediction in pursuit of the utilitarian goal of crime prevention provides appellate courts with an independent rationale for refusing to review the decisions of guidelines administration for their contribution to sentence disparity.

Appellate courts cannot be expected to address the de facto disparity that can be caused by categoric overprediction and the underlying trade-offs between predictive efficiency and fairness unless a legislature outlaws incapacitative strategies altogether by adopting a sentencing policy based on just deserts. Under a just deserts sentencing policy, sentencing guidelines focus on past events to establish ranges of sentences based upon the seriousness of offenders' criminal behavior. Furthermore, punishment has to be proportionate to the seriousness of that past behavior. In determining the seriousness of an offender's behavior, sentencing rulemakers and sentencers who wish to depart from the guidelines' ranges can only consider the severity of the current offense and the number and severity of the offender's previous convictions.[17]

From these basic principles of just deserts, appellate courts can derive workable standards to regulate extraordinary sentences and rulemaking decisions in a guidelines system. First, the concept of proportionate punishment provides a standard under which courts can apply the traditional method of legal reasoning by analogy to the problem of determining whether or not sentences outside the guidelines are justified because they are similar to other extraordinary sentences (see Levi, 1948: 1). Analogy is possible under a theory of just deserts because the factors relevant to sentencing are limited to mitigating and aggravating circumstances in the present offense and the nature and extent of the offender's criminal record.

This does not mean that the task of reviewing sentences outside the guidelines will be an easy one. There will still be "apples and oranges" problems. For example, does a robber with ten prior robbery convictions who obtains property by verbal threat deserve the same extraordinary sentence as a first-time offender who shoots a robbery victim? The answer is necessarily subjective and will be somewhat imprecise. However, this is the kind of question that appellate courts are accustomed to dealing with in the process of developing, refining, and applying general rules in order to resolve specific cases. Cases will be sifted and sorted into categories of similarity over time. The limited number of factors relevant to desert and the commonly shared, if rough, sense of what constitutes serious behavior, make the task possible. By comparison, the nearly infinite variety of factors that can justify individual predictions of future behavior under sentencing policies of incapacitation or rehabilitation makes reasoning by analogy impossible.

Second, just deserts theory "prohibits raising or lowering a particular offender's punishment because of his predicted likelihood of recidivism or his supposed need for treatment" (von Hirsch and Hanrahan, 1979). This relatively bright line between past and future sentencing considerations provides a standard for the appellate courts to review the reasons for extraordinary sentences and the rules of guideline administrators. Instead of calling upon appellate courts to evaluate idiosyncratic sentencing decisions and the technical judgments underlying categoric risk prediction, a just deserts policy directs the courts to identify the decisions and strategies that apparently disregard the seriousness of past behavior as presumptively contrary to the legislature's sentencing policy. The appellate court's burden of ferreting out and questioning the value judgments of guidelines administrators under a policy of incapacitation is, in effect, replaced by a burden on guidelines administrators to justify rules that cause sentence variations apparently unrelated to the seriousness of past behavior. As a result, a legislature can reasonably expect its appellate courts to reduce the amount of sentence variation in a penal system and increase the public accountability of sentencing administrators.

Thus, a legislature's choice between a policy of incapacitation and a policy of just deserts will not only affect the levels of sentence variation and sentence disparity in a sentencing guidelines system; its choice will also determine whether sentencing administrators or appellate courts will oversee the distribution of punishment and the allocation of resources in a guidelines system.

Minnesota's new sentencing guidelines system demonstrates that the regulatory benefits of guidelines can be preserved without the incapacitative strategies that will baffle the public and the appellate courts, and without the threat of a kind of sentence disparity that is immune from judicial review. The Minnesota guidelines system operates under the following policy statement:

> The purpose of the sentencing guidelines is to establish rational and consistent sentencing standards which reduce sentencing disparity and ensure that sanctions following conviction of a felony are proportional to the severity of the offense of conviction and the extent of the offender's criminal history. Equity in sentencing requires (a) that convicted felons similar with respect to relevant sentencing criteria ought to receive similar sanctions, and (b) that convicted felons substantially different from a typical case with respect to relevant criteria ought to receive different sanctions.

The sentencing guidelines embody the following principles:

> (1) Sentencing should be neutral with respect to the race, gender, social, or economic status of convicted felons.
>
> (2) While commitment to the Commissioner of Corrections is the most severe sanction that can follow conviction of a felony, it is not the only significant sanction available to the sentencing judge. Development of a rational and consistent sentencing policy requires that the severity of sanctions increase in direct proportion to increases in the severity of criminal offenses and the severity of criminal histories of convicted felons.

(3) Because the capacities of state and local correctional facilities are finite, use of incarcerative sanctions should be limited to those convicted of more serious offenses or those who have longer criminal histories. To ensure such usage of finite resources, sanctions used in sentencing convicted felons should be the least restrictive necessary to achieve the purposes of the sentence.

(4) While the sentencing guidelines are advisory to the sentencing judge, departures from the presumptive sentences established in the guidelines should be made only when substantial and compelling circumstances exist.[18]

In fairly straightforward language, Minnesota's sentencing policy emphasizes the need for standards to reduce disparity and promote equity that are based on the theory of just deserts. However, as the rules and commentary that follow this policy statement indicate, Minnesota's system preserves the essence of guidelines methodology. In developing the guidelines, data on prevailing sentence and release practices were compiled and analyzed and a set of relevant sentencing factors developed to structure the sentencer's discretion without totally eliminating it.[19]

The two dimensions of a just deserts sentence, the seriousness of the current offense and the number and seriousness of crimes for which the offender was previously convicted, appear as the two axes of Minnesota's sentencing matrix table. The table, or "Sentencing Guidelines Grid," includes presumed ranges for prison sentences, as well as a "dispositional line" that creates a "presumption in favor of execution of the sentence" for cases falling below and to the right of the line and a "presumption against execution of the sentences" for cases falling above and to the left of the line.[20] In other words, the Minnesota sentencing guidelines regulate "in/out" felony sentencing decisions, as well as decisions setting the length of incarceration.

Under the "Criminal History Score," the extent and severity of an offender's criminal record are categorized in detailed grades of blameworthiness, including the custody status of the offender at the time of the current offense, the number and kind of criminal convictions, and his or her juvenile record.[21] By adopting the just deserts principle, that an offender's previous criminal convictions are relevant to assessing the blameworthiness of his or her current offense, Minnesota's guidelines retain a factor that also happens to be one of the most powerful predictors of recidivism (see von Hirsch, 1981: 591, n.1; von Hirsch and Hanrahan,

1979: 23). However, predictive factors that are unrelated to desert and that increase the potential for disparity, such as "age at commitment," "admitted or documented heroin or opiate derivative abuse problem," or "verified employment or full-time school attendance for six months during the two-year period prior to commitment," are explicitly rejected by the guidelines.[22]

Proponents of incapacitative guidelines might criticize Minnesota's system on the grounds that it will permit covert and unregulated incapacitative strategies under the guise of just deserts. To a limited extent, this is true. Within the narrow ranges of Minnesota's presumptive sentences, incapacitative strategies in fixing the specific sentence would be tolerated. But when presumptive sentences are aggravated or mitigated, or when extraordinary sentences are imposed outside the guideline ranges, these sentences would not be upheld unless they were supported by reasons based on the policy of just deserts. However, as in the case of prior criminal convictions, the fact that a desert factor also has predictive power would not be a basis for objecting to its use.

In fact, Leslie Wilkins and other prominent guidelines penologists, such as Don Gottfredson and Peter Hoffman, accept the validity of a guidelines system such as Minnesota's:

> It seems that there may be little conflict between two apparently quite different options in model building. We know that the weightings and methods for deriving equations do not seem to make much difference to the power of prediction. . . . We know also that equations that have different sets of items included provide equally good predictive performance—there is no particular set of items or weights which is clearly optimum in terms of predictive power. . . . It is, therefore, highly probable that equations could be found that reflected only the just-deserts theory, and that, at the same time, proved equally as predictive of success or failure as did equations that utilized items that were not justified by this theory. In operational terms, this could mean that the distinction between a predictive model and a just-deserts model could be moot! . . . Clearly, those who would advocate the just-deserts approach could not find any reasonable grounds to reject a set of guidelines merely because the means for quantifying the prior criminal record happened to be predictive [Gottfredson et al., 1978: 136].

Two other features of Minnesota's guidelines are worth noting. First, Minnesota's guidelines policy takes an important practical step in dealing

with a crucial sentencing issue involving both equity and resource allocation that is usually not framed in terms of disparity, unless the concept of
disparity is expanded to include similarly situated offenders in the other
countries of the world with which we like to compare ourselves.[23] This
country's relatively high rates of incarceration, long prison terms, and
overcrowded prisons are the direct result of our criminal sentencing
practices. However, these practices also reflect the citizenry's desire to
punish that exceeds its willingness to pay. No theory in our jurisprudence
of sentencing supplies a practical answer to the question "How much is
too much?" Principles of "parsimony" or the "least restrictive alternative"
represent a valid concern about excessive punishment and prison overcrowding without providing practical limits (see Morris, 1974: 61).

The Minnesota legislature has addressed this problem by directing its
Sentencing Guidelines Commission to "take into substantial consideration . . . correction resources, including but not limited to the capacities of
local and state corrections facilities."[24] With this simple phrase, the
legislature has assigned the responsibility for monitoring the rates and
lengths of prison sentences and for controlling prison populations. It has
also provided the outer limits under which the guidelines system can begin
to distribute punishment among offenses and offenders and to allocate
resources among programs and facilities.

The overall level of punishment in Minnesota's penal system may still
be too high, or perhaps too low. However, the legislature's directive to the
sentencing commission recognizes and regulates an activity at the front
end of the criminal system that has already been going on informally at
the back end: Sentences are shortened to control prison population. It
may be cynical public policy, but it is also realistic public policy to
acknowledge that the taxpayers' pocketbooks, together with the humanity
of corrections' authorities and the constitutional interpretations of the
courts, actually determine the quantity and quality of punishment that
our penal systems generate. Sentencing guidelines can then proceed to
distribute this punishment in a relatively fair and rational way.

Second, although Minnesota's statement of sentencing policy serves as a
model for a just deserts sentencing guidelines system that can be regulated
by judicial review, the process under which the statement was written
ought not to be part of the model. Minnesota's statement of sentencing
policy was not written by the legislature but by its Sentencing Guidelines
Commission. The Minnesota legislature enacted statutes that created the
commission and directed it to establish sentencing guidelines.[25] However,
aside from specifying policy limits in terms of current correction

resources, the legislature left it up to the sentencing commission to develop a specific sentencing policy, subject to review and ratification by the legislature within a specified period of time.[26]

This legislative oversight approach to policymaking provides the insulation from partisan politics that simplifies the task of deciding how to punish. However, there are several reasons why a legislature should formulate a sentencing policy and adopt it in statutory form. First, a legislature may never get around to a serious review of the sentencing policy formulated by an administrative agency, given the controversial nature of the subject and the lengthy agenda of most legislatures. Second, policy questions of equity and resource allocation that are implicated by decisions to rehabilitate, deter, incapacitate, or blame, as opposed to decisions to implement policy by making specific sentencing rules, ought to be resolved in the open by the public's elected representatives. Third, courts are likely to give a policy developed by the legislature more weight in imposing sentences, in the first instance, and in reviewing those sentences and the rules made by the guidelines' administrators on appeal. Finally, a legislative statement eliminates the possibility of administrative actions changing sentencing policies when one theory of punishment proves ineffective or loses its luster. To ensure that sentencing guidelines are respected and enforced, a guidelines system needs the political legitimacy and the force of law that a statutory policy statement provides.

In adopting a sentencing policy based on just deserts, a legislature does not have to conclude that the only justification for criminal punishment is the taking of "an eye for an eye, a tooth for a tooth." It is simply deciding that sentences that take an eye for a tooth, with the prospect of protecting society, are impermissible. Instead of settling the affirmative case for retributivistic punishment once and for all, a sentencing policy based on just deserts forbids the practice of determining the nature and extent of actual sentences on the basis of elastic utilitarian concepts such as deterrence, incapacitation, or rehabilitation. It is "a handy tool left lying around by the retributionists that can be used to advance certain goals of the criminal law—not those that have to do with preventing anti-social behavior, but those that have to do with limiting the damage done to other important social values as the criminal law goes about its inevitable but ambiguous business" (Packer, 1968: 112-113). In other words, the just deserts concept of proportionate punishment is an important "limiting principle" on the power of the state to punish its citizens (Packer, 1968: 66).

The purpose of a just deserts sentencing policy is not to provide the sole justification for the imposition of criminal sentences. It is unnecessary for legislators to deny that sentences protect the public because they deter some and incapacitate others. Corrections programs can continue to operate in prisons and communities, with the hope that some offenders will be rehabilitated. These objectives will continue to be important byproducts of criminal punishment.

A just deserts sentencing policy will not tell us if our criminal sentences are too high or too low across the board. Rates and amounts of punishment will probably continue to be set by the parsimony of taxpayers and the constitutional interpretations of courts. A just deserts policy also carries the risk that it will be interpreted as a mandate for vengeance and longer prison sentences (see Orland, 1978: 29; but also see von Hirsch and Hanrahan, 1981: 289). Furthermore, because of a metaphysical quality to the concept of proportionate punishment, some disparity will survive out of disagreements over what aggravates or mitigates and by how much.

What the just deserts concept of proportionate punishment offers is a fair and manageable guide to the construction of a scale of actual sentences in which sentence variation is kept to a minimum. More importantly, in the hands of a reviewing court, the concept becomes a limiting principle that checks the power of the state to punish its citizens and increases the likelihood that punishment will be distributed fairly and rationally.

In a system in which available resources and our knowledge about what we are doing are so limited, perhaps the equitable distribution of punishment and rational allocation of resources is all we should expect from a criminal sentencing policy.

The case for a legislative sentencing policy based on just deserts demonstrates again that the reduction of sentence variation depends ultimately on judgments of value over the proper objectives of criminal punishment. Even with a full array of procedural safeguards, sentence variation will continue to be a prominent feature of our penal systems unless theories of punishment that condone or conceal variable sentencing treatment are excluded from their sentencing policies. No amount of judicial review can eradicate sentence disparity in a system that openly pursues the crime prevention strategies of deterrence theory at the expense of equal sentencing treatment as a matter of sentencing policy; nor will sentence review assure that like cases will be treated alike in rehabilitative or incapacitative systems where sentences are based on idiosyncratic decisions made through first-hand observation or expert judgment.

The case for just deserts is also based on the premise that the methods chosen to administer a sentencing system should be consistent with our representative form of government. The decisionmaking process in a sentencing guidelines system should be legitimated by public understanding and by provision for governmental checks and balances. If a guidelines system is to accomplish its regulatory function, the criminal justice community and the public must understand the methods it employs and feel confident that the system is being held in check by the processes of government. This is the primary significance of a legislative sentencing policy based on a theory of just deserts.

Despite doubts about the affirmative case for taking one person's eye in exchange for another's, the just deserts concept of proportionate punishment provides a standard that the public can comprehend and that reviewing courts can apply. The concept admittedly lacks precision. However, it grounds a sentencing system in the historical facts of offenses and offenders' criminal records that can be understood by the average citizen and verified and evaluated by the appellate courts.

By comparison, an incapacitative guideline system focuses on propensities for future criminal conduct and employs a technology that is becoming increasingly incomprehensible to citizens and courts alike. The methodology of categoric prediction makes it likely that, without a degree in criminology and a mastery of statistical science, the average citizen will view the allocations of punishment it produces as incoherent and unfair, and that the average appellate judge will regard the value judgments it requires as technical and final. Such a system presents the prospect of guidelines administrators, without the electoral mandate of legislators or the institutional detachment of judges, making the final, controversial, and unchecked decisions of what is a fair distribution of punishment and a rational allocation of corrections resources.

Adoption of a guidelines sentencing system represents the single most important step in regulating sentencing practices and reducing disparity. The administrative structure of the system, with a sentencing commission as the centerpiece, supplies the same insulation from political whim that has made the parole system a sometimes useful, if covert, mechanism to standardize sentences. However, this kind of insulation also represents a lack of political accountability that has increasingly proved fatal to systems of parole.[27] The workings of a guidelines system, with its matrix tables of severity ratings and criminal history scores, too easily conjure up popular images of the therapeutic state in *A Clockwork Orange* (Burgess, 1962) or *1984* (Orwell, 1949), and give rise to claims of "sentencing by computer," ignoring demands for political accountability. If a sentencing guidelines system is to survive amid the political pressures and competing objectives in a penal system, it needs the popular support that a comprehensible legislative sentencing policy can bring and the institutional checks that the appellate courts can provide. This kind of political accountability is the ultimate value that a sentencing policy of just deserts and judicial sentence review can promote in the process of reducing sentence disparity.

NOTES

1. Some states, such as Connecticut and Massachusetts, have adopted special systems of judicial review in which panels of trial judges sit to review sentences. Evaluating the merits of this system of sentence review is beyond the scope of this chapter (see American Bar Association, 1968: 28-29).

2. Parole boards and trial judges are both considered "sentencers" for the purposes of this chapter. The parole release decision is as important as the judge's sentence in the formal process of determining actual punishment in most felony sentencing systems (see Wilkins et al., 1978).

3. Professor Davis also pointed to the U.S. Parole Board as an outstanding example of unstructured discretion (Davis, 1969: 126).

4. For a proposal to regulate the prosecutor's contribution to sentence variation, see Schulhofer (1980: 733).

5. See, e.g., Oregon Revised Statutes 144.785(1) and Oregon Administrative Rule 255-35-035.

6. The legislatures of Illinois, Minnesota, Oregon, Pennsylvania, and Washington have enacted guideline systems in the past few years (see Singer, 1979: 137-166).

7. There is a substantial evidence of widespread judicial opposition to structuring sentencing discretion (see Robin, 1975: 201; Zalman, 1977: 284-285).

8. Minnesota Statutes, Section 244.11 (1978).

9. Fortunately, from the perspective of those who designed Minnesota's guidelines system to regulate sentencing practices and reduce disparity, the appellate courts of Minnesota have given great weight to the sentencing guidelines in determining whether or not sentences are excessive or lenient, and disparate, in spite of Minnesota's vague review statute (see, e.g., State v. Bellanger, 1981).

10. H.B. 440 (1981); Section 21, ch. 137, Washington Laws of 1981.

11. 18 P.C.S., Section 1386(c) (1978). The guidelines adopted by Pennsylvania's Commission of Sentencing are subject to legislative veto (18 P.C.S., Section 1385(b)).

12. Model Sentencing and Corrections Act of the National Conference of Commissioners on Uniform State Law, Section 3-208(b).

13. This language is taken directly from Section 706 of the Administrative Procedure Act (see 5 U.S.C., Section 706, 1977).

14. If a legislature wishes to send an even clearer message concerning the variation in the intensity of sentence review, it could adopt a "clear and convincing evidence" standard instead of the "clearly erroneous" standard:

The appellate court shall modify a sentence outside the guidelines' ranges to conform to those ranges unless it concludes from the facts contained in the record below that there is a clear and convincing evidence to support the sentence [see Addington v. Texas, 1979].

15. Supp. to Ill. Rev. Stat. ch. 38, par. 1005-5-4.1 (1977).

16. The most persistent and prolific proponent of contemporary just deserts theory is Andrew von Hirsch (see von Hirsch, 1976; von Hirsch and Hanrahan, 1979).

17. Under the classical principles of retributivism first expressed by Kant, desert was solely a function of the conduct involving the current offense. Consideration of an offender's prior convictions in determining proportionate punishment is a principle of the modern theory of just deserts (see Fletcher, 1978: 459-461; von Hirsch, 1981).

18. Minnesota Sentencing Guidelines and Commentary of the Minnesota Sentencing Guidelines Commission 1 (revised August 1981).

19. Id. at 2-10.

20. Id. at 11.

21. Id. at 3-10.

22. Id. at 13.

23. This country probably has the longest average prison sentences in the Western world (see O'Donnell and Curtis, 1977: 54-55).

24. Minnesota Statutes, Section 244.09, subd. 5(2).

25. Minnesota Statutes, Section 244-09.

26. Minnesota Statutes, Section 244.09, subd. 12.

27. Maine has abolished parole. California, Indiana, and Illinois have abolished parole release. Several other states have recently considered these options (von Hirsch and Hanrahan, 1979: 1).

CASES

ADDINGTON v. TEXAS (1979) 441 U.S. 418, 99 S. Ct. 1804

BULLINGTON v. MISSOURI (1981) 451 U.S. 430, 101 S. Ct. 1852

HARRIS v. BOARD OF PAROLE (1980a) 288 Or. 495, 605 P.2d 118

HARRIS v. BOARD OF PAROLE (1980b) 47 Or. App. 289, 614 P.2d 602

HARRIS v. BOARD OF PAROLE (1979) 39 Or. App. 913, 593 P.2d 1292

JUREK v. TEXAS (1976) 428 U.S. 262, 96 S. Ct. 2950

PEOPLE v. COX (1979) 77 Ill. App. 3d 59, 396 N.E.2d 59

RUMMEL v. ESTELLE (1980) 445 U.S. 263, 100 S.Ct. 1133

STATE v. BELLANGER (1981) Minn., 304 N.W.2d 282
STATE v. DINKEL (1978) 34 Or. App. 375,579 P.2d 245
STATE v. WALDRIP (1975) 111 Ariz. 516, 533 P.2d 1151
UNITED STATES v. Di FRANCESCO (1980) 449 U.S. 117, 101 S. Ct. 426
UNITED STATES v. UNITED STATES GYPSUM (1948) 333 U.S. 364, 68 S. Ct. 525

REFERENCES

ALLEN, F. E. (1978) "Address: the decline of rehabilitative ideal in American criminal justice." Cleveland State Law Review 147.

ALSCHULER, A. W. (1978) "Sentencing reform and prosecutorial power: a critique of recent proposals for 'fixed' and 'presumptive' sentencing." University of Pennsylvania Law Review 126.

American Bar Association (1968) Standards Relating to Appellate Review of Sentences. Project on Minimum Standards for Criminal Justice.

BULLOCK, H. A. (1961) "Significance of the racial factor in the length of prison sentences." Journal of Criminal Law 52.

CAMPBELL, A. (1978) Law of Sentencing. Rochester, NY: Lawyers Co-op.

CASSOU, A. and B. TAUGHER (1978) "Determinate sentencing in California: the new numbers game." Pacific Law Journal 9.

COBURN, D. (1971) "Disparity in sentences and appellate review of sentencing." Rutgers Law Review 25: 207, 214-215.

COFFEE, J. (1976) "The repressed issues of sentencing: accountability, predictability, and equality in the era of the sentencing commission." Georgetown Law Journal 66.

DAVIS, K. (1976) Administrative Law of the Seventies. Rochester, NY: Lawyers Co-op.

——— (1972) Administrative Law Treatise. Rochester, NY: Lawyers Co-op.

——— (1969) Discretionary Justice: A Preliminary Inquiry. Baton Rouge: Louisiana State University Press.

DAWSON, R. O. (1969) Sentencing: The Decision as to Type, Length and Conditions of Sentence. Boston: Little, Brown.

DIX, G. (1969) "Judicial review of sentences: implications for individual dispositions." Law and the Social Order 69: 369, 404-405.

FLETCHER, G. (1978) Rethinking Criminal Law. Boston: Little, Brown.

FRANKEL, M. (1973) Criminal Sentences: Law Without Order. New York: Hill & Wang.

FRIENDLY, H. (1973) Federal Jurisdiction: A General View. New York: Columbia University Press.

GARDNER, M. (1976) "The renaissance of retribution—an examination of doing justice." Wisconsin Law Review 76.

GAYLIN, W. (1974) Partial Justice. New York. Alfred A. Knopf.

GOTTFREDSON, D., L. WILKINS, and P. HOFFMAN (1978) Guidelines for Parole and Sentencing: A Policy Control Method. Lexington, MA: Lexington Books.

GOTTFREDSON, D., P. HOFFMAN, M. SIGLER, and L. WILKINS (1975) "Making paroling policy explicit. Crime and Delinquency 21.

HART, H.L.A. (1973) Punishment and Responsibility: Essays in the Philosophy of Law. Oxford, Eng.: Oxford University Press.

HOFFMAN, P. and J. BECK (1974) "Parole decision-making: a salient factor score." Journal of Criminal Justice 2.

HOFFMAN, P. and M. STOVER (1978) "Reform in the determination of prison terms: equity, determinacy and the parole release function." Hofstra Law Review 7.

LEVI, E. (1948) An introduction to Legal Reasoning. Chicago: University of Chicago Press.

LIPTON, D., R. MARTINSON, and J. WILKS (1975) The Effectiveness of Correctional Treatment: A Survey of Treatment Evaluation Studies. New York: Praeger.

MARTINSON, R. (1979) "New findings new views: a note of caution regarding sentencing reform." Hofstra Law Review 7.

MONAHAN, T. (1978) "The prediction of violent criminal behavior: a methodological critique and prospectus," in A. Blumstein et al. (eds.) National Research Council Panel on Research on Deterrent and Incapacitative Effects, Deterrence and Incapacitation. Washington, DC: National Academy of Sciences.

MORRIS N. (1974) The Future of Imprisonment. Chicago: University of Chicago Press.

O'DONNELL, P., M. CHURGIN, and D. CURTIS (1977) Toward a Just and Effective Sentencing System: Agenda for Legislative Reform. New York: Praeger.

ORLAND, L. (1978) "From vengeance to vengeance: sentencing reform and the demise of rehabilitation." Hofstra Law Review 7.

PACKER, H. (1968) The Limits of the Criminal Sanction. Stanford, CA: Stanford University Press.

ROBIN, G. (1975) "Judicial resistance to sentencing accountability." Crime and Delinquency 21.

SCHULHOFER, S. (1980) "Due process of sentencing." University of Pennsylvania Law Review 128.

SIMON, F. (1971) Prediction Methods in Criminology. London: Her Majesty's Stationery Office.

SINGER, R. G. (1979) Just Deserts: Sentencing Based on Equality and Desert. Cambridge MA: Ballinger.

UNDERWOOD, B. (1979) "Law and the crystal ball: predicting behavior with statistical inference and individualized judgment." Yale Law Journal 88.

VON HIRSCH, A. (1981) "Desert and previous convictions in sentencing." Minnesota Law Review 65.

——— (1976) Doing Justice: The Choice of Punishments. New York: Hill & Wang.

——— and K. HANRAHAN (1981) "Determinate penalty systems in America: an overview." Crime and Delinquency 27.

——— (1979) The Question of Parole: Retention, Reform or Abolition? Cambridge, MA: Ballinger.

Washington Law Review (1973) "Discretion in felony sentencing—a study of influencing factors." Volume 48.

WILKINS, L., J. KRESS, D. GOTTFREDSON, J. CALPIN, and A. GELMAN (1978) Sentencing Guidelines: Structuring Judicial Discretion. Final Report of the Feasibility Study. Albany, NY: Criminal Justice Research Center.

WOLFGANG, M. and L. RIEDEL (1973) "Race, judicial discretion and the death penalty." The Annals of the American Academy of Political and Social Science 407.

ZALMAN, M. (1977) "A commission model of sentencing." Notre Dame Law 53.

ZEISEL, H. and S. DIAMOND (1977) "Search for sentencing equity: sentence review in Massachusetts and Connecticut." American Behavioral Foundation Research Journal 4.

Chapter 10

REDUCING DISPARITY IN JUVENILE JUSTICE
Approaches and Issues

BRUCE FISHER
CARY RUDMAN
LESLIE MEDINA

The sentencing inequities found in the adult system of criminal justice have been subject to criticism since before the turn of the last century, but because of an adherence to "individualized" justice, little corrective action has been taken. As states move away from the goal of rehabilitation toward a "justice" model of corrections, sentencing procedures are being modified. Many states have adopted some form of determinate sentencing law for adult offenders, in part to reduce sentencing disparities. Increasingly, the criticisms leveled against the criminal justice system now confront the juvenile justice system. Many observers are concerned about sentencing inequalities as manifested both in the determination of disposition at court and the determination of release from state institutions. There is currently much debate about the nature and extent of the alleged inequities, and perhaps more importantly, about whether the underlying philosophy of the juvenile justice system should also be changed to reflect a "justice" model rather than a model based on individual rehabilitation.

AUTHORS' NOTE: The information presented in this chapter is based on research conducted by the URSA Institute of San Francisco pursuant to a grant from the National Institute of Juvenile Justice and Delinquency Prevention, Washington, D.C. Bruce Fisher acted as principal investigator of the study, and Cary Rudman and

With these issues in mind, the National Institute of Juvenile Justice and Delinquency Prevention awarded a grant to the URSA Institute (UI) of San Francisco to study the release process of juveniles from state-level institutions throughout the country. During the first phase of the grant, UI staff made an extensive review of the literature of juvenile commitments and institutional release practices and analyzed the relevant statutes in all fifty states. UI staff also conducted a telephone survey in each state to identify current practices and procedures in the areas of commitment, placement, and institutional release, and to assess any legislative or policy trends in this area. This chapter, representing some preliminary findings and observations of this research project, is divided into three parts: a brief review of the relevant literature, an overview of recent statutory approaches to reducing disparity, and an analysis of policy issues in the move toward determinate sentencing and disparity reduction in the juvenile justice system.

LITERATURE REVIEW

Literature specifically addressing sentencing disparity for juveniles is scarce. This scarcity can be accounted for by two primary reasons, both of which are related to the historical goals of the juvenile justice system. First, the juvenile courts were predicated on a parens patriae model, which allows the judge, acting in the role of the parent, to utilize broad discretion in applying open-ended laws, rules, and regulations to consider the best interests of a youth in the disposition of a case. The premise of the second goal—to rehabilitate—is that dispositional and release discretion is necessary in determining when an individual is ready to be returned to society. Because the value of rehabilitation in the juvenile justice system has received widespread acceptance, the sentencing approach that rests upon the rehabilitative model, the indeterminate sentence, has long been the prevailing approach, despite occasional criticisms.

During the past decade, however, diverse groups have intensified their criticism of the inequities in the sentencing of juveniles. Civil libertarians,

Leslie Medina served as senior researchers. Barbara Allen-Hagen acts as the grant manager for NIJJDP. Robert Coates of the University of Chicago, and Mark Fraser and Elizabeth Friedman of the URSA Institute, are senior researchers on the project and helped gather the information reported in this chapter. Professor Coates, Ms. Allen-Hagen, and Donna Hamparian of the Academy for Contemporary Problems in Columbus, Ohio, read the early drafts of this chapter and each made valuable contributions to this draft.

for example, have objected to the injustices in the system, particularly to the fact that minor offenders may be committed to institutions and may, in fact, be locked up for longer periods of time than more serious offenders. Because of their concern over rising crime rates and the system's seeming inability to rehabilitate young offenders, law and order advocates have also criticized the sentencing process, particularly its apparent lack of accountability for serious juvenile offenders. Moreover, some correctional staff have become more candid about the inability of institutions to rehabilitate, and recent studies in this area have also reached this conclusion. Together, these critics have launched an attack on the disparities inherent in an indeterminate sentencing system, and have advocated a move toward more determinacy within juvenile justice.

The purpose of this review is to identify the central issues related to sentencing disparities in juvenile justice, including: conflict over the nature of sentencing disparities; a shift in correctional philosophy; a growing interest in constitutional safeguards for youths; and a movement toward the deinstitutionalization of status offenders. It is important to note that this review is not intended to be exhaustive but rather representative of the empirical research and policy positions found in the literature.[1]

Conflict Over the Nature of Sentencing Disparities

Numerous studies have examined the relationship between the disposition, current offense, prior offense history, and demographic characteristics of youths. Although the findings of those studies vary, there is substantial agreement that juveniles are subject to vast sentencing disparities resulting from the discretion inherent in indeterminate sentencing statutes.

Thornberry (1979) reviewed several studies that describe the relationship between disposition and two extralegal variables—socioeconomic status (SES) and race. The earlier studies found that race and SES were either unrelated to dispositions or were only spuriously related, since their effect could be explained by the legally relevant variables of offense seriousness and prior record. Thornberry's study, contradicting the earlier findings, concluded that "when the two legal variables were held constant, the racial and SES differences did not disappear. Blacks and low SES subjects were more likely than whites and high SES subjects to receive severe dispositions" (Thornberry, 1973: 90).

Wheeler conducted three important studies. The first study analyzed the institutional and population factors related to length of stay in state-operated correctional institutions, and the "revolving door" effect, focusing on factors related to the offender and the institutional stay (Wheeler and Nichols, 1974). The major findings emerging from this study were:

- there was no significant relationship between commitment offense and average institutional stay;
- younger offenders were found to stay longer than their older counterparts;
- large institutions in states with a high youth population showed nearly three months longer average length of stay for offenders than similar facilities in states with a low youth population;
- institutions with diagnostic classification systems tended to keep youths longer than institutions without classification systems; and
- the type of release authority—parole board or institutional staff—was *not* related to length of stay.

Wheeler's (1978) second study examined two policy issues related to indeterminate sentencing for juveniles: sentencing disparity and "prisonization." This study resulted in three major findings. First, the study revealed a strong pattern of "reverse discrimination" in "treatment" institutions. That is, white youths tend to stay longer than nonwhite youths in institutions in which treatment is the primary focus. Second, less serious and younger offenders tended to be incarcerated longer than older and more serious offenders. And third, institutional placement was an important predictor of length of stay. The study also found that many experience "prisonization"; that is, a positive relationship exists between length of stay and return to the institution.

In his third study, Wheeler (1976) conducted a quantitative analysis of factors related to institutional stay in thirty states. His study came to two striking conclusions. First, regardless of an institution's size, parole board status, or type of diagnostic classification system, no statistically significant difference in length of stay was observed. Second, and perhaps more important, no significant relationship was found between length of stay and offense and offender characteristics. However, there did appear to be a pattern of institutionalizing status offenders longer than youths committed on felony index crimes.

Finally, several other studies also focused on sentencing disparities in the juvenile justice system. Chein's (1976) study of the parole decision-making process in three juvenile correctional facilities in Minnesota concluded that the seriousness of the offense is unrelated to the length of institutional stay; parole authority decisionmaking is unsystematic and arbitrary; and commitment offense and delinquent history are the primary factors considered by the parole board, although a wide range of other factors are also considered. Crisman's (1976) study of discrimination in sentencing female juveniles concluded that many females are incarcerated for acts for which males do not receive institutional placement. Also, girls often spend more time in confinement than boys for less serious offenses. And Allen (1975), in his study of 450 boys given indeterminate sentences and placed in a maximum security juvenile institution, refuted the assumption that administrative boards are able to predict outcomes of offenders following release. All of the above-cited studies, and others like them, have formed an empirical basis for challenging the traditional correctional philosophy of the juvenile justice system.

A Shift in Correctional Philosophy

Since the late nineteenth century, the central aim of the juvenile justice system has been to rehabilitate youths through individualized treatment. Under the rehabilitative model, indeterminate sentencing was deemed necessary to assess the "progress" of each youth's treatment and to determine, on an individual basis, when each youth was "ready" for release in the community.

The traditional system is now being challenged on two fronts. First, many authorities are questioning whether the system has fulfilled its goals. Sleeth (1978-79) and McCarthy (1977), for example, note the diminishing belief that the juvenile justice system is able to rehabilitate youth. Other authorities go further, claiming that the juvenile justice system is being challenged because it has failed to demonstrate success (see Sheppard, 1977; and Page, 1979).

Second, the attack focuses on the philosophical foundations of the juvenile justice system. Sheppard, for example, challenges the rehabilitative justification for indeterminate sentencing and argues that children have a right to be "punished" for the offenses they have committed, as opposed to "treated" for what someone else perceives them to be. Other leaders in the field suggest that the juvenile justice system is already punitive in nature, without providing adequate procedural protections. Pearl West (1978), the former Director of the California Youth Authority, has stated: "One can't speak about (rehabilitation) without speaking about (punishment) because clearly anyone who is going to be locked up is going to be punished." And Sleeth (1978-79) states that "when the philosophy of rehabilitation is put into practice, the frequent result is that the juvenile offender suffers significant deprivation of his liberty for a substantial number of years, often until he reaches majority and sometimes beyond."

To the extent that there has been a shift in the philosphy of juvenile justice, there have also been recommendations for changing the sentencing procedures. Allen, after studying traditional release procedures, claims that the underlying theory of indeterminate sentencing needs reexamination. A major social policy implication of Wheeler's first study, moreover, supports the adoption of a modified fixed sentence for the juvenile offender and the removal of the status offender from the purview of the juvenile correctional system (Wheeler and Nichols, 1974).

Various national commissions concerned over the excessive use of incarceration characterizing the juvenile justice system have called for a change in sentencing structure. The primary standards groups—Institute of Judicial Administration/American Bar Association Joint Commission on Juvenile Justice Standards (IJA/ABA) (1980), National Advisory Committee on Criminal Justice Standards and Goals Task Force on Juvenile Justice and Delinquency Prevention (The Task Force) (1976), and the National Advisory Committee for Juvenile Justice and Delinquency Prevention (NAC) (1980)—agree that sentences should be legislatively adopted and judicially implemented. They also agree that sentences should be proportionate to offense severity, that dispositional limits should be established (namely maximum lengths of stay) and that judges should select the least restrictive alternative when possible.

In fact, the standards set forth complex approaches to juvenile sentencing, based on the type of offense committed and the existence of a prior offense history. Simply described, the standards classify offenses by category (five categories in the IJA/ABA and four in the Task Force) and set forth maximum periods of sanctions, depending on the type of sanction imposed by the court. For example, in the IJA/ABA Standards, the court is free to choose nominal sanctions (reprimand, warning, unconditional release), conditional sanctions (probation, restitution, and similar measures not involving out-of-home placement), or custodial sanctions (residential sanctions, whether in a secure or nonsecure facility). The standards specify a maximum length for all conditional or custodial sanctions by the court (McCullough, 1981). It should be noted, though, that while the NAC supported this conceptual framework in principle, it opted to stop short of endorsing a particular sentencing structure (NAC, 1980). The fundamental purpose of the sentencing approaches proposed by the three standard-setting groups is to increase equity in sanctions.

A Growing Interest in Constitutional Safeguards for Youth

The role of due process and equal protection in juvenile proceedings was marked by In re Gault (1967), in which the U.S. Supreme Court declared that the due process clause applied to the adjudicatory stage of juvenile delinquency proceedings. Another leading case, In re Winship (1970), held that proof beyond a reasonable doubt was also required in juvenile proceedings. Yet because rehabilitation is seen as the primary purpose of juvenile justice and not punishment or individual deterrence, indeterminate sentencing for juveniles has been constitutionally upheld in many states. Also, for the same reason, many procedural protections have not been accorded youth, including, for example, the right to a jury trial.

Now, with increasing frequency, the indeterminate sentencing system, with its lack of procedural protections, is coming under fire, and proposals for change are being made. Sheppard (1977) and Page (1979), for example, criticize the lack of procedural protections for youth. Additionally, a central theme of the IJA/ABA (1980) is the reduction of discretion of juvenile justice authorities at the sentencing and correctional stages of delinquency proceedings. These standards, setting offense-related maximum sentences and abolishing the executive's parole power, aim at protecting youth from arbitrary and capricious decisionmaking.

Movement Toward the Deinstitutionalization of Status Offenders

The deinstitutionalization of status offenders, much discussed in the literature, was a goal espoused in the 1974 Juvenile Justice and Delinquency Prevention Act as amended and adopted by the Office of Juvenile Justice and Delinquency Prevention (OJJDP). The IJA/ABA standards (1980) and the Task Force standards (1976) also set forth standards to deinstitutionalize status offenders and nonoffenders. These federal efforts promote policies that would result in a reduction in disparity by removing status offenders from institutional placement.

A DESCRIPTION OF RECENT STATUTORY AND ADMINISTRATIVE APPROACHES TO REDUCE DISPARITY

A number of states have recently taken two approaches to reduce disparity in juvenile sentencing: state legislatures have enacted statutes aimed at reducing judicial discretion exercised in preadjudicatory determinations (decisions to bind youth over to adult court) and dispositional determinations (decisions to commit adjudicated youth to the state youth correction agency for indeterminate periods of time); and state youth correction agencies have instituted administrative rules and guidelines aimed at reducing the disparity evident in agency postcommitment, length-of-stay determinations.

The following discussion is in three sections. The first section examines state statutes that limit the discretion exercised both by the judges and prosecutors in the preadjudicatory decision to bind over a youth to the criminal courts to be tried as an adult. The next section examines various state statutory approaches to minimize judicial and administrative discretion exercised in the commitment and release of adjudicated delinquents. Included in this section is the examination of serious delinquent statutes that attempt to reduce the disparity of dispositions with respect to serious or violent juvenile offenders. The final section examines administrative rules and guidelines instituted by some state youth correction agencies to reduce agency discretion with respect to postcommitment, length-of-stay determinations.

Preadjudicatory Determinations

Most states have passed legislation enabling juvenile court judges to waive or bind over statutorily defined youth to the criminal courts to be tried as adults. Although the individual state statutes differ in approach, they are similar in intent. Certain offenders, because of their age at the time of the alleged offense, the nature of the alleged offense, and/or the nature and number of prior adjudications, are deemed nonamenable to the treatment provided by the juvenile justice system. Therefore, such youths are transferred pursuant to statutory criteria to the criminal justice system. The following discussion examines four different statutory approaches by which a preadjudicatory decision to transfer a youth to the criminal courts is accomplished. The four types of statutes are: bindover/waiver statutes, concurrent jurisdiction statutes; exclusive jurisdiction (criminal courts) statutes; and statutes that lower the maximum age of juvenile court jurisdiction.

The most common state approach resulting in a youth being tried in criminal court is the bindover statute. Bindover statutes typically provide a prosecutor the right to petition the juvenile court judge to transfer a youth to the criminal courts if the youth meets specific statutory criteria. The most common criteria are: the youth has attained a certain age at the time of the alleged offense; the instant offense would be a felony, or violent felony, if committed by an adult; and the youth is not amenable to treatment in the juvenile justice system. The juvenile court judge must make a determination that the youth qualifies pursuant to the above statutory criteria. If the judge grants the petition, the youth is transferred to the criminal courts and tried as an adult. This approach leaves the decision to transfer to the discretion of the juvenile court judge.

Other approaches used by the states to effectuate the transfer of youths to criminal court are statutes creating concurrent jurisdiction over youths who at a statutory specific age are alleged to have committed an offense that would be a serious or violent felony if committed by an adult. "Concurrent jurisdiction" statutes usually allow a prosecutor, pursuant to statutory criteria, to file a petition for delinquency in the juvenile court or to file a complaint in the criminal court for the alleged commission of an act or acts enumerated in the statute. Such statutes are similar in criteria to the bindover/waiver statutes, with the major exception that the prosecutor rather than the judge has the discretion to choose the court of original jurisdiction.

Some states have statutes that exclude certain offenses committed by youth of a specific age from juvenile court jurisdiction. For example, in Louisiana, if a youth is 15 years old and is alleged to have committed either a capital crime or attempted aggravated rape, he or she must be tried as an adult in the criminal court. In such states, the legislature has removed all discretion from the judge and the prosecutor with respect to choosing the court of original jurisdiction. Such "exclusive jurisdiction" statutes have been adopted by a number of states in recent years.

Finally, there appears to be new consideration given by state legislatures in a number of states to bills that simply lower the maximum age of juvenile court jurisdiction for the commission of *any* offense that would be a crime if committed by an adult. Currently, some states, such as Connecticut, have lowered the age of juvenile court jurisdiction to 16. Some states are considering lowering the age even further, perhaps to as low as 13.

Statutory Approaches

After a youth has been adjudicated delinquent for the commission of an offense, the judge has a variety of alternatives, including sending the youth home with a judicial warning, with or without probation; placing the youth in a foster or group home; or committing the youth to the state youth correction agency for placement, usually in an institution.

In most states, the judge has total discretion to determine the dispositional alternative. In all states, individual judges, even those within the same county, may order different dispositions for youths who have committed the same offense, are the same age, and have similar backgrounds.

As a result, judicial discretion is likely to result in a wide disparity of dispositional decisions in almost every state.

In the majority of states, the judge has the discretion to issue any disposition, regardless of the offense for which the youth was adjudicated delinquent. In other words, two youths adjudicated delinquent, one for petty theft and the other for rape, could both be committed to the state youth corrections agency for placement in an institution. Not only could both be committed, but, due to the nature of commitment in a majority of states, both youths would be committed for an indeterminate period of time up until the age of majority. After commitment, the discretion to release the youths from placement would usually rest with the juvenile corrections agency.

In an effort to reduce judicial discretion exercised at dispositions, and/or agency/parole board discretion exercised in connection with the decision to release a youth from placement, some state legislatures have responded by enacting new legislation. The legislation may be of two types: statutes that prescribe the disposition and length of stay policies for *all* youth who have been adjudicated delinquent; and statutes that prescribe dispositional and length-of-stay policies for a subset of delinquents, usually labeled serious, violent, repeat, or habitual. The following discussion describes specific states' statutory approaches. The recent legislation enacted by the state of Washington comes closest to a type that creates "determinate" sentencing for *all* adjudicated delinquents. As described, even Washington state's approach still leaves room for a great deal of judicial discretion at the dispositional phase.

In fact, Washington state's juvenile justice act is quite complex and cannot be easily summarized with absolute accuracy. For purposes of general description, however, Washington state can be said to have created a statutory approach to disposition based on a youth's age, instant offense, and the severity of recent offenses. By calculating each of these variables, a set formula allows the court to assign a point score to each individual youth. Dispositions can then be determined by the point total. At the lower range, youths are classified as "minor or first offenders" and must be diverted if the statutory scheme is followed. At the high range, youths are classified as "serious offenders" and must be committed to the Division of Juvenile Rehabilitation for residential placement for a specified range of weeks if the statutory scheme is followed. In the middle range, youths are classified as "middle offenders" and may or may not be committed at the discretion of the judge. If committed, however, the statute sets forth a specific range of weeks during which such middle offenders are to be in residential placement, provided the statutory range is utilized.

Washington state's approach has been characterized by those in that state as "presumptive" sentencing, in that there is a presumption that the youth will receive a disposition in accordance with the sentencing guidelines. However, a section of the Juvenile Code allows the court to order a disposition and/or a commitment range outside the statutory guidelines if the judge declares that "manifest injustice" would result to the public or the youth if the statutory guidelines were used. At present, according to DJR officials, approximately 50 percent of the commitment orders involve manifest injustice, either to commit an otherwise noncommittable youth or to extend or lower the range of residential placement for a committable youth.

A number of states have recently passed legislation limiting judicial discretion with respect to the disposition of subsets of adjudicated delinquents. These subsets of delinquents are usually statutorily labeled as "serious, "violent," "repeat," or "habitual" juvenile offenders. For the purposes of this discussion, all such statutes will be known as "serious delinquent" statutes. They are to be distinguished from statutes that allow or mandate that certain youths be tried as adults, and from statutes that deal with young adult offenders.

Serious delinquent statutes aim to reduce the discretion exercised by the judge at disposition and, in some cases, limit the discretion exercised by state youth corrections agency personnel with respect to length of stay and placement decisions. Similar to delinquency statutes, serious delinquent statutes create a category (e.g., violent offender) with statutory criteria that the court must determine. Once the court finds that a youth is a serious, violent, or repeat offender, the statute will, in varying degrees, specify the terms of such an offender's commitment, placement, and length of stay.

In Kentucky,[2] if a youth is 16 years of age or older and is adjudicated delinquent for the commission of a class A or class B felony, the court in its discretion may commit the youth to the state youth corrections agency. However, if the court commits the youth, he or she must be institutionalized for an indeterminate period of time of not less than six months. In addition, if a youth is 16 years of age or older and is adjudicated delinquent for the commission of any felony *and* has previously been adjudicated delinquent of a felony in two separate adjudications, the court in its discretion may commit the youth to the state youth corrections agency. Again, if the court commits, the youth must be institutionalized for an indeterminate period of time of not less than six months. However, the Kentucky statute, as well as other state statutes, returns some discretion to the judge. In Kentucky, if the youth is committed as described above, the committing court may, with the consent of the state youth corrections agency and upon motion of the youth, grant probation to the youth after he or she has been committed for a minimum of 30 days.

Judicial discretion has been virtually eliminated in Illinois' Habitual Offender Act.[3] Under the act, if a minor has been adjudicated twice for an offense that would be a felony if committed by an adult, and the instant offense is one of an enumerated list of violent offenses, the youth shall be adjudged a habitual juvenile offender and must be committed to the Department of Corrections until his or her 21st birthday, without possibility of parole, furlough, or nonemergency authorized absence from confinement of any sort. However, pursuant to the statute, the minor is entitled to earn one day of good conduct credit for each day served as a reduction against his or her period of confinement. Such good conduct credit is determined by the Department of Corrections.

North Carolina also has a serious delinquent statutory provision that limits the discretion of the judge while granting discretion to state youth correction agency personnel.[4] Pursuant to the statutory provision, if the judge finds that a youth who has been adjudicated delinquent is 16 years of age or older *and* has been previously adjudicated delinquent for two or more felony offenses *and* has been previously committed to a residential facility operated by the Division of Youth Services, *and* that alternatives to commitment are inappropriate, *and* that the youth's behavior constitutes a threat to persons or property in the community, such judge shall commit the youth to the division for a definite term not to exceed two years. However, the statute allows the Division of Youth Services to reduce the duration of the definite commitment by an amount not to exceed 25 percent if the youth's behavior in the institution is satisfactory *and* the division may move for a reduction of more than 25 percent if it would be in the best interests of the youth.

Both Colorado and Delaware have serious delinquent statutes that direct the judges to make minimum institutional or out-of-home placement upon the finding that a youth is a special delinquent according to the criteria specified in the statute. In Colorado,[5] if a youth 15 years of age or older at the time of the alleged offense is adjudicated delinquent for a statutorily defined crime of violence, *or* if a youth has probation revoked for a statutorily defined crime of violence, he or she is designated a violent juvenile offender. If a youth of any age, who previously has been adjudicated delinquent, is adjudicated delinquent for a felony, *or* whose probation is revoked for the commission of a felony, he or she is designated a repeat juvenile offender. Upon adjudicating a youth a violent juvenile offender, the court shall commit or place the youth out of the home for not less than one year. Upon adjudicating a youth a repeat juvenile offender, the court shall commit or place such a youth out of the home for not less than one year. However, a repeat juvenile offender may be released by the committing judge upon a showing of exemplary behavior.

Delaware[6] has a serious delinquent statutory provision that applies to a youth who has been adjudicated delinquent of an offense that would be a felony if committed by an adult *and* within 13 months of said adjudication is adjudicated for a subsequent offense that would be a felony if committed by an adult. Any youth designated a serious delinquent shall be committed by the court to the Department of Corrections for institutional confinement for a period of not less than six months. Furthermore, such a youth may not be released from institutional confinement without a court determination.

All of the serious delinquent statutes discussed here provide for a youth who meets specific statutory criteria to be committed to the state youth corrections agency and, in some cases, institutionalized for a minimum period of time. These statutes do not address the *type* of institutionalization (e.g., secure or nonsecure). Two states, New York and Georgia, have instituted serious delinquent statutes that give the judge wide discretion to find that the youth qualifies, but once that judicial determination is made, the two statutes detail not only the length of commitment but the type and length of residential confinement as well.

Both the New York and Georgia statutes dictate restrictive placement for youth who fall under the respective statutes. In New York,[7] there are statutorily enumerated acts that are divided into Designated Class A felonies and Other Designated felonies. If a youth is 13, 14, or 15 years of age, or, in some cases, 14 or 15 years of age and is adjudicated for the commission of a class A or other designated felony, he or she may be subject to restrictive placement. After adjudication and prior to disposition, the court considers the following criteria before ordering a disposition of restrictive placement:

- the needs and interests of the youth;
- the record and background of the youth;

- the nature and circumstances of the instant offense, including whether any injury was inflicted by the youth on another participant;
- the need for the protection of the community; and
- the age and physical condition of the victim.

If the court, after considering these criteria, finds that restrictive placement is required, then the court *must* impose it. For a youth who has been adjudicated for a designated class A felony, restrictive placement means that he or she shall be committed to the Division for Youth for five years and be placed initially in a secure facility for not less than 12 months.[8] After the period of secure confinement, the youth must then be placed in a residential facility (secure or nonsecure) for 12 months. If a youth is adjudicated for an other designated felony, restrictive placement means that such youths shall be committed to the Division for Youth for three years and be placed initially in a secure facility for not less than six nor more than 12 months. The youth is then placed in a residential facility (secure or nonsecure) for an additional period of not less than six nor more than 12 months. All of the above is made part of the court's dispositional order. Included in the dispositional order are instructions about extensions of placement, as well as prohibitions against transfer and release during and subsequent to the first two segments of placement.

Georgia[9] has a similar serious delinquent statute, in that once a youth is found to be subject to the statute, he or she *must* be placed in restrictive custody. The Georgia statute addresses designated felony acts for which, if a youth 13 years of age or more is found to have committed them, the judge, using identical criteria to those used in New York, must determine whether restrictive custody is required. The youth is committed to the Division of Youth Services for a period of five years and is ordered by the court to be confined in the state secure institution for not less than 12 nor more than 18 months. Subsequently, the youth is placed under intensive supervision for a period of 12 months. Additionally, the court dispositional order does not allow the youth to be transferred to a nonsecure facility or released from intensive supervision without a new court order.

Administrative Approaches

Some state corrections agencies are attempting to reduce agency discretion with respect to placement and length-of-stay determinations for committed delinquents through the development of administrative rules and guidelines. As did the dispositional statutes, the administrative guidelines fall into two categories: guidelines that are applicable to *all* committed youth, and guidelines that are applicable to a subset of committed youth.

Arizona's Department of Corrections, Juvenile Services instituted length-of-programming guidelines in April 1980. The guidelines set forth maximum and minimum lengths of institutional stay for *all* youths adjudicated delinquent and committed to the Department of Corrections. The guidelines define six categories of delinquent activity. After commitment to the department, a youth is first categorized into the appropriate offense severity level by staff at the department's diagnostic center. Staff members then examine the committed youth's prior adjudications, i.e., the number and class of prior adjudications for two years prior to admittance to the department. That computation is put into a predetermined formula and a range of institutional stay is determined. The guidelines also provide an administrative process to reduce or extend the minimum and maximum length of stay imposed by the guidelines. The length-of-programming guidelines do not recommend, however, the nature of the placement (e.g., secure or nonsecure).

Massachusetts' Department of Youth Services has established a classification process, initiated on March 31, 1981, to deal with serious and chronic juvenile offenders. The process has three major components: a classification panel, a classification grid, and procedural guidelines. The classification panel reviews all committed youths adjudicated for crimes of violence against persons and having had a history of offenses. The panel uses the following criteria to determine whether the youth will be accepted for secure treatment:

- circumstances of violent offenses;
- significant aspects of past offenses;
- past performance in placement and treatment programs; and
- individual youth characteristics.

If the youth is accepted for secure treatment, the classification grid specifies a predetermined time range based on instant offenses.

Texas has also instituted placement and institutional length-of-stay guidelines. The guidelines, issued through the Texas Youth Council, are called the Case Management System. They divide all committed youth into essentially two categories: violent and nonviolent offenders. The Texas Youth Council classifies the committed youth, using the offense for which the youth was adjudicated, and then determines a length of stay and type of placement. Violent offenders are placed in Texas Youth Council secure institutions for a minimum of 12 months. Nonviolent offenders may be assigned to any residential program for a minimum of three months.

In this section we have described three basic approaches to decreasing discretion and reducing disparity in the juvenile justice system. Each of these three methods raises many policy issues, some of which are discussed in the following section.

POLICY ISSUES IN THE MOVE TOWARD DISPARITY REDUCTION FOR JUVENILES

The move toward reducing disparity in the juvenile justice system by the establishment of legislative or administrative mandates for sentencing (or for trying youth as adults) has raised a number of policy issues that were identified during UI's national survey of release decisionmaking. This discussion identifies a number of these issues.

The trend toward determinate sentencing has intensified the debate over the appropriate role of the legislative, judicial, and executive branches in juvenile justice. The prevailing approach to juvenile justice gave absolute discretion to the juvenile court judge over the dispositional (sentencing) phase of juvenile justice and absolute discretion to the juvenile corrections agency/parole board over the corrections (release) phase. As noted above, recent legislative and administrative reforms have reduced discretion in both these areas.

Survey respondents throughout the country identified the struggle for power between these three groups—legislators, judges, and correctional officers—as the underlying factor in the current debates over juvenile justice. Corrections agency staff are particularly critical of the legislature's usurpation of power over the determination of an individual youth's length of stay. Their objections, as might be expected, usually focus on the need for individualized decisionmaking rather than uniformity based on offense and prior record, variables many feel to be irrelevant to the purposes of juvenile corrections. Additionally, many juvenile corrections personnel object to the unnecessarily long periods of incarceration pre-scribed by state legislatures, arguing that institutional time must be mini-mized to avoid the negative effects of "institutionalization."

Judges seem more willing to support legislative attempts to "ration-alize" lengths of stay based primarily on seriousness of offense, although some feel that some of the mandated lengths of stay are too short. Many judges object to efforts to reduce their dispositional prerogatives, however.

In Washington state, for example, where a judge is allowed to disregard legislative mandates for dispositions he or she feels would result in "manifest injustice" to the community or the youth, approximately half the commitments to the state Division of Juvenile Rehabilitation involve the use of this "manifest injustice" section. Refusal to follow state standards was most often seen in cases where a youth would not otherwise be commitable, or where the judges wished to extend the mandated length of stay.

In adopting determinate sentencing schemes, many legislators voice criticism of both judicial and administrative efforts in juvenile justice, usually attacking judges and corrections staff alike for being "too soft" on serious juvenile offenders. A not insignificant number of legislators also appear to have criticized judges and corrections staff for institutionalizing minor or first offenders as well as status offenders. In any event, by understanding the nature of such "turf disputes" between legislators, judges, and corrections officials, reforms toward determinate sentencing can be seen as a political struggle as well as a philosophical one. Debates over the nature of appropriate dispositions and appropriate lengths of stay may, in reality, be debates over the power of district attorneys, judges, legislators, and juvenile agencies.

In their simplest terms, determinate sentencing statutes can be viewed as the usurpation by the legislature of roles previously played by the judiciary or the executive (i.e., juvenile corrections agency). In this context, many state agencies are attempting to ward off legislative intrusions into their domain by adopting administrative length-of-stay guidelines based on offense severity and prior record. Based on our survey, it appears that judges have not yet adopted this strategy in an attempt to maintain their power. However, some judges indicate that they have considered the establishment of judicially derived guidelines, countywide or statewide, for dispositions so that decisionmaking would be less disparate at the judicial level. As far as UI could discover, however, no such judicially based guidelines have been formally adopted.

Determinate sentencing approaches magnify the influence of political moods on the juvenile justice system. Many of the earliest supporters of determinate sentencing for juveniles were identified as political liberals and decried the abuses of indeterminate sentencing that too often kept minor or status offenders in correctional institutions for long periods of time. Ironically, many of these same commentators are now having second thoughts as to the wisdom of determinate sentencing as drafted by legislatures dominated by conservative politicians.

When legislatures establish laws that determine when a youth must be tried as an adult, when a youth must be committed to state juvenile institutions, and for how long such a youth must be confined, they are of necessity making political decisions. Given the political conservatism of the late 1970s and early 1980s, state legislatures have become increasingly populated by public officials committed to a "law and order" platform. As a result, many respondents in our survey were greatly worried by the actual or potential harshness of their respective state's legislative approaches in this area. Many felt that much legislation mandated unnecessarily long sentences for juveniles and/or sent too many to adult court for trial. Others felt that this would be the likely result of future legislative acts in their state.

Determinate sentencing has increased the importance of discretion exercised by police, court intake workers, and especially, district attorneys. The actual crimes charged against a juvenile offender and the actual crimes for which the juvenile is convicted have not been critical to the indeterminate-based juvenile justice system. This is because, in most states, courts can order any disposition they wish once a youth has been adjudicated a delinquent, regardless of the actual crime for which he or she has been found guilty. Thus, a minor offender can be committed for institutional placement as easily as a juvenile found guilty of several felonies. Likewise, juvenile corrections staff may keep a minor offender institutionalized for as long or longer than a serious offender if they so choose.

The move to determinate sentencing in a number of states has reduced some of this discretion. In such states, the disposition and the length of institutional stay are linked directly to the specific adjudicated offense and specific prior offenses. The actual charge for which the youth is found guilty therefore becomes a critical factor in these states. As a result, prosecutorial discretion as to which offenses to charge and, particularly, as to where to allow a guilty plea, has become a significant source of power. According to our survey, in most states in which determinate sentencing for juveniles has been implemented, the discretion that rested with judges and correctional staff has been reduced only at the cost of substantially increasing the discretion available to the prosecutor.

This fact raises a number of issues. Is increasing prosecutorial discretion in juvenile justice an intended result of determinate sentencing? Is it a desirable result? Is a system in which prosecutorial discretion significantly determines dispositions for youth and lengths of institutional stay more appropriate than one in which judges and juvenile correctional staff make such determinations? Greater experience with determinate sentencing for juveniles and continued research in the area will no doubt shed light on these issues.

Determinate sentencing for juvenile may require an expansion of due process rights for juvenile court proceedings. Historically, because the juvenile justice system was seen as rehabilitative in nature and therefore quasi-civil, as opposed to criminal, due process rights did not attach to juvenile court proceedings. In re Gault and its successor cases reversed this notion and mandated that certain rights attach at delinquency proceedings, including rights to appointed counsel, notice, and cross-examination. The courts have not, however, extended to juvenile offenders all of the rights accorded to adult offenders, such as the right to a jury trial.

The adoption of a just deserts approach to juvenile justice, with its focus on punishment for specific offenses (including specific priors), questions the notion that a juvenile court proceeding is not quite the same as a criminal proceeding in the adult court. To our knowledge, only one state, Illinois, has recognized this fact and has created a right to a jury trial for youths tried under a determinate sentencing statute. Most other states (e.g., North Carolina and Washington) have not. In New York, a court ruling stated that as a constitutional matter, the determinate sentencing law for juveniles did not require jury trials for youths tried under the statute. This discussion is meant only to raise the issue and not to set forth an involved legal analysis. Undoubtedly, this area will be the subject of much litigation in the future.

Laws mandating serious youthful offenders to be tried as adults probably do not reduce sentencing disparity. As indicated earlier, a number of states have reduced the discretion of the juvenile court judge (and, to some extent, the prosecutor) in the determination of when to bind over a youth to adult court for trial. Such laws may be referred to as "exclusive jurisdiction states," since they give exclusive jurisdiction to the adult courts to try certain youth, usually designated by specific felony offenses, and/or a specific number of prior felonies and/or a minimum age. ("Concurrent jurisdiction statutes" allow the district attorney to file certain serious cases, also designated by instant offense, prior offense and age, in either the adult or juvenile court at the prosecutor's discretion.)

Since these "exclusive jurisdiction statutes" create a consistent determination of whether certain juvenile offenders will be tried as adults or juveniles, they may be said to reduce disparity—i.e., all youths with these specific characteristics will be tried as adults. However, recent studies have suggested that such youths often receive quite disparate sentences from the adult court (see Hamparian et al., 1982). One such study indicates that youths tried as adults often receive probation from the adult court because, in that environment, they are seen as first offenders and deserving of lenience. Since others, no doubt, are given prison sentences, the sentencing of youths in adult court is, in fact, likely to be quite disparate.

It should also be noted that disparity probably exists between the sentencing of serious delinquents who do not quite meet the requirements to be tried in adult court and those young offenders who do. That is, a serious juvenile offender tried in juvenile court will likely be institutionalized for a significant amount of time in a juvenile correctional facility, while an equally if not more serious juvenile offender who is tried as an adult will often receive probation with no institutional time, or else have his case dismissed outright, often for legal insufficiencies.

Almost all determinate sentencing approaches for juveniles focus on serious offenders and do not restrict dispositional or length of stay alternatives for minor and first offenders. The majority of states that have adopted some form of determinate sentencing for juveniles have mandated sentences for serious, violent, or chronic delinquents. These laws have attempted to reduce disparity in the sentencing of this subset of delinquents. Most of these states have not, however, restricted the discretion of the court or the juvenile corrections agency with regard to the disposition of minor offenders. As a result, in most of these states, disparity in dispositions for these minor offenders appears to be as great as it was prior to the adoption of determinate sentencing statutes. Conceptually, sentencing statutes for juveniles can be drafted that mandate dispositional alternatives for a range of adjudicated delinquents, including first or minor offenders. For example, statutes could require certain youths to be diverted prior to adjudication and/or require judges to place certain youths on probation, others in community-based placement, and still others in institutions. To the extent that a statute mandates certain dispositions, including length of stay, it may be described as "mandatory sentencing," as opposed to "definite sentencing," which allows the judge total discretion to determine the appropriate disposition, but sets a definite length of stay (residential placement) if the judge opts for commitment.

As noted earlier, most states that have adopted determinate sentencing for juveniles in recent years have drafted mandatory sentencing statutes that apply only to the most serious juvenile offenders, leaving intact indeterminate sentencing approaches for all nonserious delinquents. There are exceptions, however.

Washington state's sentencing law, for example, has both "mandatory" and "definite" features and addresses minor offenders as well as serious offenders. As noted earlier, adjudicated delinquents in Washington are given a numerical score depending on instant offense, chronicity and seriousness of recent prior offenses, and age. Depending on a youth's score, he or she may be either a "minor or first offender," a "middle offender," or a "serious offender." The law acts as a mandatory sentencing law for "minor or first offenders" and for "serious offenders." It is mandatory in that the law specifies a diversion for "minor or first offenders" and commitment for a specific range of time for "serious offenders." It is definite as to "middle offenders," who may or may not be committed by the judge at the judge's discretion, but who, if committed, will be subject to a definite length of stay as set forth in the sentencing law.

The failure of most states with determinate sentencing statutes to address dispositional issues for less serious offenders seems significant. Many critics of indeterminate sentencing decried the inappropriately long periods of institutionalization of minor offenders as much as they did the inappropriately short sentences for serious offenders.[10] It appears, however, that most state legislatures are responding only to the latter issue. Since most delinquents committed to state juvenile institutions in these states are committed pursuant to an indeterminate delinquency statute rather than the determinate statute for serious delinquents, it would appear that disparity of sentencing is still widespread, even in these states.

In practice, attempts to reduce disparity in juvenile justice through determinate sentencing statutes may not significantly reduce the discretion available to juvenile corrections agencies. In states having indeterminate sentencing schemes for juveniles, a great deal of discretion is given to juvenile corrections agencies (or parole boards). These agencies usually have total discretion to determine the initial and subsequent placements of a juvenile, including the security levels of such placements, the type of treatment/rehabilitation program into which the youth is placed, and the overall length of stay. In such states, according to UI's survey, these agency decisions have usually been based on criteria other than the seriousness of the specific offense or prior offenses committed by the youth. To a large extent, these decisions are based on the needs of the youth, his or her performance while in placement, the institutional population, and the availability of alternative placements.

As promoted by their advocates, determinate sentencing statutes for juveniles would appear significantly to restrict the discretionary power of the corrections agency in deciding where and for how long a youth is confined, and to tie these decisions to the instant and prior offense history of the youth. As a result, arguably, sentencing in juvenile justice would become less disparate in that it would treat committed youths in a consistent manner, according to their present offense and prior record.

For the most part, however, the determinate sentencing statutes for juveniles that have already gone into effect have only partially reduced the discretion of the juvenile corrections agency. In most cases, although the statutes mandate a specific length of commitment, they do not mandate specific placements nor security levels. Thus, as in indeterminate sentencing states, corrections officials retain discretion as to whether the youth will spend his or her "term" in secure or nonsecure facilities, in institutions, or in community-based group homes. As a result, there may still be wide disparity in the nature of the sentences served by two youths committed for the same offense and with identical offense histories.

This point seems central to an understanding of determinate sentencing in juvenile cases. For example, in Washington state, where one of the most ambitious determinate (or "presumptive," because of the manifest injustice escape clause) statutes has been adopted, the average length of institutional stay for the large majority of youths committed to the Division of Juvenile Rehabilitation appears to be only slightly longer than it was prior to the new law. However, one of the major effects of the new offense-based sentencing scheme in Washington appears to have been on the type of placement to which youths are sent after completing their institutional stay. Prior to the new law, the majority of youths were placed in their family home subsequent to an institutional stay. Now, because many have not been in "residential placement" for the minimum period of their sentence at the time they are released from an institution, the majority of these youths are being placed in community-based, nonsecure group homes, as opposed to the family home. These group homes may, in fact, be in the same city and even the same neighborhood as the youth's family home, depending on availability. In that case, the youth may be back in the same school and the same environment as if he or she had returned to the family home.

In the case of Washington state, as well as in other states with determinate sentencing, the length of *institutional stay* may still have little to do with instant and prior offenses. The length of *overall residential placement,* however, may be directly related to these factors. However, as noted earlier, there are several states that appear to mandate the nature of the stay as well as the length. New York, for example, specifies that youth adjudicated for certain felonies and found to require restrictive placement must remain in secure confinement, depending on the felony, for a fixed period of time.

Juvenile correctional agencies are also retaining discretion over committed youths in ways other than by deciding the nature and length of differing levels of placements. Based on our national survey, it appears that juvenile correctional agencies have developed a number of administrative mechanisms that allow them to circumvent legislative requirements for minimum lengths of stay and to move and/or release youths based on the more traditional criteria of program completion, institutional population, and availability of alternative placements. This is a phenomenon that seems to exist in most states that have adopted determinate sentencing schemes, and even in those states that historically have allowed judges to affix specific lengths of stay to commitment orders. These administrative mechanisms include early furloughs, advance leaves, and other strategies that allow a youth to go home earlier than otherwise allowed by the statutes or the judge's sentence. How widespread such administrative policies are is unclear. But, according to many of our respondents, they are far from uncommon. This fact suggests, again, that in practice, determinate sentencing statutes may be implemented in such a manner that wide disparity continues, and individualized discretion is still a major factor.

One further comment on the role of juvenile corrections agencies in states with determinate sentencing statutes seems noteworthy. In a number of states, correctional staff have indicated that their early fears and antagonism toward fixed sentences as opposed to individualized release decisions dissipated after some months of experience with the new approach. These respondents still feel that rehabilitation is the primary goal of the juvenile justice system. They told us that determinate sentencing resulted in some youths (serious offenders) being kept much too long in institutional settings and thus becoming increasingly bitter, hostile, and isolated, while others (minor offenders) remained institutionalized for too short a period of time, and thus could not get maximum benefit from the rehabilitation programs offered at the institution.

Despite such criticisms, many of these repondents indicated that they had learned to live with determinate sentencing by redefining their role in the rehabilitation of youth. While working in an indeterminate system, many juvenile corrections workers came to believe that it was primarily their responsibility to rehabilitate a youth. They believed that the isolated and controlled environment available within an institutional setting created the maximum opportunity for helping a youth. As a result, many institutional staff felt a personal sense of failure if the youth again became delinquent after leaving the institution.

A surprising number of these respondents indicated that a determinate sentencing approach, which releases minor offenders earlier than they would be under an indeterminate approach, forced them to recognize the limits of their role and responsibility. Many stated that they now believe it is as much the responsibility of community-based programs, the youth's family, and other support agencies in the youth's community to "rehabilitate" the youth as it is the responsibility of institutional staff. Thus, they have come to define their role in a more limited capacity than they had held under indeterminate sentencing. Specifically, they now see their role as that of initiating the rehabilitative process and, perhaps, advocating for strong postinstitutional support services.

It is interesting to note, by the way, that attitudes of juvenile correctional workers toward the implementation of determinate sentencing schemes often appear to be a direct reversal of the attitudes of those who advocate determinate sentencing of juveniles. That is, correctional staff criticize determinate sentencing because it keeps serious offenders institutionalized for too long a period and results in the too early release of nonserious offenders. Most proponents of determinate sentencing, of course, desire to extend the length of stay for serious offenders and reduce the length of stay for nonserious offenders.

Lack of alternative placements for juveniles may cause disparate lengths of stay regardless of a state's approach to commitment and release. Conceptually, a nondisparate sentencing structure would confine offenders committing the same crime and with similar criminal histories for similar periods of time. Thus, for example, two adult offenders convicted of the same offense and with the same criminal history would be released at approximately the same time. This would occur whether or not the adult prisoner had a stable home to which he could return, or a job to begin, or for that matter, any place to go at all. As an adult, it would be his responsibility to fend for himself, and society (by statute) implicitly presumes that he is able to do so.

When a committed delinquent is ready to be released from institutional placement, he or she may or may not have any place to go. To the extent that the youth's family is not able or willing to care for the youth, the juvenile corrections system may have limited options for release of the youth. If the youth is old enough or mature enough, the youth might be released for independent living. Otherwise, attempts will be made to place the youth in some sort of residential setting, e.g., a foster home, group home, or work program. If no placements are available, and the youth is still young (under 17, for example), the youth's stay in institutional care may be extended for lack of an alternative residential setting.

This seems to pose a dilemma for the determinate sentencing of juveniles. If a youth is entitled to be released at a certain date, he or she should be released at that time. But where no home or other placement is available, can we just release a youth to the streets? Possibly, a right to release creates a right to an alternative placement. But even if such a right is established, by executive order, legislative mandate, or judicial decision, there may not be funds and resources available to provide these alternative living situations. In this case, it appears, committed youth may spend disparate lengths of stay in institutions for reasons unrelated to the determinate or indeterminate sentencing approaches of the states.

CONCLUSION

In conclusion, it appears that the 1980s will see a definite trend among state legislatures and juvenile corrections agencies to reduce disparity in juvenile justice and to minimize the discretion exercised by judges and corrections staff. This trend will accompany efforts to mandate older, more serious delinquents to be tried as adults. It also appears that this trend will result from efforts to deal more severely with serious and violent juvenile offenders, rather than from a philosophical commitment to the reduction of disparity in juvenile corrections per se.

Based on a preliminary assessment of some of these early reform efforts, it also appears that the philosophy of rehabilitation ingrained in most juvenile justice corrections workers and the limited institutional and noninstitutional resources available for committed delinquents will result in the continued presence of a great deal of individualized decisionmaking within juvenile justice, with much of the disparity in decisionmaking that has characterized the traditional, indeterminate approach. This will be true, for the most part, because of the dynamics resulting from a system's attempt to struggle with concepts of both proportionate sentencing and rehabilitation in a context characterized too often by limited resources.

NOTES

1. For a more extensive literature review, see Charles P. Smith et al. (1980: 208-228).
2. Kentucky Revised Statutes, 208.194 (1976).
3. Illinois Revised Statutes, ch. 37, s. 705-12 (1979).
4. General Statutes of North Carolina, Section 7A-652(b)(2) (1979).

5. Colorado Revised Statutes, 19-3-113.1 (1980).

6. 10 Del. C Sec. 937(c) (1977).

7. New York Family Court Act, Section 712(h)(1976) and Section 753-a(1976).

8. Many of the youths subject to this provision are, in fact, now tried as adults pursuant to New York's 1978 Juvenile Offender Act.

9. Georgia Code Ann. Section 24A-2301 (1980).

10. Wheeler's studies of juvenile sentencing in a number of states found that (1) given offender characteristics such as offense and sex, no significant variation in stay was demonstrated. However, there was a pattern of detaining status offenders longer than youth committed of felony index crimes; (2) in Ohio, "younger" and "least dangerous" were characteristics associated with longer stays (see Wheeler, 1976).

CASES

In re GAULT (1967) 387 U.S. 1
In re WINSHIP (1970) 397 U.S. 358

REFERENCES

ALLEN, H. E. (1975) "Indeterminate sentence in America—an empirical test." Presented at the 19th Annual Southern Conference on Corrections.

CHEIN, D. (1976) "Contingencies in the careers of juvenile delinquencies: decision-making in juvenile correctional institutions." Ph.D. thesis, University Michigan, Ann Arbor.

CRISMAN, N. (1976) "Female offenders." Presented at the 106th Annual Congress of Corrections.

HAMPARIAN, D. et al. (1982) Youth in Adult Courts: Between Two Worlds. Washington, DC: U.S. Department of Justice.

Institute of Judicial Administration/American Bar Association Joint Commission Juvenile Justice Standards (1980) Standards Related to Juvenile Delinquency Sanctions and Standards Related to Disposition. Cambridge, MA: Ballinger.

McCARTHY, F. B. (1977) "Delinquency dispositions under the juvenile justice standards: the consequences of a change of rationale." New York University Law Review 52.

McCULLOH, R. W. (1981) A Comparative Analysis of Juvenile Justice Standards and the Juvenile Justice and Delinquency Prevention Act, Vol. 3: Reducing Detention and Commitments: Community-Based Alternatives to Incarceration. Washington, DC: Government Printing Office.

National Advisory Committee on Criminal Justice Standards and Goals' Task Force on Juvenile Justice and Delinquency Prevention (1976) Juvenile Justice and Delinquency Prevention, Standards 14.9 and 14.13. Washington, DC: Government Printing Office.

National Advisory Committee for Juvenile Justice and Delinquency Prevention (1980) Standards for the Administration of Juvenile Justice, 3.181 and 3.182. Washington, DC: Government Printing Office.

PAGE, J. R. (1979) "Equality of sentencing between juveniles and adults: a logical extension of People v. Olivas." Pacific Law Journal 10.

The Sacramento Union (1978) Page 1, April 14.

SHEPPARD, R. E., Jr. (1977) "Challenging the rehabilitative justification for indeterminate sentencing in the juvenile justice system: the right to punishment." St. Louis University Law Journal 21.

SLEETH, V. (1978-79) "A child is a child, except when he's not: California's new approach to disposition of juvenile and youthful offenders." California Western Law Review 14.

SMITH, C. P. et al. (1980) A National Assessment of Case Disposition and Classification in the Juvenile Justice System: Inconsistent Labeling, Vol. 2: Results of a Literature Search. Washington, DC: Government Printing Office.

THORNBERRY, T. P. (1979) "Sentencing disparities in the juvenile justice system." Journal of Criminal Law and Criminology 70.

——— (1973) "Race, socio-economic status and sentencing in the juvenile justice system." Journal of Criminal Law and Criminology 64.

WHEELER, G. R. (1978) "Juvenile sentencing and public policy: beyond counterdeterrence.": Policy Analysis 4.

——— (1976) "The computerization of juvenile corrections—demystification of the therapeutic state." Crime and Delinquency 22.

——— and K. D. NICHOLS (1974) A Statistical Inquiry into Length of Stay and the "Revolving Door": The Case for a Modified Fixed Sentence for the Juvenile Offender. Columbus, OH: Ohio Youth Commission, Division of Research, Planning, and Development.

INDEX

ABOUT THE AUTHORS

IRA BLALOCK, an ordained Unitarian minister, has held a variety of positions in the public sector. Since 1975 he has been a member of the Oregon Board of Parole, and for two years he served as chairperson of the board. Mr. Blalock was also the first chairperson of the Advisory Commission on Prison Terms and Parole Standards, the first sentencing commission in the country.

MARY LOU FENILI is currently Staff Counsel to the California Board of Prison Terms. In the legislative unit of the governor's office, she participated in developing the compromise version of the legislation enacted as the Uniform Determinate Sentencing Act of 1976. Hired by the board in 1977, she served as Project Manager for the Disparate Sentence Review Project.

BRUCE FISHER is a partner in Urban and Rural Systems Associates (URSA) of San Francisco, California. Since receiving his law degree from Harvard Law School, Mr. Fisher has practiced and taught law in California, and has worked as a consultant on a variety of youth services and juvenile justice projects. He is currently directing a study of institutional commitment and release decisionmaking for juvenile delinquents funded by the Office of Juvenile Justice and Delinquency Prevention. He is also an adjunct professor at the University of San Francisco Law School where he teaches a course on juvenile justice.

MARTIN L. FORST is an instructor in the Criminal Justice Administration Department at Sonoma State University in California. Prior to his current teaching position, he served as research associate at the Center for the Study of Law and Society at the University of California in Berkeley.

He is the author of *Civil Commitment and Social Control* and co-editor of *Crime and Justice in America.*

ALEXANDER GREER is research associate on the Theoretical Studies Project of the Center for the Study of Causes of Crime for Gain at the Rutgers University Criminal Justice Research Center. He has also published articles in the sentencing area. He is currently completing his J.D./M.A. at Rutgers School of Law and School of Criminal Justice.

KATHLEEN J. HANRAHAN received her M.A. from the Graduate School of Criminal Justice, State University of New York at Albany. She is co-author of *The Question of Parole: Retention, Reform, or Abolition?* and *Parole Systems in the United States,* and has published articles in the area of sentencing and parole.

LESLIE A. MEDINA is a senior research associate for Urban and Rural Systems Associates (URSA), San Francisco, where she is currently Assistant Project Director for a Juvenile Institutional Release Decision-Making Study funded by the Office of Juvenile Justice and Delinquency Prevention. Ms. Medina received her B.A. from the University of California, Berkeley and a Masters in Public Administration from the University of Southern California. She is presently a Ph.D. candidate in Jurisprudence and Social Policy at the University of California, Berkeley, Boalt Hall School of Law.

PETER A. OZANNE is an Assistant Professor of Law at the University of Oregon and teaches courses in Criminal Law and Procedure and Trial Practice. He received his B.A. degree in Political Science and Economics from the University of Washington in 1967 and his J.D. degree from Stanford Law School in 1971. The Oregon Legislature recently appointed him to its Joint Interim Committee on the Judiciary Task Force on Sentencing, which was established to review and propose revision of the state's criminal sentencing laws.

WILLIAM PANNELL is currently Chief of Management Information of the California Board of Prison Terms. He previously served as Chief of the Operations Research Unit of the California Department of Corrections. He is the author of several journal articles on the application of statistics, mathematics, and simulation to criminal justice problems.

CARY RUDMAN is senior research associate with Urban and Rural Systems Associates (URSA) of San Francisco, where he is working on a national study of commitment and release decisionmaking for adjudicated delinquents. He is also working on the Violent Juvenile Offender Research and Development Initiative funded by the Office of Juvenile Justice and Delinquency Prevention. Mr. Rudman received a J.D. from Loyola University of Los Angeles and an LL.M. from Harvard Law School. Prior to his association with URSA, he was a Reginald Heber Smith Community Lawyer Fellow with the Legal Aid Society of San Diego, California.

RICHARD F. SPARKS is Professor at the School of Criminal Justice at Rutgers University. He is co-author of *Key Issues in Criminology* (1970) and of a major statistical analysis of criminal victimization, *Surveying Victims* (1977). Most recently, he has completed work on two research projects funded by the National Institute of Justice: Strategies for Determinate Sentencing, and Evaluation of Statewide Sentencing Guidelines. He is currently the director of another National Institute of Justice project that established the Center for the Study of the Causes of Crime for Gain.

BRIDGET A. STECHER is a Ph.D. candidate at Rutgers University, School of Criminal Justice, and an adjunct at Seton Hall University. Most recently, she was the research associate for the National Institute of Justice project to evaluate statewide sentencing guidelines and is currently the director of a project that will study the crime control effects of criminal sanctions.

FRANCES M. TERNUS is a Deputy State Public Defender in San Francisco, California. She represents indigent criminal defendants in appeals from felony convictions and in other postconviction proceedings. Additionally, she has represented over 100 prison inmates at determinate term-setting parole hearings. She received her undergraduate degree from the University of California at Berkeley and her law degree from Golden Gate University Law School.

LAWRENCE F. TRAVIS III is an Assistant Professor of Criminal Justice at the University of Cincinnati. He received his Ph.D. from the School of Criminal Justice at the State University of New York at Albany. He has previously served as research director for the Oregon State Board of Parole, and research analyst for the National Parole Institute. Among other works, he is the author of *Changes in Parole and Sentencing Decision-Making: 1976-1978* and co-editor of *Corrections: An Issues Approach*.